FISHING IN NORTHERN CALIFORNIA

Expanded & Revised Edition

Ken Albert

ISBN   0-934061-03-3

Cover Design: Electric Art Studios
     Mountain View, CA

Printed By: Delta Lithograph
     Van Nuys, CA

MARKETSCOPE
BOOKS

119 Richard
Aptos, CA 95003
(408) 688-7535

Two Other Great Books

Fishing in Southern California

This book(8½ x 11, 228 pages) is laid out just like the NorCal fishing guide. It includes How To Catch Sections on all fresh water fish as well as Barracuda, Bonito, Calico Bass, Grunion, Halibut, Marlin, Sea Bass, and Yellowtail. Plus there are sections on all major SoCal fishing waters(30 lakes, The Salton Sea, Colorado River, over a dozen mountain trout locales and the Pacific Ocean). All these waters are mapped in detail.

Bass Fishing in California

At last, a bass fishing book just for Californians - both beginners and veterans. This book explains in detail how to catch more and larger bass in California's unique waters. But most valuable, it includes a comprehensive guide, with maps, to 36 of California's best bass lakes, up and down the state. 8½ x 11, 208 pages.

Order Your Copies Today

	Price	Sales Tax	Total Price	Qty	Total Amount
___ Fishing in Northern California	$13.95	$ .90	$14.85	____	_____
___ Fishing in Southern California	$13.95	$ .90	$14.85	____	_____
___ Bass Fishing in California	$12.95	$ .85	$13.80	____	_____

Postage & Handling(1st book $1.25; no postage and handling charge on 2 or more books) . . . . . . _____ *

Check Enclosed . . . . . . _____

___ ***Special Offer**(order 2 books, any combination, and we'll pay **all** postage & handling)

Name_____

Address_____

_____

Send Your Order To: **Marketscope Books, Box 171, Aptos, CA 95001**

(Permission is granted to Xerox this page)

Contents

Continued . . .

Contents (continued)

Fishing is Still Great!

In the first edition of this book we proclaimed that fishing is great in Northern California. Well, guess what? Fishing is still great.

There are 5,000 lakes and 30,000 miles of streams in California, and the vast majority of these lakes and streams are in Northern California. And then there are the hundreds of miles of coastline, San Francisco Bay and 700 miles of waterways in the Delta. Anglers here are fortunate to have an immense variety of quality fishing opportunities;

- Thousands of mountain streams and lakes for trout.

- Numerous lakes and reservoirs for bass, trout, catfish and panfish.

- Steelhead and salmon in coastal rivers.

- Valley rivers for striped bass, salmon steelhead, shad and catfish.

- Bay waters for striped bass, sturgeon and halibut.

- Salmon, albacore, rockfish and lingcod in the Pacific.

Most of this great fishing is close-to-home, quite simple, and requires only modestly priced tackle. An added benefit, fishing is a wonderful way to share the outdoor experience with the entire family.

But the immense variety of the Northern California fishing experiences does raise many questions. Some major and others just puzzling;

- What size hook(or line) do I use for trout(or catfish)?
- Where are the bass hotspots at Folsom or New Hogan?
- If I catch a halibut(or a catfish, or a ...), how do I clean and cook it?
- When is the hot halibut season in San Francisco Bay?
- Can I fish from shore at San Pablo Reservoir?
- Where are the best spots to fish along the Sacramento River?
- What are the surest producers for largemouth bass?
- What rod and reel do I need for steelhead?
- When is the best time to go on an albacore trip?

Fishing in Northern California answers all these questions and many, many more. For all the types of fish and different locations, it tells **how** to fish, **where** to fish and **when** to fish. It tells what **equipment, tackle, rigs, bait** and **lures** to use, how to **clean** and **preserve** your catch and how to **cook** each fish.

Comprehensive NorCal fishing maps are shown on the next two pages.

RIVER and STREAM FISHING

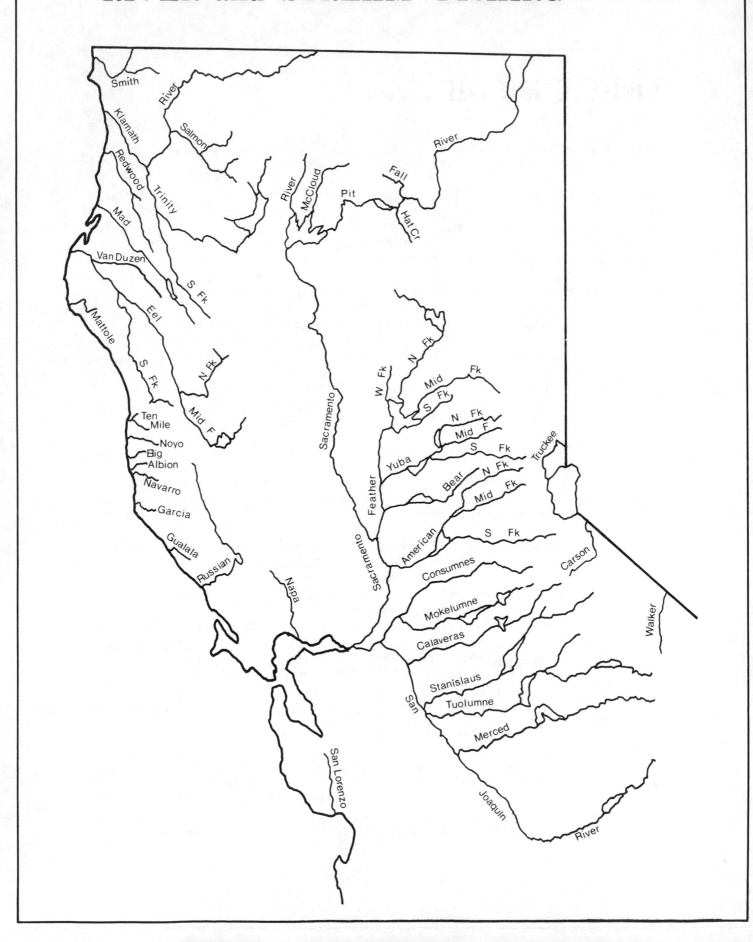

PACIFIC, BAY and LAKE FISHING

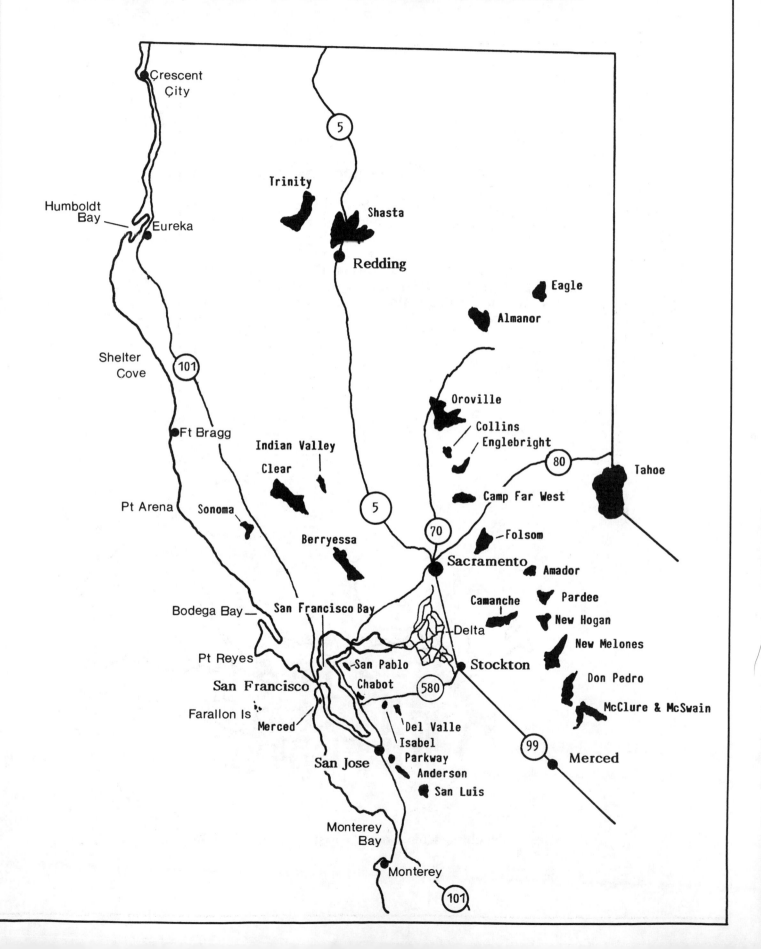

About This Expanded and Revised Edition

The first edition of this book was a winner. Outdoor writers praised it and anglers obviously had a need for it. Three big printings were sold in its 18 month life! No doubt, it would have continued to sell. But a second edition allows us to bring NorCal anglers 50% more useful fishing information. More "how-to's." More maps. More lakes. More on mountain trout. More saltwater coverage. More of everything. Quite simply, this expanded and revised edition is bigger and better. We hope you like it.

See "Teaching Kids How To Fish" section starting on Page 13.

Fishing Tips

There is one element of fishing success that can't be taught or learned. Rather, it must be self-instilled. I'm talking about self-confidence. Often "how-to" fishing articles end with a pep talk on the importance of fishing with confidence - that old Positive Mental Attitude. You know it's corny, but somehow it works.

I personally feel so strongly about the need to have faith in your approach and your tackle, that I've reversed things and put this topic first. I love fishing even when I don't catch fish. But I love it even more when I do. Often the only difference between an angler who puts fish on the line and one who just wets his line, is attitude. So fish with confidence.

Confidence will make you more attentive and more aware. It keeps your mind in gear. But, most importantly, it will encourage you to experiment, to change baits, or lures, or depths, or location until you find fish. This book tells you all you need to know to catch any kind of fish in Northern California. Just add self-confidence. The positive effects of perseverance, confidence and variety of approach can't be over emphasized.

When to Fish

There is no question that the time of year, the time of month and the time of day all impact on fishing success. More so, for some species, than others. All life moves in cycles. Fish are no different. For example, it's no coincidence, that most of California's fishing records were set in the spring months. March, April, and May are probably the best months to fish. These are the spawning months. Simply stated, here are the best times to fish;

Time of Year

Spring is best all around, followed by fall. Winter is surprisingly good. Summer, for many species is the worst. Yes, I know about summer vacations; the weather is beautiful and fishing seems to be a natural, warm weather sport, but often the fish don't know this. Or maybe they do! However, some fishing is good in summertime, especially if the proper approaches are followed. On the next page is a table that highlights the best time of year to fish for each species. It's easy to see why fishing is a four season sport in Northern California.

Time of Day

For most types of fish, during most times of the year, there is little doubt

Fishing Seasons (+=good, -=fair)

Species	J	F	M	A	M	J	J	A	S	O	N	D
Abalone			-	-	-			+	+	-	-	
Albacore								-	+	-		
Bass(largemouth & smallmouth)		-	+	+	+	-	-	-	-	+	-	
Bluegills		-	+	+	+	-	-	-	-	-	-	
Catfish		-	-	-	-	-	+	+	+	-	-	
Clams												
Crappie		-	+	+	+	-	-	-	-	-		
Halibut						-	+	+	-			
Kokanee			-	-	+	+	+	+	-	-		
Lingcod	+	+	-	-	-	-	-	-	-	+	+	+
Rock Cod	-	-	-	-	-	-	-	-	-	-	-	-
Salmon												
-Ocean		-	-	-	+	+	-	-	-			
-S.F. Bay								-	-	-		
-Rivers							-	+	+	+	+	-
-Lakes	+	+	+	+	-	-	-	-	-	-	+	+
Shad				-	+	+	-					
Sharks	-	-	-	-	-	-	-	-	-	-	-	
Steelhead	+	+	+	-				-	-	+	+	+
Striped Bass												
-Ocean						-	+	+	-	-		
-Bays			-	-	-	-	-	+	+	+	+	-
-Rivers	+	+	+	-	-	-			-	-	+	+
Sturgeon												
-Bays	+	+	+	-	-	-		-	-	-	+	+
-Rivers	+	+	-	-	-	-	-	-	-	-	-	+
Trout												
-Streams				+	+	+	-	-	+	+	+	
-Lakes	+	+	+	+	-	-	-	-	-	-	+	+

that early morning(from first light until 8 a.m.) and late evening(the 2–3 hours before dark) are the best times of day to catch fish. These are the times of day when fish are active and feeding. For some situations night time is also good. For example, bass fishing after dark on warm summer nights, using noisy, dark surface plugs(in shallow water) can be good. Also, summertime catfishing can be good from 9 p.m. and during the two hours before daybreak.

Time of Month(The Tides)

Some would say that the phases of the moon have a great deal to do with fishing success, in any environment. This may or may not be true. But, there is no doubt that tides do impact fishing success in shallower tidal waters like bays. Surf, rock and pier anglers know how tide movements effect fishing. In tidal waters, it's always best to fish on days when there is a big change between high and low tide. Waters move faster, bait and bait fish get moved around, so game fish feed more actively.

The height of the tide varies according to the positions of the sun and moon in relation to the earth. These influences are illustrated below. The best fishing is during spring tide periods. Fish the hours before, through and after a high tide change for peak action.

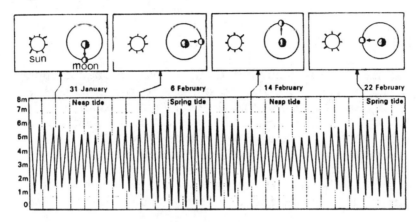

More on the Moon

There is a school of fishing thought that says that the position of the moon(or some say the moon and the sun), on a daily basis, has an effect on the feeding and activity level of fish. These peak activity periods coincide with the moon's strongest gravitational pull which occurs twice each day when the moon is directly above or below a particular point on earth. When the moon is above, it's a major period, and when it's below it's a minor period, according to the theory. These activity periods are published in California outdoor newspapers and in magazines like "Field and Stream". Or a guide can be purchased to calculate major and minor activity periods each day. If nothing else, it's fun to see if the activity periods coincide with ones own fishing experience.

Where to Fish

This book has tons of "where to fish" information in it. But there are three generalizations about "where to fish" that apply so universally, that they are worthy of special attention.

Fish on the Bottom!

To catch many varieties of Northern California fish you've got to fish on or near the bottom. This is true for:

. Bass	. Rockcrabs
. Catfish	. Salmon(in rivers)
. Crayfish	. Steelhead
. Halibut	. Striped Bass
. Lingcod	. Sturgeon
. Rock Cod	. Trout

Stream trout will rise up for food, but then retreat to the bottom. Trout near shore in lakes, are on the bottom. I'd like to emphasize the truism, "fish on the bottom" with this analogy. Most creatures that live on land, actually live on the bottom of a vast sea of atmosphere. This atmosphere is about 100,000 feet deep, yet most creatures live right on the bottom of the atmosphere. Of course, people and all fur bearing animals live on the bottom, but so do most birds and insects. Birds and insects spend most of their time in and around the ground, plants and trees that are part of the atmospheres bottom structure. Well, the same is true of most fish. Water is their air.   It provides food, shelter and security.

The primary Northern California game fish that are consistently caught in open water (not near the bottom) are salmon(in the ocean), albacore, kokanee(a land locked salmon), trout(in lakes) and some sharks.

Fish at the Right Water Temperatures

In big Northern California lakes and reservoirs, the key factor in finding fish during the summer months is water temperature. Lakes stratify into three distinct layers with the coming of summer and stay that way until fall. The middle layer of water, called the thermocline, has a large concentration of dissolved oxygen, baitfish and therefore, trout, salmon and even bass. The thermocline, which provides the right temperature for trout and salmon metabolism, is down from 10 to 80 feet, depending on season and lake characteristics.

LAKE STRATIFICATION
Surface
Epilimnion Layer
Thermocline Layer
Oxygen and Baitfish Rich
Hypolimnion Layer
Bottom

Gauges for measuring water temperature at various depths are available for as little as $5-10. Below is a chart showing the temperatures where you are likely to find fish;

Species	Optimum Temperature	Temperature Range
Salmon	55°	44-58°
Trout(lake)	50	43-53
Trout(brown and rainbow)	55-60	44-75
Bass, striped	70-72	60-78
Bass, Largemouth	70-72	60-73
Bass, smallmouth	64-66	-
Panfish	-	64-76
Catfish	-	75-80

Fish Don't Like Direct Light

This is one reason why fishing drops off when the morning sun hits a lake. But, there are things you can do. For instance, if you're catching fish in a lake early in the day, try deeper down as the light increases. Or, if you're fishing a trout stream, work the shady side. This also applies to lake shores.

Teaching Kids How to Fish

My father died when I was a teenager. But, many times he shared his love of fishing with me. In the first edition of this book, I told a very personal fishing story. It was about how my youngest son came to know and love his grandfather's old lures and tackle box. This story was special to me, but not unique. Fishing brings families together. Teach your children how to fish. Do it for them and for yourself.

Kids and fishing just seem to be made for each other. It's hard to find a youngster that won't jump at the chance to "go fishing." A good starting age is 3 to 7 years old. And we're not just talking about boys going fishing with their fathers, or older brothers. Over a third of U.S. fishing licenses are sold to women. So a lot of girls learned to fish along the way, and fathers and mothers are teaching their daughters how to fish in record numbers.

It is not easy, but children can be "turned-off" to fishing if parents don't follow some simple guidelines. I've explained them beginning on the following page.

Know the Basics - Many parents, who aren't experienced anglers, find out the basics by going fishing with friends who are veteran anglers. And don't be proud. Ask questions. And fish for the same species, in the same type of waters, where you are planning on taking your youngster. A fishing guide is another alternative. He or she can teach both parents and youngsters, at the same time. They are listed in phone books and they advertise in outdoor publications. Be sure to ask for references, and explain what you expect to achieve on the trip.

Equipment - Youngsters fishing tackle should be easy to operate, light weight, "kid-sized" and somewhat durable. Most experts recommend a spincast reel. These are closed-faced reels that cast and retrieve easily and don't backlash(or tangle the line). One hint. These reels need a little tension on the line to retrieve properly. This is usually of no concern while retrieving in water where a lure or sinker provides the tension. But for "drive-way" practice casts and retrieves in store isles, the line right in front of the reel opening should be lightly squeezed between the index finger and thumb of the non-cranking hand. This provides the needed tension so that the line pick-up mechanism in the reel can function. Damage can result if this simple practice is not followed.

Older children, say 9-11, may want to start with an open-faced spinning reel. These are the kind used by most adults. Ask the dealer to explain how to operate them.

Match the spincast reel with a short pistal grip rod. Often this combination can be purchased as a package for as little as $10-20. A good rod length is $3\frac{1}{2}$ to 4 feet. Most reels have line already on them. 8-10 pound test line is the best.

A good, well-fitting life jacket is highly recommended, for shore, pier or boat fishing. Some kids might put up a fuss, but it's an easy battle to win, and you might just be preventing an unnecessary tragedy.

Practice - And I don't mean practice at the lake or stream. Practice at home, before going fishing. Concentrate on casting and retrieving. Practice plugs are available at tackle stores, or use a small lead sinker. Kneeling behind and slightly above the youngster might be useful on the first attempts. Pick out a target and make a game out of trying to land near it. If you're going to be bait fishing it might also be a good idea to "rig-up at home. Then when you get to the water, anxious kids can start fishing right away. For kids, I like to use a small snap swivel as the first item at the end of the line. This allows quick change of lures, and easy replacement of lost bait rigs that have been pre-tied, and stored in small sandwich bags.

Where to go - Some guidelines. Go close to home. Long drives are just too much for the nervous systems of little anglers. Choose a place where fish are abundant and easy to catch. The size of the fish is secondary. Good possibilities in the Bay Area are the fish-for-pay lakes like Merced, Del Valle, Chabot, San Pablo, Isabel and Parkway. These are well stocked and employees at the lake will provide up-to-date tips and hot spots. Bay piers are also a good possibility. Call first to assess the bite. In other parts of the North State, check for public information on recent trout plants. Recent plants are usually hot spots. Finally, shore anglers need an open shoreline. The only way to keep kids from casting into trees, is to have no trees within 100 yards.

Attitude - Simply stated; don't get upset when things go wrong. And they will go wrong. Just try to solve each problem as it comes along, and provide tons of encouragement. And, by all means, when a little guy or gal gets a fish-on, don't grab the rod and land it yourself. This advice seems stupid, but in the excitement of the moment, many well-meaning parents do this very thing. Let the child try bringing in the fish alone. Give calm advice, based on instructions you communicated earlier(maybe on the ride to the fishing grounds). After a few lost fish, fate will intervene and a fish will be landed. The laughing and cheers will be worth your commitment to patience. And your little one will be very proud.

Final Thoughts - Instill positive values in your children. For example, release undersized fish(a camera will capture the thrill of even a teenie first fish), and follow other fishing regulations. Don't litter. Don't trespass. Buy a fishing license for yourself. Kids under 16 don't need one. One last piece of advice. Bring lots of favorite foods and beverages. Little anglers get very hungry.

Casting

Casting is an integral part of most fishing activities. This is true whether you bait fish with a sliding sinker rig for trout in a lake, or live bait fish for striper on a party boat. And it's also true that better, more accurate casts, catch more fish.

Casting with spinning or spincast equipment is quite straightforward, but accurate casting takes some practice. Freshwater or saltwater conventional reel rigs are more difficult to master because of backlash, but good equipment and practice will pay off here too. Novice anglers should read up on the subject at the library and observe more experienced casters whenever possible.

Flycasting is different. In spinning or baitcasting the weight that is cast is concentrated in the lure or bait. And it is the weight that pulls line off the reel. But in flycasting, the offering is virtually weightless, and it is the fly line that is the weight. Flycasting is probably the most difficult casting skill to develop. A good book on the subject is "Fly Fishing From the Beginning."

Playing and Landing

A variety of fishing techniques are needed to entice a fish to bite or strike. Once this is accomplished, whether you've got a bass or a sturgeon on the other end of your line, there is a certain commonality in playing a larger fish. Here are the elements;

1. Pull the rod up and back forcefully to set the hook. Don't be tentative. Hold the reel handle firmly, so no line is given. After setting, adjust the drag, if necessary.

2. Hold the rod tip up when playing a fish. The rod butt should be held against the stomach area. Lower the rod tip and reel in, simultaneously. Pump the rod upwards to move the fish in. Then, again reel in on the down stroke. This rod "pumping" allows you to reel in when tension on the line and terminal tackle is not at its maximum.

3. Never give a fish slack. If it charges, reel in fast. Try to guide fish away from your boat with rod tip high. But, if the fish does get under your boat, put the rod tip down into the water to prevent line abrasion or twisting around the outdrive.

4. If your fish runs, let him go against the drag. That's what it's for. Then slowly bring him back by reeling in, or if necessary, using the pumping technique.

5. Keep the rod tip high while landing. This allows the rod to act as a shock absorber and prevents the chance of slack line. Net the fish from below and in front.

Catch and Release

There is a growing awareness among anglers that the fish resource is limited. And some anglers now feel that the ultimate fishing experience is not to "take a limit" but to catch and release as many fish as possible. Of course, no one should keep more fish than they can use, or keep a fish that they don't enjoy eating.

Obviously, catch and release is a personal decision. It's also a practice that can be and should be exercised on a selective basis. Sometimes a fish shouldn't be released - for example, a badly hooked, bleeding fish, or a small rockfish that has been brought up from 50 fathoms, and is dead on arrival. For some reason, I personally don't like to take fish that are about to spawn. I know this is somewhat irrational since it's absolutely true that whenever in a fishes lifecycle you take it, you're forever preventing that fish from spawning. But

I guess I just feel that when a fish has made it through all the hurdles and survived all the predators and all the hazards, that is has a right to spawn without me interferring. On the other hand, I don't mind taking fish that are in abundant supply or even those that are planted regularly.

When you do want to release fish, there are several things you can do to improve the chances for the fish;

1. **Use barbless hooks**(or flatten down barbs with a pliers) and **avoid fishing with bait**, if possible. If you do use bait, don't use a sliding sinker rig. Hooks with sliding sinker rigs are often very deep.

2. **Time is of the essence.** Play and release fish as rapidly as possible. A fish played gently for too long may be too exhausted to recover.

3. **Keep the fish in the water** as much as possible. A fish out of water is suffocating and, in addition, is twice as heavy. He may seriously injure himself if allowed to flop on the beach or rocks. Even a few inches of water under a thrashing fish acts as a protective cushion.

4. **Gentleness in handling is essential.** Keep your fingers out of the gills. Do not squeeze small fish...they can easily be held by the lower lip. Nets may be helpful provided the mesh does not become entangled in the gills. Hooks and lines catching in nets may delay release, so keep the net in the water.

5. **Unhooking.** Remove the hook as rapidly as possible with longnose pliers. If the fish is deeply hooked, cut the leader and leave the hook in. Be quick but gentle - do not roughly tear out hooks. Small fish are particularly susceptible to the shock of a torn-out hook.

6. **Reviving.** Some fish, especially after a long struggle, may lose consciousness and float belly up. Always hold the fish in the water, heading upstream. Propel it back and forth, pumping water through its gills. When it revives, begins to struggle and can swim normally, let it go to survive and challenge another fisherman.

Rods and Reels

How-to-catch each of the major sports fishes in Northern California is described in detail in this book. There are 19 of them in all. Rod and reel recommendations are made in each section. But, not only are the most desirable rod and reel combinations noted, but so are alternatives that often work just as well. So, happily, you don't need 19 rod and reel sets to enjoy all the fishing experiences in this book.

Often, one rod and reel is useful in several types of fishing. For example, a boat rod and conventional saltwater-sized reel can be used for salmon trolling, striper trolling, strugeon, halibut, lingcod and rock cod. This may even be over kill in some situations, since a lightweight spinning outfit can be used to troll or cast for average striper(6-10 pounds). This same light spinning out-fit can be used for trout(both lake and stream), bass casting, panfishing, even steelhead in smaller coastal streams. In fact, an angler doesn't even need a fly rod and reel to fly fish, but don't tell avid fly anglers this. A casting bobber on spinning equipment will deliver a fly. See Catching Trout(in streams). And talking about stream trout fishing, one hot item now is the mini-spinning outfit - a 5 foot rod and tiny reel. It's fun to use but spinners can also usually be delivered effectively using a 7 foot rod and normal sized reel filled with 4 pound test line.

Fortunately, rods and reels of good quality(not gold-plated, but good quality) are not that expensive. But, before considering a specialized rod and reel, first consider using what you've got on hand. Look at what others are using when you get to the water. I'm always surprised at the variety. Besides, the fish doesn't know what's on the other end of the line. Good line, tied well, a decent drag and know-how, will land most fish.

Knots, Hooks, Line and Swivels

A good fishing knot is one that stays tied and one that doesn't weaken the line too much. There are many knots that fit these criteria, but most veteran anglers use only one or two basic knots. The best overall knot is probably the improved clinch knot. It can be used to tie hooks to leaders, swivels to line, etc. There are two versions;

An often neglected item is the fishing hook. It's important to keep them sharp. Inexpensive little sharpeners are made just for this purpose. Both bait hooks and lure hooks get abused, in use, and in tackle boxes, so do sharpen them up regularly.

The designation system used in fishing hook sizing can be confusing for those who don't deal with it regularly;

. Large hooks(1/10 and up) increase in size as the number increases. (So a 4/0 is a larger hook than a 2/0).

. Small hooks(1 and down) decrease in size as the number increases. (So a 6 is a larger hook than a 10).

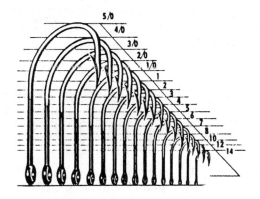

A leading hook manufacturer(Eagle Claw) makes the following hook size recommendations;

. Panfish: Bluegill   - 8 down to 12
            Crappie   - 4

. Bass: Smallmouth - 3/0 down to 4
            Largemouth - 8/0 down to 4
            Striped   - 3/0 up to 10/0

. Catfish: up to 5#   - 4 down to 12
            large   - 4 up to 8/0

. Trout: Rainbow   - 5 down to 14
            Brown   - 5 down to 14
            Steelhead   - 2 up to 6/0

. Salmon   - about 6/0

Good quality fishing line is a wise investment. And many anglers replace the line on all their reels at the beginning of each fishing season. Monofilament is appropriate for most fishing, and consider the fluorescent feature. It helps immensely in seeing where your bait and line are.

Swivels are available in a number of shapes and sizes. Their primary purpose is to prevent lure twist. Some models have eyes on both ends, while others, called snap swivels, feature a locking device on one end. It is very handy for quickly changing lures. However, the action of some finely tuned lures, like premium brand imitation minnow type lures, may be inhibited by using a snap swivel. Tie these lures directly to the line. One tip. Even the highest quality swivels, are very inexpensive. Cheap foreign swivels often fall apart, and sometimes don't swivel. So buy good quality.

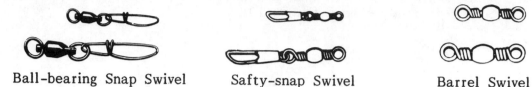

Ball-bearing Snap Swivel   Safty-snap Swivel   Barrel Swivel

Fish Locating Electronics

A sonar unit(either paper or video) is the eyes and ears of any angler operating from a boat. This device prints out a profile of the shape of the bottom and the shadows of bait schools and individual large fish. Actually, the flasher-type depth sounder provides the same information, but this equipment requires more experience and judgment to use effectively. Chart recorders are very helpful in both saltwater and bay bottom fishing for rock cod, lingcod, striper and strugeon and for freshwater bass and trout fishing. There's little doubt that the proper use of a boat mounted chart recorder gives the angler an edge-it allows him to "almost" see the fish.

Maps

First, let me emphasize that none of the maps included in this book(or in any fishing book, for that matter) are to be used for navigational purposes. Their only intent is to indicate where the fish can be found. Navigational maps for coastal and bay waters are available at marine and boating stores. These are published by the National Oceanic and Atmospheric Administration(U.S. Department of Commerce).

There are other good maps that are especially useful to anglers;

    U.S. Forest Service Maps - especially useful in determining which land is publicly owned.

    U.S. Geological Survey - good for detailed topographical features, and for locating out-of-the-way fishing spots.

    U.S. Bureau of Land Management - for streams and lakes in this agency's jurisdiction.

Park Scenic Maps - both federal and state parks publish maps that can be quite helpful.

Hal Shell's Delta Map - comprehensive map of the entire Delta waterways including facilities.

Topographical Maps - these are very useful for underwater lake terrain and mountain topography.

Regulations

Fishing regulations in California are simple and straightforward, but they are also detailed and specific. A Fish and Game Commission publication, "California Sport Fishing Regulations" is available free at any location where fishing licenses are sold. This is a fact-filled, well-organized brochure that has all you need to know about current regulations. Read it over and know the rules. I'm always bothered when I see a young child on a camping trip unknowingly violating regulations that are designed to protect the young fish. A stringer full of 10-12" dead stripers caught in the Delta in July is not the youngsters fault, but their uninformed parents.

Organizations and Publications

Some of the most active fishing organizations and some of the best publications for up-to-date Northern California fishing information are;

- Fishing & Hunting News
  Northern California Edition
  511 Eastlake Avenue E
  Seattle, WA 98109
  (206)624-2738

- The Fish Sniffer
  P.O. Box 930
  Elkgrove, CA 95624
  (916)685-2245

- California Angler Magazine
  179-C Roymar Rd.
  Oceanside, CA 92054
  (619)967-1952

- United Anglers of California
  1360 Neilsen Street
  Berkeley, CA 94702
  (415)526-4049

- California Striped Bass Assoc.
  P.O. Box 9045
  Stockton, CA 95208

California Angling Records

Athletes always say "records are made to be broken." Maybe that's **still** true of fishing records, too. Eighty percent(or 21 out of 26) of the records listed on this page were set in the 1970's and 1980's. Seven were set since January 1980!

Species	Weight (lb+oz)	Where Caught	Date
Albacore(tuna)	73-8	San Diego	Nov 82
Bass, largemouth	21-3½	Lake Casitas	Mar 80
smallmouth	9-1	Trinity Lake	Mar 76
Catfish, blue	36-13	Lake Jennings	Aug 77
channel	41	Lake Casitas	Aug 72
flathead	55	Colorado River	Apr 80
Halibut, California	53-8	Santa Rosa Island	May 75
Kokanee	4-13	Lake Tahoe	Aug 73
Lingcod	53	Trinidad	1969
Panfish, bluegill	2-10½	Lake Los Serranos	May 76
black crappie	4-1	New Hogan Lake	Mar 75
white crappie	4-8	Clear Lake	Apr 71
Rockcod, cabezon	23-4	Los Angeles	Apr 58
Salmon, chinook	88	Sacramento River	Nov 79
coho	22	Paper Mill Creek	Jan 59
Shad, American	7-4	American River	May 82
Shark, blue	231	Santa Cruz Island	Aug 74
bonito	298-8	Anacapa Island	Jul 70
thresher	527	San Diego	Oct 80
Steelhead*	27-4	Smith River	Dec 76
Striped Bass	65	San Joaquin River	May 51
Sturgeon	468	San Pablo Bay	Jul 83
Trout, brook	9-12	Silver Lake	Sep 32
brown	26-5	Lower Twin Lake	May 83
lake	37-6	Lake Tahoe	Jan 74
golden	9-8	Virginia Lake	Aug 52
rainbow*	27-4	Smith River	Dec 76

*Rainbow and steelhead are not separated

Introduction to "How to Catch..."

Many fishing books are jam packed with interesting, colorful information. But they have one glaring shortcoming. They never answer the question "how". Our purpose in the next 22 sections is to remedy this problem. So if you want to know "how to catch . . ." just look in the appropriate section. The explanations are simple, straightforward, complete and understandable. And the fish are in alphabetical order for easy reference. And here they are . . .

Abalone
Albacore
Bass(largemouth)
Bass(smallmouth)
Bass(striped)
Bluegill
Catfish
Clams
Crappie
Crawdads
Halibut
Kokanee
Lingcod
Rock Fish
Rock Crab
Salmon(in the Ocean)
Shad
Sharks
Steelhead and Salmon(in Rivers)
Sturgeon
Trout(in Streams)
Trout and Salmon(in Lakes)

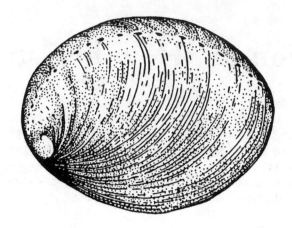

How to Catch...Abalone

Abalone is a rock-clinging, single-shelled creature that inhabits shoreline waters (especially where there are concentrations of rocks and kelp) all along the Northern California coast. It has a large, fleshy foot and sensory projections on its underside. Most all seaside gift shop browsers have seen an eye-catching display of abalone shells. And those who have ordered them on restaurant menus know how delicious it is. But it's possible for anyone, with some insight and a little luck, to enjoy catching, preparing and eating abalone. That's what this section and each of the other "How To Catch" sections is all about.

Fishing Techniques

There are three basic techniques for taking abalone;

1. Rockpicking - searching the rocky shore on foot.

2. Free diving - diving near shore with a snorkel only(no aqualung).

3. Scuba diving - diving with an aqualung.

North of Yankee Point(at Monterey), only rockpicking and free diving are allowed. So scuba divers are not permitted to take abalone anywhere along the Northern California coast from Monterey to Bodega Bay to Fort Bragg to Cresent City, near the Oregon border.

Rockpickers operate at low tides. Preferably a minus low tide and a calm ocean.

They start about an hour before the low tide and quit before the incoming tide threatens a soaking or being stranded away from shore.

The basic technique is to comb an area looking for abalone attached to rocks. Often it is best to feel under water in crevices and cracks that other rock-pickers have missed.

Free divers operate in the water. The wise ones in pairs, taking turns diving down to rocky bottoms in 5-30 feet of water. Abalone are pried off the rocks with a metal bar. Since this can fatally injure the abalone, it is best to be sure the abalone is of legal size before prying it off. Rockpickers must also make this judgment. To pry the abalone off the rock and avoid injuring it, slip the bar under the abalone. Then lift the handle end up, pushing the tip of the bar against the rock. This prevents injury to the abalone foot. If it is undersize, hold the abalone back on the spot where it was taken until it grabs hold itself.

Free diving lessons are available at selected locations along the coast. No one should attempt to free dive without proper instruction.

Tackle and Equipment

The equipment needed for rockpicking and free diving are an abalone iron(of legal dimension), a fixed caliper measuring gauge, a state fishing license, a catch bag(or at least a gunnysack), neoprene boots, neoprene gloves and an inflatable buoyancy vest. In addition, for free diving, you'll need a wet suit, hood, snorkel, mask, fins, knife(for escaping from kelp) and a weight belt.

Where to Fish

Abalone can be found all along the Northern California coast from Monterey to the Oregon border. Good areas are scattered all along between Santa Cruz and Fort Bragg. North from Fort Bragg to Westport are the best bets. Check with dive shops and experienced abalone rockpickers and divers for more specific information.

Cleaning and Cooking

Cleaning abalone is different from most other sea food, but it is not actually difficult. Insert the abalone iron between the meat and the shell, at the pointed end of the abalone. Now, pop out the meat. Next, trim away the flanged edges and all the intestines. A pot scrubber can then be used to rub off the black skin. Scrape off the suction cups with a knife. Now it's time to tenderize the meat. Before slicing, pound it with a big mallet. Then slice it 1/8 to 1/4 inch thick. Use the mallet again for a final tenderizing. The end of a bottle may also be used for tenderizing. Most people feel that the only way to prepare abalone is quick pan frying. Tenderized steaks are usually floured, or dipped in egg and sauteed over high heat for less than 1 minute on a side. Fry only enough to heat clear through and slightly brown.

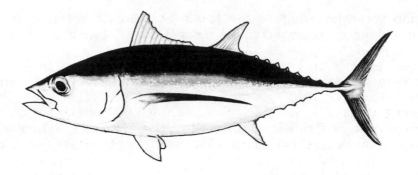

How to Catch...Albacore

Albacore, or long-finned tuna, often take commercial fishing boats a couple
of hundred miles from shore. Commercial boats stay out until their freezers
are full. Fortunately, there is a time each year when albacore come close enough
to shore(35-50 miles usually), so that sport fishermen can get in on the fun.
These fish migrate up the coast of California, typically hitting the waters off
Monterey and San Francisco about late August. Good fishing, following their
arrival, may last for as little as a week or two, or may extend for several months.

There are years when albacore fishing gets hot as close as ten miles from shore.
These are the only times most sport fishermen consider albacore fishing in their
own boats. At other times it's probably best to venture out on a well-equipped,
fast, large party boat especially rigged for albacore. Typically the boats leave
in the wee hours of the morning(about 3a.m.) and are back in port by 7p.m.
Cost ranges form $50 to $75. There are also overnight one day($125) and two
day($250) trips available.

Fishing Techniques

Trolling is the most popular technique for taking albacore. But, before we get
into trolling specifics, a word about where to troll. After all, it's a big ocean!
First, albacore congregate and feed in warmer water. Most experts look for
water in the 63-65°F range, with 60°F being the minimum. The second good
fish finder is bird activity. Birds actively pursuing bait fish means that albacore

may be doing the same thing. When birds are spotted, run the boat through the edge of the activity, not through the center. No need to chance scattering the bait fish and feeding albacore.

Albacore trolling is characterized by;

- . Trolling close to the boat(the theory goes that the wake looks to the albacore like a bait fish feeding frenzy). Put the lure right in the white water wake of the boat, about 50 to 70 feet behind the stern.

- . Fairly rapid boat speed(perhaps 7-10 knots) to move along the feathered or rubber-skirted jig at a good pace.

- . Party boat captains usually troll in square grids of about 20 minutes per leg until fish are located. A zig-zag pattern is also a good approach.

The other method of albacore fishing is used on party boats and some private boats, after a school of fish is located by trolling. The boat is stopped, and scoops of bait fish(usually anchovies) are tossed into the water to raise the albacore up to the surface. This technique is called chumming. Fishermen drift live bait near the surface. Since albacore move in schools, it's always a good idea for even private boats to try drift fishing after a trolling hook-up is landed. Frozen anchovies often work, even without chumming. Drift, facing the wind, so as not to put the rig under the boat. Casting out a Salas or similar jig can also work.

Tackle and Equipment

Albacore are big, fast, open-ocean sport fish. They are one of the most sought after game fish in California ocean waters. A good fish averages 15-30 pounds, with some ranging up to 40 pounds or more.

Essential equipment includes;

- . Large, iced, fish storage box(or cooler, or a plastic trash container) and a good-sized gaff.

- . a 6-6½ foot medium to heavy trolling rod(roller-tipped, a 4/0 to 6/0 size reel filled with at least 300 yards of 50-80 pound monofilament line. This heavy equipment is needed to quickly land the first fish, so chumming and drift fishing can begin before the school disappears.

- . For drift fishing, a light to medium action, fast-tapered, 7 foot rod mated to a conventional reel capable of holding 300 yards of 25-30 pound test line is suggested.

Lure and Bait

The most productive albacore jigs;

Description: Chrome plated or abalone-pearl head and a natural feather or vinyl skirt.

Colors: Dark colors(like black, purple, green and yellow) during darker periods. Light colors(like red and white, red and yellow) in bright periods.

Size: 4-10 ounces.

The preferred bait is live anchovies. The best are 3-4 inches long, green backed (they seem to be friskier), with no scale toss, or other signs of deterioration. For surface fishing, hook the anchovy through a gill cover. For deeper action, nose hook the anchovies and use a 1 or 2 ounce rubber-core sinker about 30 inches up the line. Use the sharpest hooks money can buy. Nickle-plated Gamakatsu hooks in No. 4 and No. 6 are a good choice.

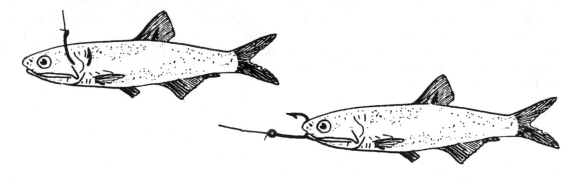

Where to Fish

It varies. But two of the better albacore grounds are Soap Run and Pioneer Sea Mount. These are both 35-55 miles out, off the coast of Davenport.

Cleaning and Cooking

Albacore is most often steaked. Make sure the dark flesh is removed from each piece.

Like salmon, albacore has a relatively high fat content. Also, like salmon, the most popular way to prepare it is barbecuing. The smoke seems to add to the flavor. Poached albacore tastes like canned tuna, but even better. Poached albacore may be stored in a refrigerator for several days, or frozen for a short time. Sauteing albacore is also popular. These strong tasting fish work well in recipes with spicy or tomato-based sauces.

LARGEMOUTH BASS

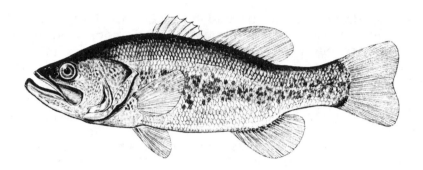

How to Catch...Largemouth Bass

The largemouth bass is one of Northern California's most popular warmwater game fish. It's found in nearly all suitable lakes, sloughs, farm ponds and most of the lakes featured in this book. But these fish are not native to California. It is believed that the Northern-strain largemouths were first planted in California in 1879. The locale was Crystal Springs Reservoir, in San Mateo Co.

In 1959, Florida-strain largemouths were first planted in some Southern California lakes. This strain reaches much greater weight than the Northern-strain. World class Floridas are in the 20 pound plus range, whereas 10-12 pound Northern-strain are trophy size. But now, Northern-strain, Florida-strain and hybridized populations are found in many Northern California lakes. Experts say that it is almost impossible to tell the strain of a caught fish since the young can exhibit the features of either parent's strain.

But it's certain that Florida-strain fish are making an impact on NorCal bass fishing records. The states record(21 lb.- 3½ oz.) was taken at Lake Casitas in Southern California in March 1980. But Northern California anglers are gaining. In December 1984 Harold Nakutsu caught a 15 lb.- 13½ oz. bass in Lake Amador to break the NorCal record. And then in April 1986, Tim Kimura set a new NorCal record with a 17 lb. - 1¼ oz. fish, again at Amador. By the way, the Florida-strain bass grow faster, live longer, spawn earlier, but are more difficult to hook.

If you want to know more about California bass fishing than is presented here, see **Bass Fishing in California**(Marketscope Books, 1987.)

Fishing Techniques

Bass fishing is best during the spring and fall. But ironically, probably most people fish for bass in the warm summer months. Why not? Family vacations fit best when the kids are out of school. And the weather is comfortable "out on the lake." Don't get me wrong. Bass are caught in the summer. But it takes more effort, since the fish are usually down deeper.

The basic technique used in bass fishing is casting and retrieving a plug, a spoon, spinnerbait, a jig, a plastic worm or a live bait. Of course, the retrieve approach must match the lure. All types of casting equipment can and is used, including baitcasting, spinning, spincasting and flycasting. More on this in the Tackle and Equipment section.

Successful bass fishing centers around the answer to three questions. Where to cast? How to cast? What to cast? Here are some guidelines;

- Bass are almost always on or near the bottom, or near underwater cover like a fallen tree. The "bottom" could be near shore(say in the spring) in 2 feet of water, or it might be in 40 feet of water on the slope of a sunken island.

- Largemouth prefer to be near structures, whether it be a rocky fall-off, a sunken log, a weedbed, standing timber, a rocky point, etc.

- Largemouth bass prefer a water temperature of about 70°F. This means that in the spring and fall, bass are likely to be nearer shore, in shallow seventyish water. When the surface temperature is well above 70°, bass hold out deeper, but do make feeding forays into shallower water, primarily at night.

- If you(or someone else) catches a bass at a particular spot, and the lake temperature conditions don't change, the spot will probably produce more bass.

- At an unfamiliar lake, seek information about "good spots" from other anglers, bait shops, marinas, etc.

- Cast your offering so it lands near structures, or will be retrieved near structures. For example, put it next to a pile of boulders that are partially submerged, or right by a fallen tree. Retrieve parallel to a submerged log, not across it. Try inlets where streams flow into lakes.

- Retrieve slowly. Seventy to eighty percent of the time, a slow retrieve is best. But, if it's not working, don't hesitate to try a rapid retrieve. A combination may be in order also. For example, a few quick turns of the reel handle just after the offering lands(to get the bass's attention), followed by a slow retrieve.

. Retrieve everything, except surface plugs, near or on the bottom. Since the bass are on the bottom, you've got to put your offering on the bottom. Afterall, we live and eat on the "bottom" of the atmosphere, so doesn't it seem natural for some fish(particularly bass) to live and eat on the bottom of their "atmosphere."

. With plastic worms and jigs, "feel" the bottom during your retrieve. No doubt this practice will result in some lost rigs, but it will also result in more bass. Using snagless, or near snagless, offerings as described later, will minimize loss.

. Cast quietly. In fact, fish quietly. Minimize engine noise, oar lock noise, "scraping tackle box along the floor of the boat" noise, and so on. Bass fishing is akin to stalking.

. Catchable-sized bass feed mostly on smaller fish(like shad, minnows, bluegill, etc.), crawdads and worms. This means that offerings that are successful look and act like swimming fish, moving crawdads or worms.

. At times, bass strike out of reflex action. Sometimes they attack an offering the instant it hits the water. At these times, you could be casting anything and it would work.

. Many professional bass anglers feel that bigger bass come on bigger bait.

Lures and Bait

Many an otherwise sane person is driven absolutely crazy by the immense selection of bass plugs, jigs, spoons, spinnerbaits, plastic worms. etc. And professional bass-tournament fishermen seem to own at least one of everything, based on the size of the tackle boxes in their boats!

But, don't despair. You don't need one of everything to take bass. Largemouth bass offerings fall into 7 categories;

1. Crankbaits   5. Jigs

2. Surface Plugs   6. Plastic Worms

3. Spinnerbaits   7. Live Bait

4. Spoon Jigs

It's probably a good idea for a serious bass angler to have a sampling of the basic offerings in each category, but that isn't even necessary. For example, some bass fishing experts say that one or two types account for more bass than all the others combined. These two are plastic worms and spinnerbaits.

Crankbaits

Crankbaits are a broad category of lures, mostly plugs, that get their name because the reeling speed determines how much the lure dives, vibrates and wobbles. Most of these lures have plastic, fish-shaped bodies. They also have a plastic tip, the size, shape and angle of which imparts action to the reeled lure. Many have 2 sets of treble hooks which provide a good chance to hook a striking bass. But this also increases the chance of snags, so crankbaits are best used in open water. Crankbaits work, to one degree or another, almost all year long in such structures as sloping points, along shorelines, in shallow flats, etc.

Crankbaits either float at rest, sink slowly or sink rapidly. The most common way to fish these lures is to first jig it for a moment before beginning the return. Then reel fast to get the lure to the bottom. Now slow down enough to either drag the lure along the sloping bottom or bump it along, or return steadily right over the bottom. Crankbaits are designed to be fished parallel to the shoreline so you can keep the lure near the bass, and at the prescribed depth for the longest time.

Popular bass crankbaits include Bomber Model A's, Rapala Fat Rap and Storm Wiggle Wart. Shad and crawdad styles are popular.

Surface Plugs (and Stickbaits)

Surface plugs are top-water lures that simulate a sick or injured baitfish, frog or other creature. They float both when still and when retrieved. Most surface plugs have an action designed into them using blunt ends, propellers, dished-faces, etc. The proper retrieve for most of these is slow, erratic and stop-and-go. But before retrieving, many anglers will just let it sit in the target area for up to a minute or two, just twitching it, to send out vibrations and small ripples around it. Popular surface plugs include Devil's Horses, Rebels and Rapalas.

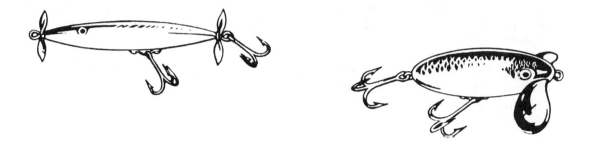

There is another class of surface plugs called stickbaits that are unique because they don't have any action built into them. Probably the most famous of these is the Zara Spook. The action needed to make a stickbait work must come from the skill of the angler. This takes several hours of practice to develop. Articles and bass books can be found at your local library to show you how to do it. The reading and the practice may be worth it because stickbaits have one profound advantage over other surface plugs. They can be kept in the target area longer because very little forward motion is required to give them the action needed. So a stickbait in skilled hands may catch more fish than other surface plugs.

The prime season for surface plugs is in the springtime spawning season when bass are in shallow water, especially in early mornings and late evenings. They are also good in summertime, in shallow water, after dark.

Spinnerbaits

Spinnerbaits are one of the most productive of all bass catching lures and are simple to cast and retrieve. They are good all year, especially in water up to 10 feet deep. Use them along brushy structures, in flooded trees or fallen trees. Most spinnerbait designs are semi-weedless so hangups are not a constant concern. Veteran anglers vary the return to change depth and action, but in most cases the slower the retrieve the better.

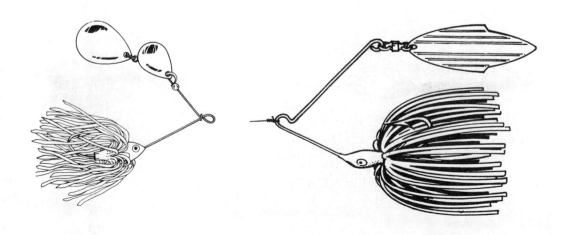

Here are some tips. The best, all around colors are probably white or chartreuse (yellowish). Spinnerbaits with two easily rotating blades seem to produce better. Spinnerbaits can be hopped along the bottom like a jig. In this style of fishing, blades that flutter freely on the downfall bring strikes. The size of spinnerbaits should approximate the length of the bait fish in the area. Skirts can be trimmed to accomplish this.

Now, the best tip of all. Add a plastic worm or pork rind on the hook of the spinnerbait. It produces more strikes from bigger bass. Probably because it keeps the lure up in the water, even with a slower retrieve.

Spooning

Jigging a spoon is a little-practiced largemouth technique, that is easy and effective. It's a great method to take bass from late autumn through early spring. That's when largemouths seek warm water down deep in Northern California reservoirs. It can also work in mid summer when bass go deep to find water cooler than surface temperatures.

A wobbling spoon is dropped down over the side of the boat, and then raised up and fluttered down at whatever depth the bass are at. The more flutter the better on the down drift. Work the jig in about a 3-5 foot, up and down range. Hopkin's 75 and Haddock Structure Spoons in about the 1/2-3/4 ounce range are about right. Fish can be taken in depths between 30-60 feet with this approach.

Jigging

Jigging, typically with a skirted leadhead jig, is somewhat more complicated than spoon-jigging, but it is a very productive technique. The jig is cast out or flipped out(more on this later) and then allowed to drop to the bottom. The most common retrieve is to skip the jig along the bottom in short, sharp jerks. Imagine you're dragging the jig along the bottom from a drifting or steadily trolled boat. That's about how you want your jig to act. Most strikes occur on the initial drop or on the ensuing flutter downs. Garland Spider Jigs and Haddock Kreepy Crawlers are popular.

Weedless Jig(with pork rind)

Non-weedless Jig

The most famous jig rig in Northern California bass waters is the "pig-n-jig." It's a 3/8 to 1/2 ounce, skirted jig(usually dark colored, like brown) with a weedless hook. A pork rind(or plastic trailer) is put on the hook. The rind makes it look more like a crawdad and also slows the rigs descent. When you move the Pig'n Jig off the bottom, don't just let it drop, let it down and be alert for a take. Keep slack out of your line to feel the strike and watch your line for unnatural movement.

Plastic Worms

Some people claim that each year more largemouth bass are taken on plastic worms than on all other artificial lures combined. This could well be true. Plastic worms do have several special advantages over other lures;

1. They can be fished at all depths of water.
2. They have outstanding action at different retrieve speeds.
3. Weedless rigging is a snap.
4. They're inexpensive, so anglers don't mind risking them in heavy cover.
5. They can be rigged in different ways for different situations. For example, in shallow spring spawning waters, they can be fished weightless. They can also be rigged with a dropper or a sliding sinker.

Here are three popular rigging styles;

Texas Style Rig

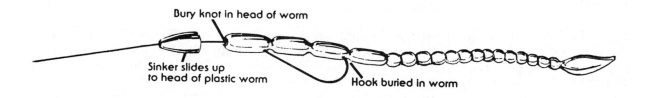

Bury knot in head of worm

Sinker slides up
to head of plastic worm

Hook buried in worm

Carolina Style Rig

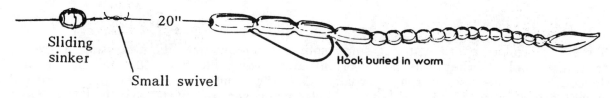

Sliding
sinker

20"

Small swivel

Hook buried in worm

Dropper/Dual Weedless Hook Rig

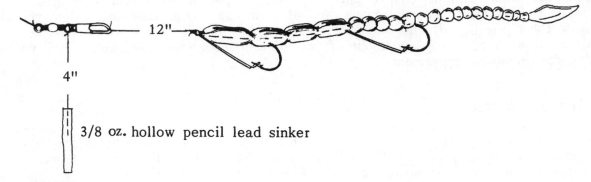

12"

4"

3/8 oz. hollow pencil lead sinker

Plastic worms(from 4-6" long) are worked along the bottom, much the same as in jigging. Work them slowly and erratically, like a night crawler twisting and drifting in the current. Dark colors, like purple and brown are most productive. Plastic worms can also be used for vertical jigging, like spooning.

Live Bait

Live bait bass fishing isn't all that common anymore. That's strange, in a way, because live bait was the only way bass were caught before plugs, spinnerbaits and all the other artificials came along. For instance, I have several live frog harnesses in my collectables. It holds the little guy in a swimming posture and would be great for casting and retrieving a frog without putting a hook through it. I've never even thought of using it.

But, other live bait are a different matter. Especially live crawdads. These critters are the way to go it you want to catch a really big largemouth bass. Here's one way to rig them;

18"

Some anglers prefer to just put some splitshot up the line about a foot or two from the hook. Others use no sinker at all. Use a #6, 8 or 10 sized bait hook, depending on the size of the crawdad. Cast them out gently. Let them sink and slowly crawl them along the bottom. When you see a twitch, that is the largemouth picking up the crawdad. As the fish moves off with the bait, the belly will come out of your line. Let the bass run a few feet and then set the hook hard. Don't allow any slack in your line when playing the bass. Fish rocky points, dropoffs and ledges. Spring is the best time to catch the lunkers on live crawdads.

Casting and Flipping

Accuracy is the measure of a good cast. Consistently accurate bass casters will hook more fish. Besides the traditional overhand cast, often a sidearm or even a underhand cast is called for to reach the target(when casting under an overhanging branch, for example) and to gently put the offering on the water. The three keys to accurate casting are practice, practice and practice.

Flipping(or Flippin') is a specialized casting technique. It's used to delicately put a jig or plastic worm on the water, especially near or in heavy cover. Spring-time shallow water bassing is prime flipping time. In elementary terms, the standing angler strips line off the reel, much like a fly angler, as the offering swings from the rod tip like a pendulum. On a forward swing the jig is flipped out and gently "put" on the water. Accuracy is critical as is an almost ripple-free landing. Weedless offerings are a rule. And in order to fight the bass in close and keep it out of cover, heavy equipment is used. Specialized flipping rod(about 7½ feet) is matched with 15-25 pound test line.

Tackle and Equipment

Today, many bass anglers use what is known in the trade as a bass boat. These boats were popularized in Bass Derbys. They are about 16-20 feet long, with pedestal seats, large outboard motors, an electric trolling motor(used for maneuvering, not trolling), several depth finders, a fish box, flashy-sparkling finish and on and on.

These boats are fun and functional, but the good news is that you don't need one to catch your share of bass. The bad news is that successful bass fishing probably does require some kind of boat that can be manuevered along an irregular shoreline. Many kinds of boats will do, from an inflatable to a canoe, to a dingy, to a row boat, to an aluminum boat, to a small stern-drive cruiser. Shore fishing for bass is possible. And some lakes, like San Pablo have good shore bass angling. But, covering very much promising structures at most lakes, on foot, is difficult.

To find promising bass territory, during all seasons, you'd best be equipped with maps of the lake, a thermometer that works well under water and a depth sounder. A flasher type will do, but a graph recorder is preferred.

Now for the tackle itself. Here, there is a great deal of lattitude. The possibilities include;

- Spinning equipment - 6-7 foot, light to medium action spinning rod. Open-faced reel with 10-12 pound monofilament line.

- Spincasting equipment - 5-6 foot pistol-grip, light to medium rod. Closed-faced spinning reel with 10-12 pound monofilament line.

- Baitcasting equipment - 5-6 foot pistol-grip, light to medium rod(can be used with spincasting reel). Baitcasting reel(some have magnetic anti-backlash mechanisms) with level-wind feature, star drag and 10-12 pound monofilament line.

What lures to use with these rods and reels? Beginners and once-in-a-while anglers should probably have a good selection of spinnerbaits, crankbaits and a surface plug or two. These are the easiest to retrieve with good action, and catch a lot of fish. A few wobbly spoons for spoon jigging in deep water are also handy. More experienced anglers wouldn't be without a good selection of plastic worms and leadhead jigs.

Professional bass anglers often put scent formulas on all their lures. It adds attracting odors and covers up human odors. Next to vibration, bass probably respond most to odor. This is an inexpensive way to improve your chances. Tests indicate that the color of ones lure is also important in producing strikes, depending on the water clarity. There's a new electronic instrument called a Color-C-Lector on the market that tells anglers which color offerings to use at a given depth in a particular water clarity. Results have been promising. It's worth looking into.

Cleaning and Cooking

Bass can be scaled, gutted and beheaded. But, many prefer to fillet them. This is the easiest way to remove the scales and skin. Any muddy flavor is in the skin.

Bass is mild and flaky. It can be cooked in a variety of ways including sauteing, broiling, poaching, baking and frying. But, in any case, do remove the skin before cooking.

Where to Fish

The top largemouth lakes in Northern California are highlighted in the Lake Section of this book. But don't overlook farm ponds, irrigation ditches and sloughs near home.

How to Catch...Smallmouth Bass

Smallmouth bass are plentiful in many Northern California reservoirs and rivers. Smallmouths are similar, in many respects, to largemouths. But they are also different in some ways that are important to the smallmouth bass angler.

Smallmouths, according to the best historical information, were planted in the Napa River and Alameda Creek in 1874. Following this introduction to California waters, smallmouths were soon released in many other NorCal streams and rivers. They flourished. The addition of dams on these free-flowing waterways restricted the movement of smallmouths, but did not inhibit their successful adaptation. In fact, as NorCal reservoirs aged, it favored the smallmouth over the largemouth. Smallmouths prefer open, rocky shoreline areas and clear water, which is just what's left after the brush, trees and other organic matter decomposes in a newly flooded reservoir.

The California record smallmouth was caught in 1979, at Trinity Lake. It weighed 9 lb.- 1 oz. This is monster size for a smallmouth. Anything over 4 pounds is bragging size. Many smallmouth anglers insist that they're better fighters, pound for pound, than largemouths. And for those who prefer stream fishing for trout, smallmouth provide another flowing-water fishing alternative.

The smallmouth, or "bronzeback" is easily identified by its brownish, almost bronze cast, with vertical dark bars. And in contrast with the largemouth, the upper jaw does not extend beyond the eye, and the dorsal fin has a very shallow notch.

Fishing Techniques

The approaches used for smallmouth fishing have much in common with largemouth angling. But there are critically important differences. It's these differences that this section highlights.

Tackle: Most smallmouth bass anglers scale down their line and lures to match the smaller size of the bronzeback. 6 and 8 pound test monofilament is typical, but largemouth rods and reels are used, with several exceptions. For example, fly rodding for smallmouth in rivers and streams with popping bugs and streamers is great sport. And some anglers use ultralight spinning equipment.

River Fishing: The overriding rule is to fish for smallmouth in the same way you would for stream trout. Stream bass prefer undercut banks, tangles and large boulders in midstream. Walk in an upstream direction to fish smaller streams. But you can float larger rivers like the lower Feather. Cast your offering above the target and allow it to flow to the target area. Try to match the local food supply, be it helgrammite, crawdad, or even lamprey eels. Small minnow imitation plugs, like Rapalas and Rebels that float at rest and shallow-dive on retrieve are good stream producers, as are streamers and poppers.

Habitat: Lake smallmouth are most often found over rocky points, over submerged gravel bars and near shale bank drop-offs. But coves and waters with stumps showing just above the water can also produce, in lakes like Trinity. Smallmouths prefer water that is somewhat cooler(mid-60's) than largemouths, so they spawn deeper(say 8 to 15 feet) and sooner than largemouths in the same waters. Cast surface lures early and late in the day, work plastic worms and jigs along the bottom and use crankbaits and spinnerbaits at different speeds and depths next to cover.

Bait and Lures

Baits are proportionally more productive for smallmouth than for largemouth. Department of Fish and Game creel census checks show that minnows are the best overall bait for smallmouths. Anglers often fish them with a small split shot about a foot above the bait hook, using a bobber. Other productive baits include crawdads, nightcrawlers, helgrammites and crickets. One caution. Crickets are not allowed in some lakes. But the whole array of artificials also produce smallmouths. Cast surface lures early and late in the day. Work plastic worms and jigs along the bottom and use crankbaits, spinners and spinnerbaits at different speeds and depths next to cover. Shad and minnow immitations are good crankbaits. The Gitzit, a small, lead-head jig with a plastic tail, is a very effective smallmouth lure.

When and Where to Fish

Shasta and Trinity Lakes are probably the premier smallmouth fisheries in the state. These lakes are at their peak for larger fish in February and March. A little farther south, some of the best smallmouth waters are Almanor, Black Butte, Collins, Folsom, Oroville and Pardee. In the Bay Area, Putah Creek, the Russian River and Lake Berryessa are good. Pine Flat, New Melones, Don Pedro and Lake Nacimiento have their spring peak in March and April. The lower Feather River is good smallmouth water, especially in April and May when flow limits are often low(in the 2500-4000 CFS range).

Cleaning and Cooking

See Largemouth Bass Section of this book.

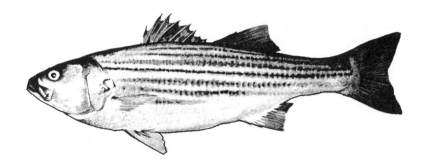

How to Catch...Striped Bass

One could write a book, and several people have, on the subject of striper fishing. This is the case because many techniques are used to catch stripers, depending on the location, the season of the year and the preferences in approach of different anglers. Our purpose here is to present the basics of the most successful approaches.

Striped bass were first introduced to California from the East coast, in 1879, near Martinez. Twenty years later, the commercial catch alone was averaging well over one million pounds per year. In 1935, commercial fishing was stopped because of the dwindling population. Currently, the striper population is good, but not nearly as good as it was 20 years ago.

The life cycle of the striper is important to be aware of because it has much to do with when and where to fish. Stripers spawn in the fresh waters of the Sacramento(from Sacramento to Colusa) and San Joaquin(between the Antioch Bridge and the Middle River) Rivers from about April to mid-June. After spawning, these fish move back down into saltwater, or the brackish waters of the San Pablo and San Francisco Bays. Stripers move back up into the Delta starting in September and these early arrivals winter over for the spring spawn. Striped bass range in size up to 40 pounds, or more. The average catch is probably 6-10 pounds. What this all means, as far as where the stripers are at any given season, is summarized in the table on the following page.

The stripers habits and lifecycle, of course, are all separate from the striper fishing that exists in several reservoirs(e.g. San Luis, New Hogan). Impoundment populations exist because of planting programs of young stripers, or through young fish migrations through aquaducts.

Table: Prime Fishing Locations for Striped Bass

Location	J	F	M	A	M	J	J	A	S	O	N	D
Ocean						X	X	X				
S.F. Bay						X	X	X	X	X		
Delta	X	X	X	X	X	X			X	X	X	X

Trolling

Trolling for stripers is probably the most popular technique. It allows you to cover a fairly wide area, if you're not sure where the fish are. Trolling is also suggested if the tides are not favorable. That is, the best striper fishing usually occurs on a large(greater than 5.0 feet) incoming tide, after a low, low tide(say 2-3 feet, or even minus). If these tide conditions don't exist, trolling may be the best bet.

The key to successful striper trolling is to keep your offering near the bottom. Most often the bass are laying close to the bottom. The most notable exception to this is probably lake striper, where surface trolling is often productive. Of course, the main problem with trolling on or near the bottom is snags. But many experienced striper trollers look at losing lures to snags as part of the cost of successful fishing. The truth is that if the stripers are on the bottom, that's where you've got to troll or else you'll just be wasting fuel.

Often in the Delta and Bays, the stripers are in 8-25 feet of water. In these depths, it's important to get your offering well back behind the boat. The engine noise and wake spooks the fish, but if you're out far enough(say 50-140 yards) from the boat, the bass have time to return before the lure passes through their area.

The best trolling speed is 3-4mph. Once your rig is out, check the tip of your rod. It should be twitching constantly. This is the action from your lure. Adjust the boat speed to get this effect.

The rig you troll depends a lot on the depth of water you're trolling in. Use the rig that keeps your offering near the bottom. In shallow water(8-10 feet), a deep diving plug, spoon or jig can be tied directly to the line or attached using a snap swivel. In deeper water(10-20 feet), use one of the two rigs shown on the following page:

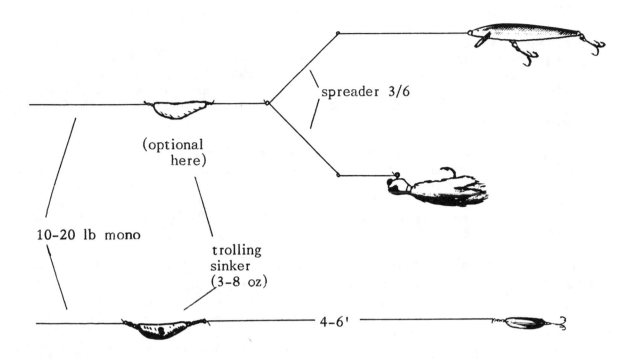

spreader 3/6

(optional
here)

10-20 lb mono

trolling
sinker
(3-8 oz)

4-6'

Deep Troll

For this type of trolling(say in the deep water channel of the Sacramento, or San Joaquin Rivers), if this is where your sonar tells you the fish are, you'll need to use diving planes, lead core line or downriggers. This type of equipment and approach is described in the Ocean Salmon and Lake Trout and Salmon Sections of this book.

The most popular trolling offerings are;

- Rebel, Rapala and Bomber lures(5-6 inches, 3 treble hooks, jointed, deep-diving, minnow-type plugs).

- Spoons(Pet, Hopkins, Kastmaster, size 3-4 inches).

- Bug Eye Jigs(2-3 oz.) - used on short leader or spreader to provide depth.

Set the drag on your reel just firm enough to prevent line from being taken out. Set the clicker in the "on" position. A singing clicker means a strike. The trolling action will have set the hook. Tighten down slightly on the drag before playing the fish.

Bait Fishing

Bait fishing can be done from a boat or from shore, although it is probably more productive from a boat(because more promising areas can be reached). As with trolling, bait fishing is best on a big changing tide. Fish often feed on the edge of drop-offs at these times. Fish the upstream edge of an incoming tide and the downstream edge on an outgoing tide. The edge of a shallow flat or sandbar is often good.

Boat anglers usually anchor and then cast out a sliding sinker rig with a big bait hook. Stripers aren't shy so a partially visible hook is no problem. The reel is left in the free spool position. Watch the tip of your rod at all times. Point your rod at the fish and play out 5-10 feet of line on the slightest nibble. Next, the fish will hit hard. Set the hook solidly by raising the rod to a vertical position quickly.

Both shore and boat anglers should use enough lead on the rig to prevent the current from drifting it.

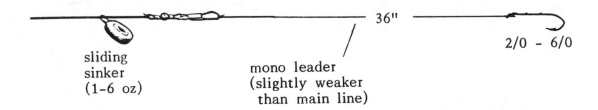

sliding
sinker
(1-6 oz)

36"

mono leader
(slightly weaker
than main line)

2/0 - 6/0

Popular striped bass baits include threadfin shad, anchovies, sardines, shiners, bloodworms, mudsuckers, bullheads, ghost shrimp and grass shrimp. Local bait shops will know which are most effective depending on location and season of the year. Live bait fish are hooked just below the dorsal fin, with the hook entering on one side and exiting on the other side of the fish. Once a live bait fish dies, the hook may be put in more securely, often with the leader secured to the tail by a half-hitch knot. Dead bait fish are often mutilated, or butterflied(opened vertically from throat to tail, folded over and then threaded through the curve of the hook several times) to put blood and oil into the water. For large sardines, fillet off a side flank. Cut it in half for enough bait for 2 hooks. For bloodworms, some experts suggest always keeping the hook tip covered with worm.

Casting

Casting for striped bass can be done from shore, from a boat or in the surf.

In tidal waters, casting is most productive on rapid, incoming tides. And like largemouth bass casting, it is often best to cast around and about structures such as bridge columns. ½ oz. Hair-Raisers, Cordell Spots and Lucky 13's are good.

In lakes, feeding birds are a key to stripers feeding on shad near the surface. Surface plugs(shad patterns) and ½ oz. Krocodiles or Kastmasters are effective.

Surf casters also depend on the feeding birds to tip off the location of the stripers. Common offerings are Rebel and Rapala lures.

Surf, Drift and Pier Fishing

Surf fishing is a popular approach for taking stripers along the Pacific coast, especially from the Golden Gate Bridge south to Half Moon Bay. Drift fishing is used to catch striped bass in San Francisco and San Pablo Bay. Pier fishing at several San Francisco and San Pablo Bay piers and particularly at Pacifica Pier, can be productive for stripers.

Each of these three techniques is described in detail in separate secions of this book.

Tackle and Equipment

Striper fishing can be done with a wide variety of tackle. Light weight black bass tackle can be used for casting or bait fishing. Medium weight spinning equipment, or free spool/star drag conventional reel-light action rods are used for trolling. Light spinning equipment can also be used for trolling. Some feel this is the most exciting way to take stripers in the 4-12 pound range.

Where to Fish

See the San Francisco Bay, Central Valley River and Lake Sections of this book.

Cleaning and Cooking

Smaller stripers are usually filleted. Large ones(above say 10 pounds) can be steaked. Striped bass fillets or steaks are white, mild in flavor, low in fat and especially good eating. Barbecuing, broiling, poaching, baking and frying are all good approaches.

How to Catch...Bluegill

Bluegills are the most abundant panfish in California waters. They're in virtually all warm water lakes in Northern California. These fish are fun to catch and are very enjoyable eating. And in many locations, they are abundant, so there is no need to feel guilty about taking them. They reproduce with great success and heavy populations can crowd out large sportfish.

Bluegill angling is easy and relaxing fishing. And it is especially enjoyable for youngsters. Give them a rod and reel, a can of worms and a little dock and they're set for hours of fun and adventure.

Finding Bluegills in a Lake

The easiest time to find bluegills is when they spawn in shallow water in spring (March-April-May). They'll be in 4-6 feet of water over sand or gravel bottoms. Be careful not to spook them if the water is clear.

In summer, bluegills behave like bass, moving to submerged channels, under docks, over bars, to weed-beds or drop-offs. It's at these times that it may be necessary to fish 10-20 feet down. A drifting, rowed or trolled boat with baits suspended at various depths can often find them. Bluegills are always in schools, so when you find one, you've found a bunch. Any type of fishing tackle (spinning, spincasting, baitcasting, cane pole) is fine.

Bait Fishing

This is probably the most popular approach especially for kids. Some of the best baits are redworms, cricketts and small grasshoppers. Commercial dough-type baits also work. A bobber is most often used, to keep the bait off the bottom and to signal a bite. From boat, shore, or dock you can use a bobber rig;

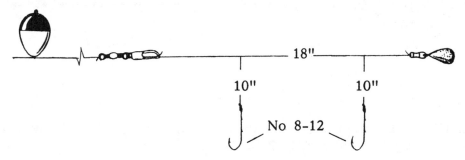

From a boat or dock you can use the same bobber rig or take it off and fish straight below the pole or rod tip.

Still fishing, or bait fishing for bluegills might be somewhat of a misnomer. Most experts agree that a slight movement of your bait is desirable. With any rig, flick the rod tip frequently to move your bait. Another principle is to change depths, if action is slow. Frequently, large bluegills are down deeper than most bobber anglers suspect.

Fly Fishing

Flycasting for bluegills is enjoyable and productive. A medium action, $7\frac{1}{2}$-$8\frac{1}{2}$ foot rod is suggested, but any will do. A wide variety of offerings will produce depending on the lake, the time of year and the time of day;

.   Panfish poppers - swim them slowly along in a stop and go fashion.

.   Rubber or plastic-legged spiders.

.   Mosquitos, Ants, Wooly Worms, Black Gnats(in size 10 or 12).

.   Bucktail streamers, size 8.

.   Nymphs(black and white, white, brown, etc.).

.   Indiana spinners(2 blades, #8 hook).

A casting bobber is a small bobber, usually made of clear plastic that is attached to monofilament line. Because of its weight(some allow you to let in water to make it even heavier) it allows anglers to cast poppers, flies, etc., using spinning, spincasting or baitcasting equipment. So you can enjoy "fly fishing" without having to use a flyrod and reel.

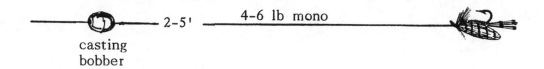

casting
bobber

Where to Fish

Bluegills can be found in just about any waters holding bass or other warm-water species. See the Lake Fishing Section of this book.

Cleaning and Cooking

Since bluegills are small, most people clean them in the traditional way. Scale them by rubbing a knife or scaling tool from the tail of the fish towards the head. Next, cut open the belly, starting from the anus, and remove the guts. Finally, cut off the head. Rinse them off and they're ready for the pan.

An alternative is to fillet them. This yields small fillets, but eliminates skin and bones in the cooked fish. See instructions on filleting in the Fish Cleaning Section of this book.

Sauteing the whole fish or individual fillets is most popular. See Crappie Section for an excellent recipe.

WHITE CATFISH

CHANNEL CATFISH

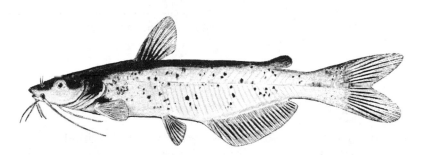

How to Catch...Catfish

Catfish are widespread and abundant in Northern California lakes, rivers, sloughs, canals and farm ponds. And despite their unappetizing appearance, and somewhat negative image, catfish are very good eating(catfish are not as difficult to clean as one might suspect, either). The delicious meals provided by catfish are attested to by the existence of hundreds of catfish farms, primarily in the Southeastern U.S., where these fish are raised and sold to restaurants and foodstores.

Fishing Techniques

Catfishing means still fishing. And catfishing means warm weather fishing since these critters like warm water and are most active when lakes, ponds and rivers warm up in the late spring, summer and early fall. Boats are not needed for catfishing. Simply find a spot on shore where you have enough room to cast out your weighted rig. Let it sink to the bottom. Snug up the line. And wait for the prowling whiskerfish to find your offering. A bank, a dock or a pier where you can sit on a comfortable chair makes things perfect.

The best catfishing and the largest catfish(they can go up to 5, 10, or 20 pounds or more) are often caught after dark. From dark to midnight and the several hours before sun-up are particularly good. But many catfish, including big ones, are caught on lazy summer afternoons.

Bring several baits along. If one doesn't produce, try something else. Often, this single maneuver can make all the difference.

Tackle and Equipment

Any rod and reel combination that can cast out a rig with a ½ - 6 oz. sinker will do just fine. These include specialized bass fishing tackle, light to medium spinning equipment and surf casting equipment. In some situations, you'll probably be better off with a longer rod(say 7-8 feet), so longer casts are possible.

Use monofilament line, at least 10 pound test. But heavier line is no problem, say 15-20 pound test.

Bait and Rigging

Catfish will eat almost anything. And they feed by both sight and by smell. Their smell sensors are on their whiskers. In fact, some catfish baits are often referred to as stink baits, because at times, it seems that catfish prefer smelly offerings such as beef liver, coagulated blood, chicken entrails, etc.

In Northern Calfiornia, some of the most successful baits are less repulsive. These include fresh clams(keep them on ice, pry them open with a knife, thread hook through hard outer edge), nightcrawlers, anchovies, redworms, sardine chunks and chicken livers.

The most common catfish rig is shown below;

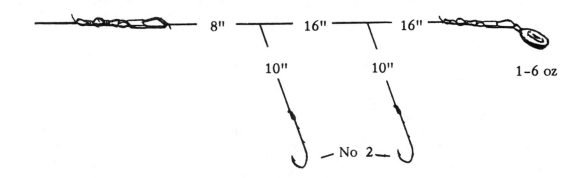

A popular alternative is the sliding sinker rig. See the Striped Bass Bait Fishing Section of this book. Some anglers use a treble hook, which helps hold on the bait. Use enough weight to get the casting distance you want and to hold the rig on the bottom, if there is a current. Some anglers prefer a dipsey sinker. It has a flat metal rim around the edge which makes it flutter up on a quick retrieve, so it's less likely to get caught in rock crevices and roots.

Where to Fish

Some of the best spots are in the lakes and reservoirs included in this book. The Delta and Sacramento Valley rivers are also very good. See the Lakes Section, Delta Section and Valley Rivers Section of this book.

Cleaning and Cooking

The first step in catfish cleaning is skin removal. To skin a catfish, cut through the skin all around the fish, just below the gill cover. Then, using a pliers, pull the skin down the fish, while holding the fishes gills. Be careful not to be poked by the sharp pectoral and dorsal fin spines. Some people nip these off with wire cutters. For larger fish, it is suggested that the fish be nailed(through the head) to a tree trunk or fence post, using an adequate sized spike. The skinned catfish can then be filleted or steaked. See Fish Cleaning Section of this book.

Catfish meat is flaky, mild, with a moist texture. It is good sauteed, fried or poached.

How to Catch...Clams

This is the only "How To Catch" section in this book that isn't really about catching. It's about digging. Digging with garden hoes, shovels, cultivators, clam shovels, clam guns or clam hooks. From an equipment standpoint, this is a very personalized sport. It's also a wet and grubby activity. Diggers either wear old tennis shoes and old pants, or waders. If you don't go the waterproof route, be sure to bring along a change of clothing. One of the best ways to get familiar with clam digging is to take a family outing to a popular clamming ground. Wander around. Watch. Ask questions. Observe the equipment and techniques. You'll have a ball.

Clamming Techniques

Clamming is probably the most popular in Northern California in late fall and early winter. During this period a tide chart is all that is needed to tell you when to go. The best time is a minus low tide. This is when the ocean rolls back to expose the prime clam beds. Clams are not found on long stretches of exposed beach. They need protected waters. Good clamming grounds include Humboldt Bay, Tomales Bay, Bodega Bay, Half Moon Bay and Elkhorn Slough (at Moss Landing).

Besides digging equipment, clammers also need a measuring device, fishing license, plastic bucket or burlap sack. The type of clams that are found depend on where you dig. Cockles are especially prolific in Tomales Bay,

Half Moon Bay and the Ano Nuevo Area(don't dig in the state reserve here). These small(minimum size limit is 1½") are found in rock and sand mix, only about three to four inches below the surface. Washington and horseneck(gapers) are smooth and reach a maximum length of 5". They are found at Elkhorn Slough, Tomales and Bodega Bays.

For horsenecks, diggers are out on the tide flats during minus tides looking for small siphon holes in the sand. These are feeding holes. When a bubbling hole is spotted, dig down. Somewhere down there is a clam. The favorite tool for these larger and deeper species is a clamer shovel. It can dig a narrow, yet deep hole rather easily. Clam hooks can also be used. One caution. Never put clams in a galvanized bucket. An electrolytic action may be set-up, ruining the clams.

Where to Dig

Humboldt Bay has Washington, horseneck and cockle clams. The most productive area is the South end of the bay. Cockles are the main quarry at the North end of the bay. Bodega Bay completely drains on a minus tide. The West side is particularly good for clamming. Tomales Bay clammers have immense areas to work, but the Western shoreline in Tomales Bay State Park is a favorite. Half Moon Bay is good just inside the North and South ends of the harbor. At Elkhorn Slough clammers can be seen digging in the area East of Highway 1. Be aware of clamming regulations. They differ by location and species.

Cleaning and Cooking Clams

The best way to get sand out of clams is to keep them in saltwater for 2 or 3 days. Change the water several times during this period. Don't use fresh water. Another way to clean clams is to freeze them. When they thaw, they'll gape open and the sand can be quickly rinsed out. Cockles are a favorite for eating. Many people steam them and then dip them in butter sauce(maybe add garlic). Washington and horseneck clams are excellent when fried. Overcooking of any clam should be avoided to prevent toughness.

BLACK CRAPPIE

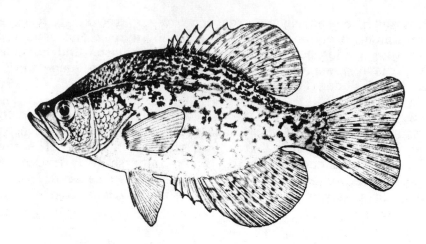

How to Catch...Crappie

Crappies(pronounced krŏp'-i) are the king of the panfish. Both black crappies and white crappies can grow quite large(the state records are black crappie-4 pounds, 1 ounce and white crappie-4 pounds, 8 ounces). Most crappies average a pound or even less. A 2-pounder is bragging size. Crappies provide fun and relaxed fishing on light tackle and are excellent eating fish.

Black crappies are the most wide spread of the two types, and do best in clearer water. Adult crappies are fish eaters, so they need an abundant supply of forage, like shad, to do well. Surprising to some, crappies also need a good deal of fishing pressure, otherwise they overpopulate their lake and all are stunted. So enjoy catching and eating crappies, it's good for the fish and good for the angler.

Finding Crappies in a Lake

The key to successful crappie fishing is finding them. These are school fish that cluster in different parts of a lake depending on season, water temperature, reproductive cycles, underwater contours, etc.

Crappies are easiest to find, and to catch, when they move into shallow water to spawn. This happens when the water temperature reaches about 60-65°. March, April and May are the likely months. These fish like heavy cover to accompany the shallow water. Look for water 3-8 feet deep with sunken trees, tule beds, cattails, lily pads and undercut rocky banks. This is much like the cover used by largemouth bass. Shore anglers do well in spring, as the fish move in close.

In summer and winter, crappies are harder to find, so stringers get skimpier, or empty. But they are still there and eating. Here's some ways to find them. Look in deeper water. They're usually down from 10-20 feet, in water that deep, or deeper. They like underwater islands, underwater stream beds, ledges, etc. Often they are in deeper water just adjacent to where they were in the spring. One way is to troll a jig or minnow across likely spots with lines of various depths. Mark the spot and depth when you get a hit. Troll slowly with oars or electric motor, or drift. Graph recorders also will do the job, for those who have them.

Fall crappies are not quite as deep as in the summer. Say 8-16 feet. And early and late in the day, crappies, like bass, move into shallower water to feed. So, even in summer, the first angler on the lake, or the last to call it a day, may fill a stringer with crappies in shallow water.

Jig Fishing

This is, by far, the most popular method of taking crappies - all year long. A word of caution before getting into the technique of this approach. It's easy to spook schools of crappies(especially in shallow water) so fish quietly and keep a low profile. And don't, for example, slide an anchor or tackle box along the bottom of your boat. Approach likely spots slowly and carefully.

Crappie jigs, or mini-jigs, are in the 1/32 to 1/8 ounce size range. Most are little leadhead jigs with a bright colored feather covering the hook end. Eyes are often painted on the head end. Some, like Sassy Shad Jigs have rubber bodies that imitate swimming shad.

Tie these jigs directly on about a 4 or even 2 pound test line. Light line gives the jig better action. Short, accurate casts are called for, from boat or shore. But since you'll be casting into cover, expect snags and expect to lose some jigs. Allow the jig to sink to the desired depth and then retrieve either smoothly and slowly, or impart a twitching action with the rod tip.

A small, clear casting bobber can be added up the line from the jig, if it's too light to cast the desired distance. The bobber will also prevent the jig from going deeper than it is set below the bobber. See Fly Fishing for Bluegill for illustration of casting bobber. Boat anglers, when directly over a school of crappie, can drop a jig straight down, and then twitch it around.

Crappie jigs come in many colors. Here are some guidelines. Light colors, like white, work well on clear days in clear water. Yellow is better on overcast days and at dawn and dusk. In off-colored water try dark colors like brown and blacks. Experiment with different styles and color. These jigs are inexpensive. Some times color doesn't even seem to matter.

Bait Fishing

Crappies love minnows, so if you prefer live minnow fishing, this is the way to go. Bait can be fished from shore, dock, or boat. Most anglers use a bobber. A typical rig is shown below;

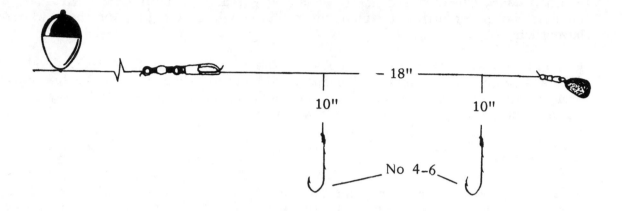

Minnows are best hooked up through both lips;

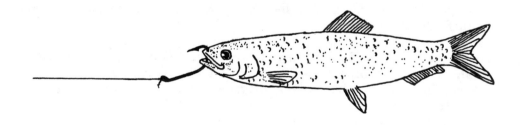

Most experts agree that a slight movement of your bait is desirable. Flick the rod tip frequently to move your bait. Another basic principle is to change depths, if the action is slow. Frequently larger crappies are deeper down than most bobber anglers suspect.

Tackle and Equipment

Just about any light freshwater tackle will do, from light spinning, to spincasting, to bamboo poles, to long fly rods. Actually the lighter the tackle the better, since it will help cast out the light jigs and baits. Ultra-light spinning tackle is popular. The only other thing you'll need is a stringer.

Where To Fish

Crappies are found in abundant supply in many Northern California lakes. See Lake Fishing Section of this book. Some of the lakes that are known for fine crappie fishing are Clear Lake, Camanche, Berryessa and Black Butte.

Cleaning and Cooking

Many people clean crappie in the traditional way. Scale them by rubbing a knife or scaling tool from the tail of the fish to the head. Cut open the belly and remove the guts. Finally, cut off the head. Rinse them off and they're ready for the pan.

An alternative, for good-sized fish, is to fillet them. This yields a little less meat, but eliminates skin and bone in the cooked fish. See instructions on filleting in the Fish Cleaning Section of this book.

Sauteing the whole fish or individual fillets is most popular. Dip them into sifted flour and sprinkle with salt, pepper and parsley and lemon flakes(if desired). Melt butter in a hot skillet, toss in the fish and turn until golden brown. Here's another recipe: Pieces cut from fillets can be battered and deep fried, and are also delicious.

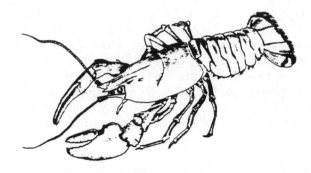

How to Catch...Crawdads

Why fish for crawdads, or crayfish, or crawfish anyway? Quite simply, because they're delicious - like mini-lobster! And besides, they're easy to catch and a snap to prepare. California crawdads can reach about 6 inches long and vary in color from brownish, to redish, or greenish. Although there is no minimum size limit, most anglers return smaller crawdads(say less than 2-3 inches), since the amount of edible meat on these is slight.

Fishing Techniques

The easiest way to catch a batch of crawdads is to use one or more wire traps. These traps have funnel-shaped openings that allow the crawdad to get in, but not out. Crawdad traps are available in many bait and tackle shops. They go for about $15.00 to $20.00, but can be purchased on sale for as little as $10.00.

These traps are baited with a piece of chicken, or liver, or a can of dog food (fish flavored is good). Perforate the dog food can with a can opener. Secure the can or other bait in the middle of the trap with a line or string. All you do is lower the trap to the bottom on a rope and wait. Crawdads are most active at night and prefer rocky areas(that provide a place to hide). Undercut river banks in shady areas are also good. If evening or night fishing is not convenient, do try it in the daytime. I've seen many crawdads caught when the sun is up.

Another technique, popular with kids, is to lower a strip of bacon or piece of liver into the water using a string or fishing line. Lower it to the bottom and wait a while. Once in a while, slowly raise up the bait and ease a landing net under it, right near the surface. Usually the crawdad will hang on to the bait long enough to be caught in the net. A boat dock or tied-up houseboat is a great place to "catch crawdads" using this technique.

Caught crawdads can be stored alive for up to a day in a bucket, covered with a damp towel or gunnysack. This is important because crawdads are cooked alive(like lobster!), at least they are live when cooking starts.

Tackle and Equipment

You'll need;

   - A bucket(to keep your catch in).
   - A crawdad trap or two, or ...
   - A pole and line(or rod, reel and line).
   - Bait(dog food, chicken leg, bacon, liver).

Where to Fish

The Delta is very good. Many lakes, ponds and streams are also good. See the Lake Sections of this book for more details.

Cleaning and Cooking

Crawdads don't need to be cleaned. Most people cook them whole(the edible meat is in the tail and pinchers). But, some people just remove the tails and cook them. If you do this you can remove the tail by twisting and pulling it off, where it meets the body. Then grasp the middle of the three flippers at the end of the tail. Twisting and pulling it will pull out the black entrail string that runs along the top of the meat under the tail side. If it doesn't come out, don't worry. You can easily remove it after cooking, when the shell is removed.

The first step in most crawdad recipes is cooking for about 10 minutes in boiling saltwater. The shell is bright red when crawdads are done. A whole crawdad can then be eaten like small lobster. Or you can clean out the meat(use a nutcracker and nut pick) and use in your favorite Newburg sauce or saute it.

Here's one popular recipe. Heat a little butter in a skillet and add fresh-pressed garlic, sweet basil, finely chopped fresh parsley, a touch of olive oil and pepper. Now add about a fourth cup of white wine, a bowl full of boiled and shelled crawdad claws and tail meat and saute for a few minutes. Serve over rice for a gourmet treat!

CALIFORNIA HALIBUT

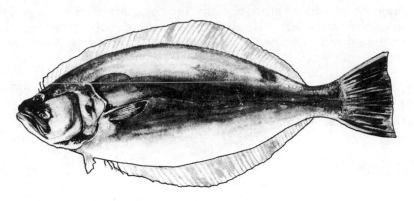

How to Catch...Halibut

California halibut is a flatfish and can range in size up to 50-75 pounds. The typical keeper is from 10-20 pounds. Adult halibut move into shallower water in the late spring and summer to spawn. Young fish swim upright, but during their first year, one eye migrates to the other side of the head and they begin to swim in a horizontal position. Also, the side with the two eyes(the top) turns dark, or sand-colored, while the bottom-side turns light.

Halibut live right on the sandy bottom. A ruffling of fins and tail kicks up a cloud of sand, that settles back on the fish, hiding it from both its predators and its prey. Only its two eyes are noticeable above the sand.

Calfiornia halibut fishing is primarily shallow water fishing. Because of this situation, it is possible to catch halibut from piers, by surf casting on beaches, or from a boat. In all these cases, the basic idea is the same, get your offering down on the sandy bottom and keep it moving.

Halibut feed most actively during moving current, especially on an incoming tide. The 2 or 3 hours before a high tide are often the best. And even slack water at high tide can be productive. Halibut do school, so if one is hooked, chances are there are more in the same location.

Fishing at the right time of year is critical to success. Summertime is when the halibut are in the shallow water. June is not too early in some locations, and July and August are usually good. Weekly fishing reports in newspapers highlight the best time.

Shore Fishing Techniques

Both pier and surf anglers can and do catch halibut, although, admittedly, the vast majority are taken from party and private boats. Two elements are essential for successful shore fishing;

1) Be there when the fish are there. Halibut move, depending on the whereabouts of anchovie schools and spawning patterns. The key is to keep up on local action.

2) Keep your offering moving. Halibut ambush moving forage fish. So your offering must do the same. This requires a constant cast and retrieve pattern. Slow retrieves are usually the most productive.

There are special sections in this book that address pier fishing and surf fishing, not only for halibut, but for all inshore saltwater game fish. See these sections for specific information.

Boat Fishing Techniques

There are two primary boat fishing techniques. The first is trolling. Most trollers use equipment similar to that needed for non-downrigger salmon trolling. Trollers work the surf line in 20 feet, or less of water. A large landing net or gaff is required. You should also have a fish billy. A sharp blow midway down the body is recommended. When trolling a deep diving lure, attach it to a good snap swivel and troll it out about 50 feet. behind the boat. Adjust boat speed so lure touches the bottom now and then. Slow trolling is best. Trolling rig is shown below;

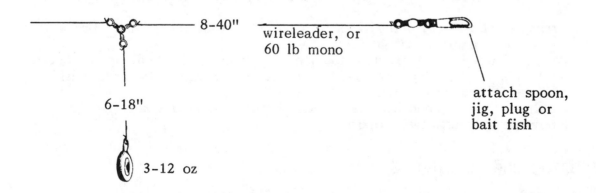

Trollers can cover a good amount of bottom. But many anglers prefer drift fishing. This technique is used extensively for halibut and striped bass in San Francisco Bay. Because of its popularity, a separate section in this book has been set-aside to detail Drift Fishing. Check-it-out for all the specifics.

Lures and Bait

Common bait and lures used for halibut are;

- Anchovies, shiners, small perch – live, hooked through the lips for drifting. Hooked on a salmon rig when trolling.

- Hair Raisers

- Pet Spoons

- Kastmasters

- Rebel minnow-type plug – about 6-7 inches.

- Bagley Bango-B deep diving plug – 6-9 inches(blue back, silver belly, bleeding gills) model has been "hot" in San Francisco Bay.

Where to Fish

There are many good fishing locations along the Pacific coast. These are described in the Ocean Fishing Section of this book. Another good source of information is coastal bait and tackle shops.

In San Francisco Bay, some of the best places to fish for halibut on an incoming tide are;

Crissy Field – Best in June, July and August. Drift parallel to shore in about 10-20 feet of water.

Alcatraz Island – Fish the shoal on the West side, July thru September, in 20-45 feet using anchovies. On incoming tides boats drift towards the island.

Treasure Island – Fish the flats North and West of the island. Use anchovies or shiners in 20-40 feet.

Angel Island – There are two spots here. Point Knox Shoal on the Southwest side of the island at 20-50 feet. Racoon Strait between the island and the Tiburon Peninsula.

Farther South, a good area is the flat between **Oyster Point** and **San Francisco International Airport**.

Cleaning and Cooking

Smaller halibut can be filleted. Larger ones are steaked. If you can get a decent-sized steak out of your halibut, then steak it. Even when filleting, the tail section can be steaked. When filleting, first make a vertical cut(the fish is laying flat) along the lateral line down to the spine. This allows you to "lift off" two manageable-sized fillets from each side of the fish.

Halibut is dense, mild, somewhat sweet and low in fat. Popular cooking methods include broiling, barbecuing, poaching, frying and baking. The fillets can be sauteed.

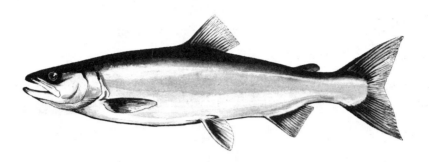

How to Catch... Kokanee

Kokanee are a land-locked sockeye salmon. They were originally planted in Western reservoirs in the late 1940's. Today, the kokanee fisheries are quite active in selected Northern California locations. Kokanee reach adulthood in about 4 years, the same as for other salmon. They spawn in late summer or fall, in lake tributaries. Kokanee can reach a length of 16 to 20 inches or more, but the overcrowding of the species(and resulting need to share a limited food resource), generally results in mature kokanee in the 8 to 14 inch range. Even at this modest size, they are a desirable catch because they taste great.

Plankton is the main food source of kokanee, so fishing for them requires an offering that provides color and movement to get their attention. They are a school fish, so once one is located, the chances of catching more, are good.

Fishing Techniques

The almost universal technique for catching kokanee is trolling. Like other salmon, kokanee prefer cold water. About 50°, in fact. This means that when a lake is stratified the kokanee are down deep. However, in spring and late fall, kokanee can be trolled for near the surface.

The approaches used for kokanee trolling have much in common with lake trolling for trout. In fact, identical equipment and rigging is used. Lake trolling is described in detail in the section Trout in Lakes. Rather than repeat all this information here, let's just highlight the few differences and the key points to success;

- . The most popular lures are nickel/red head, fire/pearl, rainbow and pearl/red head. Small spoons are most popular; Needlefish and Super-duper, size #1.

. In very cold, clear water, it is possible to troll near the surface using this type of rig;

. However, when kokanee are down more than 10 feet(the usual situation) the rig below is typical;

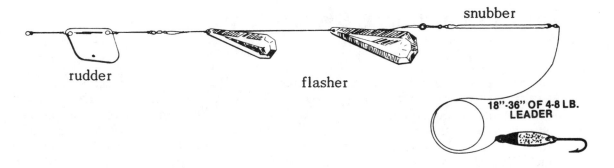

rudder   flasher   snubber

. A rubber snubber is necessary because kokanee have soft, delicate mouths. The snubber absorbs the shock of the strike.

. A diving plane or lead core line can be trolled down to about 40 feet. Downriggers are better suited below 40 feet.

. Use the same trolling techniques as used for trout; troll slow, work in an S pattern and vary your speed often.

. A depth sounder can locate the school of kokanee and tell you what depth to troll.

. Many kokanee anglers add a single kernel of white corn, a small pinch of worm, a salmon egg, or a short piece of red or white yarn to the hook of their lure. Try it if action is slow.

Where to Fish

Lake Tahoe, Donner and Bullard's Bar can produce kokanee in the 14 to 20 inch size bracket. Mature, smaller fish(8 to 12 inches) are the rule in lakes like Whiskeytown, Pardee, Bucks, Ice House, Camanche, Echo and Stampede.

Cleaning and Cooking

Most anglers clean and prepare kokanee the same as they would smaller trout - see Trout(Stream) Section. Kokanee have a very mild salmon-type meat.

How to Catch...Lingcod

Guess what? Lingcod aren't a cod. Lingcod are actually a greenling, and are rockfish. But they're much larger and tougher than other rockfish. Lings can reach upwards of 5 feet and weigh up to 70 pounds.

Fishing Techniques

Lingcod can be caught at any time of the year. And many are caught by rock cod fishermen, particularly while fishing in deep water(200-400 feet). In fact, at times a large ling will strike a small rock cod that has just been hooked.

Dedicated lingcod pursuers, however, choose to fish in fall and winter. Three of the best months are December, January and February. During this period, lings are more active, and move in shallower water to spawn.

Lingcod fishing, like rock cod fishing, is bottom, drift fishing. It is done over rocks, or reefs. Once the rig has been lowered to the bottom, it should be jigged up and down. Try to stay just off the bottom, to prevent snags.

Tackle and Equipment

You'll need a gaff(lings will tear up a landing net), a fish billie(to subdue this fish that has sharp teeth and fins) and a needlenose pliers(to take out the hook).

The tackle you'll need is the same as needed for deep water rock fishing; a medium heavy to heavy roller-tipped, 6-7 foot rod, a 6/0 or 4/0 ocean reel, a 30-50 pound monofilament line.

Lures and Bait

The most commonly used lure for lingcod is the chrome hex bar with treble hook. The appropriate lures range from 6-15 ounces, depending on ocean conditions, and lings preference. Some fishermen remove the strong treble hook that comes on this lure and replace it with light wire treble hooks. The light hook bends and gives when hung-up in the rocks, before the line breaks, thus saving the expensive(about $5.00) hex bar.

Many lingcod fishermen prefer bait fishing. The best bait is whole fish. Good choices include sandabs, rock cod or squid(some anglers cut the dorsal fin off rockfish used as bait. They say it makes the bait more appetizing). It's best if the bait is alive, or at least freshly caught. 7-10 inches is a good size. Use a two hook rig. The end hook goes through the bait fishes upper lip (or through both lips) and the other hook goes into the side of the fish near the tail.

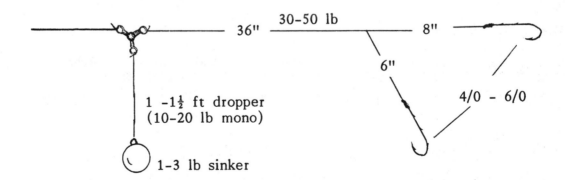

36"   30-50 lb   8"

6"

1 -1½ ft dropper
(10-20 lb mono)

4/0 - 6/0

1-3 lb sinker

Where to Fish

See Ocean Fishing Section of this book.

Cleaning and Cooking

Lingcod are most often filleted. Larger ones can be steaked. Lingcod fillets or steaks are lean and mild tasting. Lingcod meat(depending on the age of the fish and where it is caught) is often green, but turns white upon cooking. Thick fillets or steaks can be barbecued or broiled. They are also suitable for poaching or frying. Thinner fillets can be sauteed. Lingcod is rather dense, so it takes somewhat longer to cook.

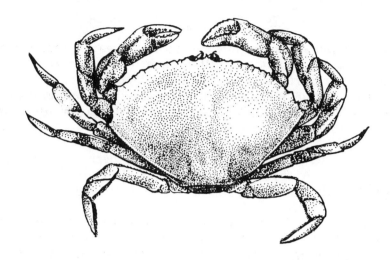

How to Catch... Rock Crab

Anglers who fish in the shallow Pacific waters near breakwaters and wharfs are often frustrated by rock crabs steeling their bait. Rather than getting mad at these plentiful pirates, why not get even - by catching them and eating them? These relatives of the Dunganess crab have large pincers that are just as tasty.

Fishing Techniques

Rock crab fishing is simple and leisurely. All you need is a hoop net and about 75-100 feet of rope(nylon or clothesline will do). Rock crab nets are sold in many fishing tackle shops for less than $20. Ask the shop how to attach the rope to the particular net you purchase.

The most common bait is a fish carcass . . . or what's left after a large rockfish has had its fillets removed. They come either fresh or fresh frozen, at bait shops(especially those on or near popular public wharfs) and fish markets. Frozen squid are also a good bait.

One rule of thumb holds true; the more bait in the net, the more rock crabs you'll catch. Crabs find the bait by smelling it. So more bait gets more smell into the water.

The fish carcasses are tied to the bottom of the net. Once out on a jetty or a wharf, simply lower the baited net into the water, all the way to the bottom. With a little experience you'll realize how often the net should be raised up to the water surface for checking. When a rock crab is spotted in the net, quickly raise it up all the way. Remove it from the net(but avoid the pincers) and place it in a bucket of sea water. Lower the net and haul up some more.

Timing will improve your catch. Crabbing is often best just before and after the peak of high tide. A three hour period centered around high tide is recommended. Winter months are most popular for sport crabbing.

Rigging and Equipment

You'll need a hoop net, 100 feet of rope or line(strong enough to lower and raise the net) and a large bucket. Also take a measuring device and fishing regulations along so you don't take undersized or illegal crabs.

Where to Fish

Piers, wharfs and rocky breakwaters or jettys along the Pacific coastline are most popular. Good spots include Moss Landing, Pillar Point Harbor, San Francisco Bay near Fort Baker, Bodega Bay and Humboldt Bay.

Cleaning and Cooking

Rock crabs are cooked and eaten like lobster. Most of the meat is in the pincers. Cook crabs in boiling water until shells turn red(about 10 minutes).

How to Catch...Rockfish

Rockfish are a group of ocean-dwelling, bottom fish, often called rock cod. They are fun to catch and delicious to eat. Varieties of rockfish go by names such as blues, reds, yellowtail, cabezon and browns. Rockfish run up to 7-10 pounds, but average 2-4 pounds. These fish are quite ugly, with large mouths and sharp pointed fins, but they produce delicious fillets.

Fishing Techniques

Rockfishing for most anglers means drift fishing from a boat. It can be done as close as ½ mile from shore to as far out as the Farallon Islands, or other offshore reef areas.

The technique is quite simple. With the use of a depth sounder, locate the boat over a rocky bottom. Often the best location is one where a depth is changing, either on the upslope of a canyon or on the changing slope of a reef.

Now just lower your rig over the side until you feel the weight hit the bottom. Put the reel into gear, and crank up a foot or two. Check for the bottom, by lowering your line frequently, to avoid drifting into snags, or letting your bait move too far from the bottom. Jigging(moving your offering up and down a few feet) is also a good idea. The motion catches the eye of the rockfish.

Sometimes rockfish are also caught alongside kelp beds in the shallows near shore. Again, fish near the bottom and reel in fast to keep the fish from snagging in the kelp.

Tackle, Equipment and Rigging

The heft or weight of the tackle needed for rockfishing depends primarily on the depth of water you're fishing in. See next page for helpful chart.

At the end of your line, fasten a heavy swivel snap. To this, attach a rock cod rig or shrimp fly rig with 6/0 size hooks. Many anglers prefer the shrimp fly rig since they have feathers that add to the attractiveness of the offering. Shrimp fly rigs can be purchased in most ocean fishing-oriented bait and tackle shops for less than a dollar each. They typically have 3 hooks and a snap swivel at the end to attach the sinker.

	50-100 Feet	300-400 Feet
Rod:		
-length	6-7 feet	6-7 feet
-stiffness	med-med. heavy	med. heavy-heavy
-guide	(roller tip helpful)	(roller tip)
Reel:	med. ocean baitcasting	Penn Senator 114 6/0
Line:	25-40 lb. mono	40-80 lb. mono
Sinker:	4 oz. - 1 lb.	½ - 2 lb.

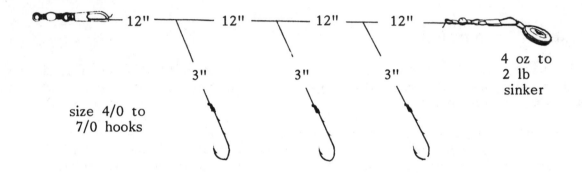

Bait

The most common bait for rockfishing is cut-up squid pieces. Cut the pieces large enough to cover the hook. Other common baits are pieces of small rock-fish and anchovies. At times fish can be hooked using bare shrimp fly rigs. But bait adds an odor that is often helpful in enticing a bite.

Where to Fish

See Ocean Fishing Section of this book.

Cleaning and cooking

Rockfish are almost always filleted. Since almost all varieties of rockfish(or rock cod) have very large heads, the yield of fillets can be as low as 20-30% of fish weight. Rock cod meat is lean, has low fat content and is mild tasting. These fillets lend themselves to the cooking method of choice including sau-teeing, broiling, poaching, frying or baking.

KING SALMON

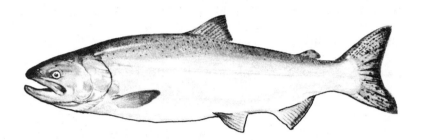

How to Catch...**Salmon** (in the Ocean)

Both king(chinook) and silver(coho) salmon are caught in Northern California ocean water. But kings are by far the most common. The salmon in California salt water were spawned naturally, or in hatcheries, in tributaries of coastal rivers like the Klamath, Trinity and Sacramento. About 60% of California ocean caught salmon originate in the Sacramento River system(including the Feather and American Rivers).

Only one single, barbless hook(either manufactured that way, or with the barb flattened using a pliers) is allowed per rod. Undersize fish(called shakers) should be released without netting or handling. A needle-nose pliers is needed. This prevents the fragile, protective membrane on the body of the fish from being broken. Grasp the leader about 2 feet up from the hook. Next grasp the hook shank with the pliers(or slide a rod or stiff wire into the curve of the hook). Now, raise and rotate the hook upside down. The salmon will drop off into the ocean.

It's obviously easier for a salmon to throw a barbless hook, so slack line condition must be avoided when playing a fish. Once a keeper salmon is netted, it should be clubbed between the eyes, with a hammer handle or fish club, to subdue it. Most seasoned fishermen gill and gut salmon when caught, and then store them in an iced fish box or cooler. The tail is clipped to distinguish from commercially caught salmon.

Fishing Techniques

There are four primary techniques for taking salmon in saltwater:

1. Trolling with a diving plane.

2. Trolling with a cannonball sinker with sinker release.

3. Trolling with a downrigger.

4. Mooching - Basically drift fishing with bait. This method is growing in popularity. Position the boat so as to drift over the top or along the side of a bait school.

Trolling

The most common method for taking ocean salmon in California waters is trolling, or pulling a lure or bait through the water using boat movement. Since king salmon especially, are often found 10 to 100 feet below the surface, methods must be employed to take bait or lures to these depths. That's where diving planes, cannonballs with sinker releases and downriggers come in.

Diving Plane - A weighted, air foil device that uses the motion of the water to dive and takes the terminal tackle with it. After a salmon strike, the diving plane neutralizes its position, allowing the rig and fish to rise up to the surface.

Cannonball-Sinker Release - This approach relies on the heft of a steel or lead cannonball of 1, 2, or 3 pounds to take the rigging down. The cannonballs are attached to a sinker release mechanism which releases the weight when a salmon hits, allowing the fish to rise and fight.

Downrigger - A pulley and boom(manually or electrically activated) which lowers a 10 pound weight on a steel cable. A clip holds the rod's fishing line and releases it when a salmon strikes.

Trolling with a diving plane or cannonball-sinker release works like this. With the boat at trolling speed(2-4 knots) lower the terminal tackle in the water, check lure action, then let out about 24-40 pulls of line(this puts the hook at about 15-20 feet deep). Other rods should be deeper or shallower until fish are located. Put on clicker and then set drag just tight enough to hold the line. Put the rod in a holder. The singing drag will signal a strike. The pull of the salmon will drop the weight or open the diving plane, allowing the fish to rise and fight. Some anglers maintain trolling speed while fighting the fish. This minimizes the chance of slack line and a thrown hook. The landing net should always be placed from the front, forward and under the fish.

Trolling with a downrigger has several advantages. It allows deep trolling (50-100 feet) without the use of heavy rods/reels and line. And the downrigger "tells you" exactly how deep you're trolling, so successes can be duplicated. Downriggers cost between $100-300 and probably are not necessary, or some say, desirable if the fish are at 10 to 40 feet. Beyond 40 feet they are very useful. Downriggers are also very useful for trolling for trout and salmon in lakes during the summertime when these fish are 50-100 feet down.

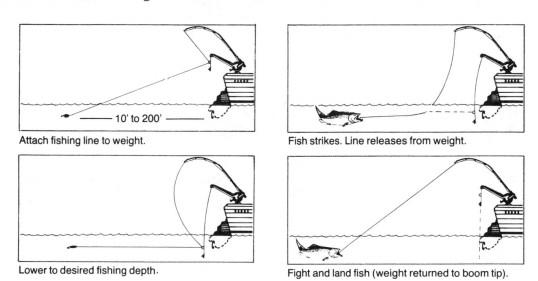

Attach fishing line to weight.

Fish strikes. Line releases from weight.

Lower to desired fishing depth.

Fight and land fish (weight returned to boom tip).

Mooching

Mooching, or drift fishing, for salmon can be very effective and quite exciting if you can locate the fish. Feeding birds are one clue as are a "boil" of bait fish on the surface. Fish locators are also helpful to select the proper depth to fish. Often, mooching is done just off the bottom, with a whole anchovie rigged on a 1/0 or 2/0 hook. At other times, moochers are successful nearer the surface. Pre-tied, two-hook mooching rigs are available at coastal tackle outlets. How to hook bait for mooching is a matter of preference; anglers often hook the end hook through the tail and the upper hook through the back, but in the Pacific Northwest, where mooching has been honed to a real science, the mooching rig illustrated below is used;

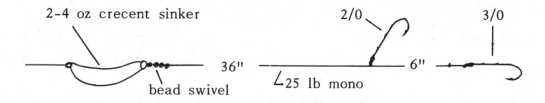

2-4 oz crecent sinker

bead swivel

36"

2/0

25 lb mono

6"

3/0

See top of next page for baiting instructions.

Start by pushing end hook through roof of mouth to just behind the head of the bait. Push the second hook through the same hole. Hook end hook through the bait just in front of the dorsal fin underneath the backbone. Pull line tight so that the top hook is secure in the head and the end hook secure in the back.

Use only enough weight to hold the bait down at a 50-60° angle. Dangle the offering. Lift the rod tip, come up a few cranks, wait. Lower it and repeat the process. Often the salmon will "bump" the bait a few times before striking solidly. Don't set the hook until a substantial strike is felt.

Another mooching rig that works is to tie a ½ ounce jig(like a Hair Raiser, Worm-Tail, Shim or Jet Tail) directly to your main line. Then bait the jig with a whole anchovie or anchovie fillet. Work it along the bottom.

Tackle and Equipment

No matter which approach you use you should have a large cooler with ice, fish club or hammer, needle-nose pliers and a large landing net.

For trolling with a diving plane or weight you'll need a medium heavy or heavy boat rod with roller tip, about 6 feet and a saltwater trolling or casting reel that can hold 300 years of 25 pound test monofilament line. Spinning reels or levelwind reels are not generally used.

The terminal tackle with diving plane includes a dodger to attract salmon;

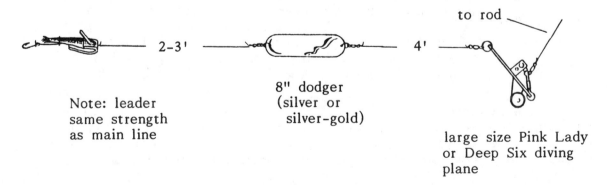

2-3'

Note: leader
same strength
as main line

8" dodger
(silver or
silver-gold)

4'

to rod

large size Pink Lady
or Deep Six diving
plane

Terminal tackle with cannonball-sinker release is illustrated on the next page.

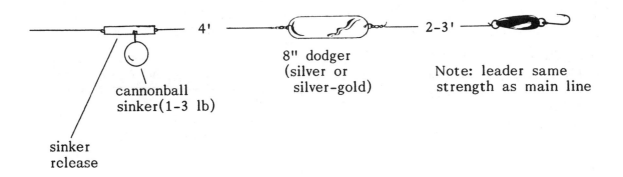

4'

8" dodger
(silver or
silver-gold)

2-3'

Note: leader same
strength as main line

cannonball
sinker(1-3 lb)

sinker
release

For trolling with a downrigger you'll need the downrigger, baitcasting or spinning rod of 6-8 feet and a baitcasting or spinning reel that can hold 200 yards of 10-20 pound monfilament line.

For mooching you'll need the same types of rod/reel combinations used for downrigging.

Lures and Bait

The most popular bait for ocean salmon is anchovies. They are purchased frozen, laying flat on a plastic tray, from bait shops. For trolling, the anchovie is either rigged on a crowbar hook or on a plastic bait holding rig.

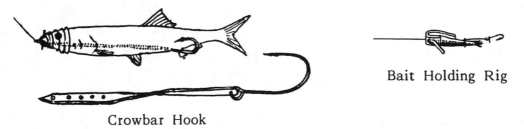

Bait Holding Rig

Crowbar Hook

It's crucial that the anchovies, when trolled, roll or wobble, like a wounded bait fish. Without practice or specific experience, this is difficult, using the crowbar hook. But, with the plastic bait holding rig(common brand names; Rotary Salmon Killer, Herring Aid), a rolling action is guaranteed because of the fin-shape molded into the plastic. Also, putting the anchovie into either of these rigs takes only a few seconds. Commercial salmon fishermen typically rig crowbar hooks in advance, because it requires patience and a steady hand.

Some Silver Spoons and lures that imitate squid can also be effective. These include Krocodile and Hopkins(1 and 2 ounce), McMahon(#4) and Apex(4½-5½ inches). Hoochie(hula skirt jig) of about 3-4 inches, in assorted colors are also popular.

Where to Fish

See Ocean and San Francisco Bay Fishing Sections of this book.

Cleaning and Cooking

Scale salmon with the jet of a water hose nozzle.

Salmon are usually filleted. Large ones are steaked. Fresh salmon and properly frozen salmon, as anyone knows who has eaten it, is out of this world. Many anglers prefer to barbecue this rich, relatively fat meat. It is also very good poached(served hot with a sauce, or chilled), broiled, baked or smoked.

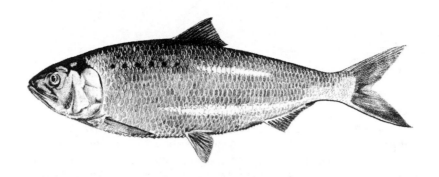

How to Catch...Shad

Veteran shad anglers consider this fish the best fighter, pound-for-pound, of all sport fish in Northern California waters. Shad spawn in the Sacramento River and its tributaries(American, Feather, Yuba) in late spring and early summer. Fishermen usually begin their shad quest in late April or early May. A typical American shad weighs-in at 3 to 5 pounds.

Fishing Techniques

Casting is the predominent technique for taking shad. Shad strike very aggressively at small, silver objects that show bright colors such as red, orange, green, white and yellow. Shad are more protective of their territory than hungry, at this time of year, so they are difficult to hook. They fight savagely, so a hook-up doesn't necessarily result in a fish in hand.

Casting is done both from shore and from anchored boats, depending on local river conditions. Shore fishing is done mostly where there is a shoal in the bend of a river. Deeper water and the availability of launch ramp facilities provides the opportunity for boat fishing.

One shad fishing technique which is commonly used, particularly at the mouth of the American River, involves fishing from an anchored boat in a relatively strong current, using a spinning or baitcasting rod. A small lead sinker is placed at the end of the line, and a weighted fly is tied on a 24 inch dropper about 18 inches above the sinker. The line is played out until the sinker just clears the bottom. It is necessary for the current to be strong enough to give the fly the proper action. This method of fishing has so many followers that space to anchor at the mouth of the American River is often at a premium. Shore anglers at the mouth of the American River successfully use spinning gear and a floating plastic bubble attached about three feet above the offering.

You can buy many types of shad lures and flies in Sacramento Valley sporting goods stores and on a weekend during a good run, even shore anglers may find it difficult to locate a place to fish. Nevertheless, the most popular method of shad angling in California, and perhaps the most rewarding, is to fish from shore with a fly rod or a spinning rod. The fly rod is used with a fast-sinking line or a shooting head. A tippet with about a 6 pound test breaking strength is desirable since the shad can be quite large. Some will exceed 5 or 6 pounds. In addition, there is always the possibility of hooking a striped bass or a large steelhead.

Let us assume you have found a likely spot on a river, just below a riffle where the fast water breaks and slows down at the head of a long pool. You wade out into the water and cast across toward the opposite bank, allowing the current to swing your line downstream. You wait a few moments as the fly at the end of your tautening line makes its way downstream and toward the bank below you. As you are ready to pick up and cast again, you hook your first shad and are in for a delightful surprise. Before long, on a typical day, you may repeat this experience again and again until you have caught and released or kept, a considerable number of fish.

If you use a spinning outfit, the shad fly is tied to the end of the line and a split shot is pinched on from 18 to 24 inches above the fly. Just enough weight is used to enable you to cast easily. Cast out across the water as you would with a fly rod, but immediately after completing your cast, reel in just fast enough to prevent the split shot from snagging the bottom.

Tackle and Equipment

Shad fishing means light tackle fishing. Equipment must be light enough and flexible enough to toss small offerings. Anyway, the light tackle makes for more challenge. Spinning, fly fishing and baitcasting set-ups are all used. Popular lures include Shad Darts, Fle-Fly and T-Killers(in white or yellow with red heads) and 1/16 to 1/8 ounce Crappie Jigs in Chartreuse, yellow, orange and white.

Where to Fish

Good areas are described in the Valley River Section. Specific locations are The Yuba River from the mouth upstream to Daguerre Point Dam, the Feather River from the mouth to fish barrier at Oroville, and the American River from the mouth to Nimbus Dam. There is also good shad action along the Russian River.

Cooking and Cleaning

Many anglers release shad because they are so bony. And filleting a shad is no easy task, even after you've seen it done by an expert. The Department of Fish and Game tried a number of years ago, to encourage the eating of shad. They did this by publishing a booklet that describes How To Fillet A Shad - In 32 Steps! Step 32 concludes, "In a little while, with some patience, you will be able to trim a shad into two boneless fillets in about 15 to 20 minutes."

Shad is mild, quite firm, with a meatlike flavor and a moderate fat level. It is good baked, poached or smoked. Some anglers prefer the shad roe.

BLUE SHARK

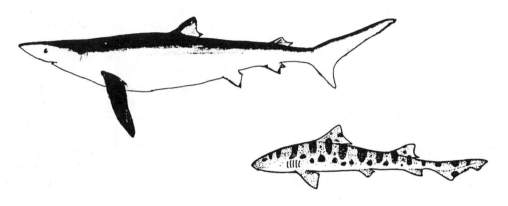

LEOPARD SHARK

How to Catch...Sharks

Shark are a misrepresented fish. All the media ever talk about are great white sharks. But there are other varieties of shark in Northern California waters. These include leopard shark, sevengill and sixgill cow shark and blue shark. What's more, the media never mentions that these sharks are becoming more and more popular among sports fishing people; popular to fish for and popular to eat.

Sevengill and sixgill cow sharks can get quite large. The largest sevengill shark caught was over 500 pounds. It's quite possible to hook fish in the 200 pound range. However, the most common shark caught in Northern California waters is the leopard shark. These can weigh up to about 30 pounds and are about 4 feet in length. The average fish is between 10 and 20 pounds.

Fishing Techniques

Most shark fishing is done from an anchored boat, using a sliding sinker rig and fishing on the bottom. It's the same approach used when still fishing for striped bass. The rig is baited up and tossed out. Depressions in the bottom or deep holes are prime spots. An incoming tide, just past slack, is a good time to fish. Always keep an eye on your rod tip(or hold your rod). When the tip moves, point the rod at the fish and then set the hook hard on the second tug.

Sharks should always be landed with a gaff. I made the mistake of landing

a relatively small leopard shark, that my son had hooked, in my salmon landing net. The shark actually bit its way out. A fish club is also needed to
dispense sharks.

Tackle and Equipment

Tackle varies, depending on the size of sharks you're after. Heavyweight shark
hunters use stiff 6-7 foot rods with roller guides, a size 6/0 conventional reel
and about 500 yards of 60-pound wire line. But these types of hefty equipment are by no means necessary or even desirable for you to enjoy shark fishing. Many shark anglers use sturgeon fishing tackle, striped bass fishing tackle,
rock cod fishing tackle or even salmon fishing tackle. Any tackle that can
handle 20 to 30 pount test monofilament line and an 8 ounce sinker will do
for most shark fishing. The two essentials, however, are wire leaders and
a fish club.

Bait and Rigging

Several types of baits are used for shark. These include anchovies, squid, salmon bellies and a bullhead-type baitfish known as a "lordfish" or "midshipman."
Non-conventional baits include chicken parts, calves liver, etc. Within this
wide array, the best are probably whole squid, pieces of salmon belly and lordfish. Squid are most readily available, but attract nuisance fish(small rays,
too small sharks and crabs).

The hook should be run through the squid several times, and check you bait
frequently. Pieces of salmon belly are difficult to come by, but work well.
Lordfish are caught as a by-product of shrimping. They work well because
smaller nuisance fish don't seem interested in them. Conventional party boat
captains often use midshipman as bait. A typical shark rig is shown below;

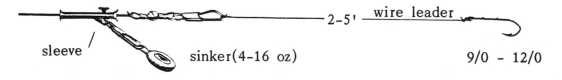

sleeve   sinker(4-16 oz)   2-5' wire leader   9/0 - 12/0

Where to Fish

Most shark fishing is done in bay waters. Good spots for leopard sharks include the area off Pt. Richmond, Hunter's Point off San Francisco and the
channel near Dumbarton Bridge in South San Francisco Bay. Good spots for

large six and sevengill sharks include "Big Hole" just west of Angel Island, "The Greenhouse" just off the Marin shoreline just south of Sausalito(look for small green building at the bottom of the cliff) and the channel from Oakland to the San Mateo Bridge in South San Francisco Bay.

Use a depthfinder and chart of the bottom, or a chart recorder to locate deep holes or underwater shelves.

Cleaning and Cooking

Smaller sharks are easily filleted. Larger sharks are generally steaked. Final trimming should remove any red meat to eliminate any chance of a fleshy taste. Remove the tough skin because it shrinks a good deal during cooking.

Shark meat is firm, white, very low in fat and has a mild to moderate flavor. Shark is well suited to baking, poaching, barbecuing, deep-frying and is a nice addition to soup, stews and casseroles. It is also delicious smoked.

STEELHEAD RAINBOW TROUT

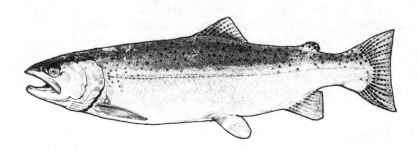

How to Catch...Steelhead and Salmon (in Rivers)

Steelhead and salmon fishing in coastal rivers and streams and in the Sacramento River system is one of the most pleasurable and rewarding of all fishing experiences. Many veteran anglers, who have fished all over the world, insist that steelhead and salmon fishing is the ultimate fishing experience, despite the wind, rain and cold. Anglers endure and overcome wet and cold because the fall and winter months are when ocean-toughened, acrobatic steelhead trout(actually a variety of rainbow trout) and large king(chinook) salmon migrate into fresh water to spawn.

Early fall steelhead are often juvenile fish that don't spawn. These are called "half-pounders" even though they run from ½-2 pounds. Mature spawning steelhead that migrate later in fall and in winter average 5 to 10 pounds, with fish in some streams reaching up to 15-20 pounds.

The migrating king salmon(some streams also have runs of smaller silver, or coho salmon) are larger fish, on average, than those caught in the ocean during spring and summer. This is because only the mature adult fish join the spawning run. They move up river to their spawning beds, spawn and die, their life cycle complete. Steelhead on the other hand, will spawn and return to the ocean several times. King salmon catches are in the 10-20 pound range with occassional fish going as high as 40 pounds. The record, caught on the Sacramento River near Red Bluff in 1979, weighed in at 88 pounds! Fresh-run salmon are bright, much like ocean-caught salmon. As spawning time comes closer, salmon turn dark, and are not good eating. These should probably be released to spawn. A fresh-run steelhead has a bright red stripe along its side, and is gourmet eating. However, as the season progresses, they turn steel blue and the meat is soft and inedible. Release these to spawn and return to the ocean.

Sometimes it is difficult to distinguish between king salmon, silver salmon and steelhead trout. Here are some basic keys;

King Salmon - On the lower jaw, the crown of the gums where the teeth project, is dark, as is the rest of the mouth. There are usually large, angular black spots on the back and both lobes of the tail.

Silver Salmon - The crown of the gums where the teeth project(lower jaw) is whitish, the rest of the mouth lining is darker. There are usually spots on the back and upper lobe of the tail, but none on the lower lobe.

Steelhead Trout - The inside of the mouth is whitish. There are teeth on the tip, but not on the back of the tongue.

Steelhead and salmon that are migrating in fresh water are not particularly interested in eating. In fact, all agree, that salmon don't eat at all. And steelhead eat little or nothing. This situation means that anglers can't rely on a fishes appetite to induce a strike. Most experts feel that steelhead and salmon strike out of instinct, curiosity, or most likely to protect their territory. They will not move far to take an offering, most stray only a few inches to either side of their hold.

In some coastal streams, particularly the Klamath and Trinity, there are summer-run steelhead. These steelhead eat and behave and often take on the appearance of rainbow trout(because they are in fresh water 6-10 months before spawning in the spring). Summer-run steelhead are caught using Stream Trout Fishing Techniques. See Catching Trout(in Streams) Section.

Some steelhead salmon anglers use boats. Others fish from shore or use waders. Boats are useful in some streams when private property limits access or where a boat can provide access to an area too steep to climb down to from a road or tract. Boat anglers can cover much more potentially good fishing spots in a day than the shore anglers can. One highly specialized and highly successful steelhead and salmon fishing technique called backtrolling, requires a boat. More on this later.

The fishing techniques, bait, lures, tackle and equipment are the same or similar for both steelhead and salmon fishing. There are several exceptions and these will be noted and explained in the sections that follow.

Some Fundamentals

All steelhead and salmon fishing techniques have one common denominator.

They are designed to get a lure or bait right down on the bottom of the stream. This is the only place the fish are, and in the winter, when they're not eating, they won't move up to take an offering. A lure or bait that's not within several inches of the bottom has almost as little chance of catching a fish as those still sitting on a shelf at the tackle shop. An old saying goes like this, "If you're not losing terminal tackle you're not fishing deep enough." Unfortunately, for our pocketbooks, but fortunately, for tackle manufacturers, this statement is all too true. Happily, there are rigs and approaches that minimize the loss due to hangups, and these are emphasized here.

We know that salmon and steelhead are on the bottom of the stream or river. The next question, where along all that bottom are we most likely to find them? Here are the choice spots;

- At a tributary stream mouth(in fact, some of these are so productive that they are closed to fishing for a certain period each year. See individual river regulations).

- Just off the main current of a river in water 3-8 feet deep. Not in the very fast water, but not in backwater either.

- At the head or tail end of a deep hole. Salmon in the Sacramento River system are pursued in holes deeper than 10 feet.

- Along a deep side channel.

- Just above or below a riffle.

- A few feet behind a slick formed by the current breaking around a boulder(this includes submerged boulders and bridge pilings and abutments that are "artificial" boulders).

- The tidal basin of the river or stream and the upper limit of high tide in any stream. Pools and holes in these sections are good.

- In small streams steelhead hold along and under sweeps of overhanging brush and foliage.

- Along underwater ledges, cliffs or undercuts.

- In the fall, early run steelhead are frequently in riffles themselves. In small coastal streams steelhead will often hold in shallow water (a foot or so) above or within a riffle.

There are a number of approaches used to catch steelhead and salmon. Here is a rundown of each.

Drift Fishing

For those readers not familiar with coastal river fishing terminology, a brief explanation is in order. Drift fishing, in this usage, has nothing to do with a boat. Drift fishing refers to drifting a bait or lure along in the current of a river. Most anglers do this from shore or while wading out, but it sometimes is done from an anchored boat. It is actually very similar to the bait fishing approach used for trout in streams in the summertime, except the terminal tackle is heavier because the water is faster and deeper, and because the fish are larger and stronger.

The lure or bait is cast upstream at about a 45° angle and then allowed to drift downstream into likely holding areas. Slack line is taken up as the drift proceeds. A key is to use the proper weight so that the offering moves freely, yet stays on or near the bottom. A weight that is too heavy will freeze or even hang-up, while one that is too light will move off the bottom. The perfect amount of weight is that which will result in a tap-tap-skip action as it makes frequent contact with the bottom and then bounces up a bit before striking again.

Strikes are often soft in this type of fishing. The fish just mouth the offering, but don't hit it or run with it. Often, fish are lost because the angler can't differentiate between a bite and the feel of the bottom. Any momentary slowing or stopping of a drift lure or bait, should be assumed to be a take. Respond by setting the hook hard.

There are several different weight systems that drift anglers use, depending on personal preference. In all systems the weight is 18-24 inches up from the lure or bait. Leaders are the same weight as the main line. These are the popular alternatives;

Lead Cinch – These are basically 3-way swivels, with rubber tubing attached to the middle swivel. They are available in stores. A pencil lead weight(3/16" diameter is most popular) of varying length is inserted into the tubing. It slips out to free the rig from a snag.

Hollow pencil lead is fastened(crimped) to the knot dropper at the swivel. If hung up, it will pull away from the lead if not crimped too tight.

3-way swivel with dropper - Use when larger weight is needed.

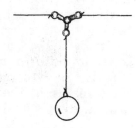

For smaller streams a simple choice is to use a rubber core sinker. Tie the hook to the main line and put the sinker on about 18" up the line. Have a selection of sinker sizes with you.

Lures and Bait

The choice of bait and lures is very wide in drift fishing. Here are the most popular;

Salmon Roe, tied in dime to quarter sized red Maline bags with thread. These are put on a special steelhead baitholding hook. Hook size #1 is good. Bags can also be put right on a regular hook.

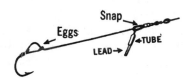

Nightcrawlers - Thread on the hook. Let an inch or so at the end dangle free.

Drift Bobbers - These are not regular bobbers but buoyant lures, usually bright colors and often rotate in the water to send off vibrations. Some slide on the leader of the hook, after a bead to enhance rotation. Others come with metal shafts and their own treble hook. These are very productive and have replaced roe as the main offering of many anglers. Popular ones are Okie Drifters, Spin-N-Glo and Glo-Go.

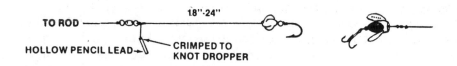

Yarn - Yarn can be fished alone, but usually it is added to roe or drift bobber rigs. Good colors are red, orange and cerise. It enhances the offerings appearance, and gets tangled in the fishes teeth(preventing deep hooking and helping signal bites). Some can also be tied to the line above the drift bobber.

Single Salmon Egg Rig - For small coastal streams, use a hook size that is entirely engulfed by the egg. Large white eggs are good. Fish with as little weight as possible(a few split shot a foot up from the hook). This system can often catch big fish.

Plunking

Here we have another "steelhead" word, that simply means stillfishing. Here the anglers intentionally put enough weight on their terminal tackle so it will not drift. Bait or floating lures are used. The rod is then propped up into a rod holder and coffee is poured. Actually, many plunkers have another rod for casting to pass the idle time. Some plunkers use a sliding sinker rig(see Catching Trout in Lakes), while others use the same rig as drift anglers. Bait and lures are also the same as for drift fishing.

Casting

Casting is simply that. Weighted spinners or spoons are cast up and across the stream and then returned. This is an active approach but since retrieves are by necessity near the bottom, they result in frequent hang-ups and loss of lures. Of course, drift fishing also results in hang-ups, but typically less costly offerings are used and rigs are used that often result in only partial loss of terminal tackle.

A small snap swivel should be used at the end of your main line to attach casting spoons and spinners. Wobbling spoons of about 1-3 inches long(e.g. Kastmaster, Daredevil) striped, dotted or solid bright flourescent hues, or in nickel, bronze or copper, are favorites. Mepps or Mounti-type spinners in nickel, brass or copper are good in size 4 and 5.

Choose the size to meet water conditions, so that the retrieve is natural and near the bottom. Heavy spoons are best in fast water. Light and narrower ones are best in quieter water. In roiled waters or at low light levels, spinners are preferred.

Backtrolling

Backtrolling is probably the most productive method of taking steelhead and salmon. It necessitates a boat. Here the anglers face the boat upstream and apply just enough power to allow the boat to slowly move downstream. A deep-diving plug, weighted plug or weighted bait is trolled off the back of the boat. Since the current is moving much faster than the boat, it takes the offering deep down in the current. The backtroller slowly works back and forth across a promising hole, then drops downstream a few feet and works across again. This approach is not recommended for anglers who are not experienced at river current boat handling.

. Steelhead backtrollers use Hotshot(size 10, 20 or 30) or similar lures tied directly to the line.

. Salmon backtrollers use Flatfish, or similar M-2, T-50 and T-55. Bags of salmon roe are tied to the treble hooks and a sardine fillet is tied to the underside of the lure.

24-30" 20 lb leader (lure)

12", 15 lb dropper

2-6 oz sinker

Float Fishing

Drift fishing requires experience and skill, in getting the offering right on the bottom and in detecting subtle bites. Some anglers, if they're not too self-conscious, add a float or bobber to their rig to minimize these difficulties. A float set at the right distance, holds the terminal tackle off the bottom, but right near it. Take up slack line as the bobber floats downstream, and set the hook if the bobber pauses or dips.

Fly Fishing

Fly fishing equipment and techniques can be used for fall and winter run steelhead and salmon. But, it is the exception rather than the rule. Specialized knowledge and skill is needed. If you intend to pursue this area, check out some steelhead and fly fishing books from your public library.

Water Conditions

Water conditions have an effect on your lure selection and fishing technique.

Muddy Water - Use roe, salmon eggs or nightcrawlers, anything with a scent. Use larger, more garish colored drift bobbers and use drift bobbers that spin fast to make vibrations.

Off-Colored Water - Use drift bobbers and artificial eggs. Ideal steelhead and salmon water is milky-green color, dropping and clearing after a freshet. Fish during a new rain - fish are stimulated.

Clear Water - Use small offerings and more subdued colors. Spoons and spinners work good.

Tackle and Equipment

Tackle used in steelhead and salmon fishing can be quite specialized, but for most situations, basic equipment is sufficient. Here is a rundown;

- **Rod** - Most drift and plunker anglers use a 8-9 foot, medium action (or medium-light action) spinning or baitcasting rod, with a 2 hand grip. A sensative tip is essential. For fishing wide tidal areas from shore, some anglers use surf casting equipment. Backtrollers generally use about a 6 foot baitcasting, boat rod with medium-heavy action and a sensative tip.

- **Reels** - Spinning reels need to be large enough to hold 200 yards of 10 pound monofilament line and have a good drag system. Ditto for baitcasting reels. Baitcasting reels are typically levelwinds with free spool and star drag.

. **Line** - Monofilament is almost universal. A 10 pound test is most common for steelhead and smaller salmon. For larger salmon 20 pound line is common.

Other equipment and riggings that are needed;

. Substantial landing net(for boat anglers). Shore anglers beach their fish.

. File - to continually resharpen hooks - they get dulled on rocks, gravel, etc.

. A needle-nosed pliers - to remove hooks.

. Knife - to gut and gill fish.

. Chest high waders.

. Warm clothing, a waterproof jacket and hat, and polarized sun glasses.

Where to Fish

See Coastal Rivers and Valley Rivers Sections of this book.

Cleaning and Cooking

Smaller fish are filleted. Larger ones are steaked. For cooking instructions see, Catching Salmon in Oceans and Catching Trout in Streams.

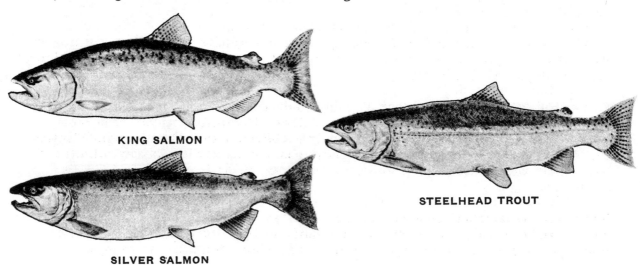

KING SALMON

STEELHEAD TROUT

SILVER SALMON

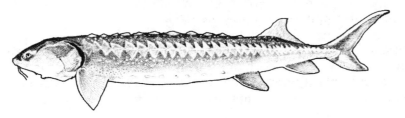

WHITE STURGEON

How to Catch...Sturgeon

Of the 16 species of sturgeon, two live in local waters(San Francisco Bay, San Pablo Bay, Suisun Bay, the Delta, Sacramento River). Green sturgeon(sometimes locally referred to as yellow) are the least prevalent. Greens have long slender snouts and grow to about 7 feet in length and 350 pounds. White sturgeon(actually grey) have a more blunt nose and can grow even larger.

Fishing Techniques

Sturgeon fishing is done almost always from a boat at anchor. And the almost exclusive approach is still fishing. Because of this it's important to drop your bait in a promising location. There are prime sturgeon fishing spots throughout the Bays and Delta.

Sturgeon fishing is best on a strong, incoming tide and at the turning of this tide. Most sturgeon are caught in 10-20 feet of water, often at drop-offs. Chart recorders are very helpful in locating these contours and actually "seeing" the sturgeon themselves. But, many sturgeon are caught by anglers who don't have chart recorders. Try a location. Move on in half an hour if there is no action.

Sturgeons are bottom feeders. In fact their mouths hover over the bottom and literally suction, or vacuum in the food, so bait must be right on the bottom. A sturgeon's initial "bite" is very soft which dictates two things;

1. A sliding sinker rig.

2. A rod tip that is sensative enough to detect the light movement as the sturgeon picks up the bait and moves slightly as it suctions it in.

Many sturgeon anglers cast out or lower in their offering, tighten up the line after the bait sinks to the bottom, and then lean the rod against the transom of the boat(the rod butt on the floor). Then, when a tap is detected, the angler lifts the rod up and points the tip directly at the fish. A big pull means to set the hook hard. Several pumps are probably in order. Sturgeons have tough mouths.

Tackle and Equipment

As mentioned above, a rod with a sensative tip is recommended. But, some anglers prefer heavy action rods. These also work fine, especially if the angler likes to hold the rod and sense the bite by keeping the line between the thumb and index finger. The rod should be 6½-8 feet long and have a long butt below the reel mount to lend leverage while playing the fish.

Most sturgeon anglers use conventional ocean-weight fishing reels. But, relatively heavy spinning reels with a good drag and the capability to hold 250 yards or so of 30 pound line will also work.

A landing net will work for sturgeon that are only a foot or more over the legal limit(40 inches). Beyond this a gaff or snair is probably required.

Bait and Rigging

Two or three hook sturgeon rigs can be purchased at many Bay Area bait shops. 6/0 size hooks are recommended. These leaders use wire line. Attach the rig to your line with a strong snap swivel.

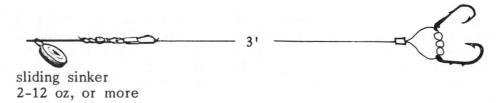

sliding sinker
2-12 oz, or more

Grass shrimp are the most common bait. Mud and ghost shrimp are also used. Two people need about 1 pound of bait. Load up each hook with bait.

4 or 5 shrimps may be needed. The bigger the wad the better. Live or fresh bait is most desirable. You can slide shrimp up the hook leader. Some suggest putting shrimp on the hook, tail first.

Anchovies and clams can also be used for bait. Some use a small hair net to hold their baits in a glob.

Where to Fish

See San Francisco, the Delta and Sacramento River Sections of this book.

Cleaning and Cooking

Many anglers put caught sturgeon on a heavy rope stringer and then bleed them while still in the water. Cut the fish deeply behind each gill.

The first item on the cleaning agenda is to gut the fish. Next, slice off the sharp spines along the sides, top and bottom. Slice through the skin on the back and belly and along the rear or the gill cage. By hand, or with a pair of pliers, pull the skin off each side. Now, cut off the head and make a deep cut around the fish right in front of the tail. You can now remove the spinal column in one piece. Finally, steak the fish and fillet the tail section. Trim off the red meat along the sides and next to the spinal column.

Sturgeon can be cooked in many ways. Baked or barbecued, lightly floured and pan-fried in butter, or smoked. The flesh is lean, compact, almost meat-like and quite rich.

RAINBOW TROUT

How to Catch... Trout (in Streams)

We are blessed by the numerous, fine trout streams in Northern California(many of these are described in the Mountain Trout Fishing Section of this book). Stream trout fishing is appealing because it can be the type of experience you personally want it to be. It can be accessible or remote, challenging or relaxing, simple or complicated.

Many people have a stereotype in their minds of the typical trout angler. It includes a flyrod, hip-high waders, a vest decorated with multicolored flys, a hat with more multicolored flys, a landing net hanging from the waist, all topped off with a Norman Rockwell-like wicker creel. This, of course, exactly describes some trout fishermen. But, forget this stereotype. Stream trout fishing can be productive and enjoyable, not only for the avid, well-equipped fly fisherman, but for everyone. You don't even need to use a flyrod, if you don't want to.

The purpose of this section is to describe, in detail, several of the basic ways to catch stream trout, regardless of the type of fishing you prefer and the type of tackle you have.

There are several different types of trout in Northern California streams. The most common are rainbow. Most are planted, but some are native. Others include the German brown trout, the brook trout and the golden trout.

Some Fundamentals

Stream trout fishing, no matter what equipment is used, focuses on casting a fly, spinner, spoon or bait into a likely place in the stream and then retrieving it in as natural a manner as possible.

Other fundamentals;

- Trout always face upstream, watching for food to be delivered to them by the moving water. So your offering should be presented in the same manner - moving from upstream to downstream.

- Trout are very leary and easily spooked. Since they're facing upstream and smelling the water that comes from upstream, always move upstream as you fish. This way, you're less likely to be detected. Move quietly and stay out of the line of sight of likely trout hangouts. Keep your shadow off the water.

- In the same vane, fish on the shady side of the stream, especially in the hours just after sunrise and just before sunset.

- Casts in an upstream direction or up and across the stream are preferred over downstream casts. Downstream casts require a retrieve that is against the current and therefore, unnatural in appearances.

- Trout stay near the bottom of the stream. So your offering must move along near the bottom. The exception to this rule is when dry fly fishing. Dry flies(floating flies) imitate floating insects being carried along by the current. Trout will rise up to take these flies. Dry fly fishing is evening fishing.

- As with most fishing, early morning and evening are best fishing peiods. But, trout can be caught at any time of the day.

- Keep hooks sharp. Banging rocks and pebbles can dull them quickly.

- If you're not succeeding in whatever approach you're using(flies, spinners, bait), try other offerings until you find the one that works.

- Trout hang out behind boulders that break the current, in deep holes, in slower water near the undercut edge of a stream(especially in shaded areas), and at the head and tail of pools. Concentrate your efforts on these areas.

- When you spot an obviously expert trout angler, watch where he or she casts from, where he or she put the offering and how it is retrieved.

Often the best places to cast from are in the water. Don't let that stop you. Just be careful and carry a wading staff to probe the bottom and improve balance.

Fly Fishing

Flies, both dry(floating) and wet(sinking) are very small and light. Too light to cast any distance. In fly fishing this difficulty is overcome by using flyline that has enough weight so it can be cast. The fly, connected by a light leader to the end of the flyline "just goes along for a ride" as the line is played out and finally set on its final trajectory. The purpose of the fly reel is simply to store line that is not being used, at the moment, and to retrieve line when necessary.

Fly fishing is an art and a science. Some say it is the ultimate fishing experience. Some people **only** fly fish. Many whole volumes have been written on fly fishing. In our limited space here we cannot compete. But here are the insights that produce fish in Northern California;

- If you're having trouble handling fly fishing equipment and making a good cast, consider a fly fishing class, watch others do it, read up on the subject in specialized books, and practice, practice, practice.

- Dry flies must float. Floating solution, leader sinking solution, tapered leaders and generally good floating fly line make this possible.

- As the old truism goes, "match the hatch." Dry flies must imitate nature. Good Northern California dry flies include California mosquito, light Cahill and the Adams. Size #14 and #16 are best.

- Present the dry fly above the suspected feeding fish and let it float naturally through that feeding area.

- Dry fly fishing is an evening affair. The several hours before dark are best.

- Wet flies imitate underwater creatures such as the larva or pupa state of aquatic insects, nymphs, grubs, etc.

- Good wet flies in NorCal include #6 and #8 bee imitation, brown or black spent wing flies and light tan caddis larvae flies.

- As the fly drifts back to you, take in excessive line. Then you'll be ready to strike.

- Watch the tip of your floating fly line. If it hesitates or pauses, set the hook.

. Standard streamers(which immitate bait fish) are the matuka(in olive), the marabou streamer and the muddler minnow.

. Many wet fly devotees use two different flies at a time.

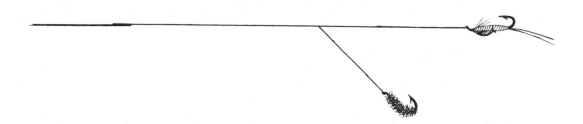

There is a great deal of variety in fly fishing equipment. One can spend hundreds of dollars or you can buy a rod/reel combination that is quite decent for less than $50.00. For starters, a 7½-8½ foot rod matched with #6 line is good. An automatic reel costs a few dollors more, but makes taking up excessive line so much easier.

Spinning

Spinning fishing means stream trout fishing using spinning or even spincasting equipment. The most popular set-ups include light spinning tackle and ultra-light spinning tackle. Ultra-light tackle is the easiest to handle and probably the most appropriate. It's capable of casting even small offerings, to sufficient distances with a 4 pound test line. Here are the fundamentals of stream trout fishing with spinning tackle;

. The most common lures are very small spinners, probably never larger than a #2. Since retrieves are with the current(you're still casting upstream), a spinner whose blade rotates freely with little more motion than current speed is more desirable. These spinners imitate swimming bait fish. A popular example of a spinner of this caliber is the Panther Marten #2, 1/16 ounce black bodied spinner. Gold blades are good for low light or overcast periods, chrome blades are recommended for sunny periods, and copper is good for not-so-clear water. Try several.

. Besides spinners, spoons are also good, like the Super Duper. Retrieval speed is critical for the success of both spinners and spoons. Test both in quiet pools. Both types put out a vibration that can be sensed in the motion at the tip of the rod. Watch for this and adjust retrieval speed accordingly. Also, frequently change return speed to give offerings a more natural swimming pattern.

. Spinners need to be worked near the bottom. Adjust your retrieval speed to achieve this. You'll hang up some spinners, but you'll catch more fish.

. Some lures are best tied directly to the main line. Others may twist the line if a small snap swivel is not used. Experiment, but if using a swivel, make sure it is in good working order and has a rounded connector at the lure end. This will insure proper action in the water.

Bait Fishing for Trout

Stream trout fishing with bait is the most flexible of all approaches. It's flexible because of the wide choice of baits that produce fish. And it's flexible because it can be done with either fly fishing equipment or spinning equipment. Some devotees even combine the two by using monofilament line on a fly rod and reel. All these possibilities are fine. Here are the fundamentals of trout stream bait fishing;

. Redworms are probably the most popular bait followed by bottled salmon eggs. Cheese and marshmallows are also popular. Then, there is a whole category of natural, live baits including crickets, beetles, grubs, larvae and pupae. Some anglers collect bait right out of the stream by using a fine mesh screen to trap bait dislodged by moving large rocks in the streambeds.

. If you're using live bait, it should be alive. So, store and transport them carefully and hook them so as not to inflict fatal damage(at least not instant fatal damage).

. A short shank #8 or #10 hook is good. Try to conceal the entire hook into the bait.

. You want the bait to drift along with the current near the bottom of the stream. Unweighted drifting is best. If you need weight to get near the bottom, use as little split shot as possible, about 8-10 inches from the hook.

. Since your bait is under water and drifting, it's not all that easy to detect bites. It helps to keep slack out of the line (while still allowing drift) and to set the hook on any sign of hesitation or pause in drift.

Using Casting Bobber for Trout

Purest fly fishermen may cringe at this approach, but here goes anyway. Some people would like to be able to cast flies or small baits without mastering a fly rod. And some can't afford fly fishing equipment. For this group a casting bobber is the answer.

A casting bobber is a small, clear plastic float that adds enough weight to a fly or a small bait to allow casting with a spinning or spincasting reel and monofilament line.

casting
bobber

2-5'

Casting bobbers are available in several sizes and configurations Some even allow you to vary weight by allowing water inside the bobber.

Fish a casting bobber rig just as you would a dry fly. If you use a wet fly or bait, allow enough distance between the bobber and the hook so your offering gets down to near the bottom. In rapidly flowing water, some split shot about 8 inches from the hook may be added.

Tackle and Equipment

Besides your choice of rod, reel, line and enticements to put at the end of it, trout anglers need several other items. Essential are both a creel(canvas ones can be purchased for as little as $5.00) or a fishing vest and an inexpensive landing net. A needle-nose pliers or other hook removing device is also essential. Small trout should be released, with as little hook damage as possible.   In fact, some trout fishermen flatten the barbs on all their hooks to facilitate catch and release. Releasing large trout is possibly even more important. It takes large ones to produce small ones.

Optional equipment for trout fishing includes polarized sun glasses, waders and a wading staff. The sun glasses help take the glare off the water and improve underwater visibility. The use of waders depends on air temperature, water temperature, the number of stepping stones in a stream and ones desire to stay dry. Wading staffs(just a light tree limb) are great to help maintain balance.

Cleaning and Cooking

Small trout(pan size) are generally just gutted and gilled(field cleaned). Larger trout are often filleted. Trout is mild, lean and sweet. It is suitable for just about any cooking approach. Sauteing is probably the most popular. The flesh of trout is tender, delicately flavored and can range in color from white to a pinkish we associate with salmon.

EAGLE LAKE RAINBOW TROUT

How to Catch...Trout and Salmon(in Lakes)

Fishing for trout in lakes is very different from stream trout fishing. This is true because the lake environment changes the behavior of trout. Stream trout are always facing upstream, confined to shallow waters, on or near the bottom, and near or behind structures like boulders, undercuts, etc. The stream determines the location and habits of trout.

Trout in lakes have different ground rules dictating their lives. Food doesn't necessarily "flow" to them, they must find it. Lake water temperatures vary by season and depth, so trout will change depth to find oxygen rich water of a comfortable temperature for them. At times they may be near the surface, and at other times they may be down 80 feet or more.

A few Northern California trout lakes also have king or silver salmon planted in them. Salmon and trout in lakes behave and are caught using the same techniques, lures and bait. Usually, anglers pursuing trout will catch an occassional salmon.

If you're catching trout in a lake, especially in the summertime, and you'd like some salmon, it sometimes helps to fish a little deeper. Research has shown that rainbow and brown trout favor water temperatures of between 55° and 60°. But, the same research determined that king and silver salmon favor 55° water, which will be down deeper.

Reading a Lake

The specifics of a lake says a lot about the location of trout. And, as many anglers have discovered, you've got to find them before you can catch them. As a matter of fact, catching trout in lakes is quite easy, once they are located. Here are the fundamentals;

.   Trout, even in lakes, relate to structures. Trout use structures to shelter themselves from predators and to keep out of direct sun. Depending on the time of year, overhanging trees, cliff areas, submerged points, coves and submerged river channels are good starting points.

.   Trout move to locate food and oxygen. The primary inlet to a lake is always a prime location. It washes in food and cool, oxygen-rich water. In cooler months, shoreline weedbeds may also provide insects and bait fish. The windward shoreline is also a good possibility. Drifting food will concentrate here. Finally, newly planted trout usually hang around the planting site for several days or more.

.   A depth sounder can be an important tool. It not only will locate struture-like underwater islands and submerged drop-offs, but it will also locate schools of bait fish and the trout themselves.

.   Trout are found down deeper in lakes in the summer months. Some Northern California lakes stratify(or divide) into three layers during the warming months and can remain in this condition until fall. The top layer is too warm and too low in oxygen for trout and salmon. They concentrate near the top of the second layer, or thermocline. In this layer there is plenty of oxygen and forage fish. This layer may be from 15-50 feet down depending on lake depth and size. Water temperature will be in the 55-60° range. A depth sounder, underwater temperature gauge or locals can all help you to determine the proper depth to fish.

LAKE STRATIFICATION
Surface

Epilimnion Layer

Thermocline Layer
Oxygen and Baitfish Rich

Hypolimnion Layer

Bottom

Fishing Techniques

There are three primary methods of catching trout in lakes;

1. Trolling – In one form or another, this is probably the most productive method of catching trout in lakes.

2. Bait Fishing – A very good method, especially for shore fishing. Can also be done from a boat, for example, at a stream inlet of the lake.

3. Casting – Also a very productive shore fishing method. Can also be done from a boat.

It is also possible to catch trout in lakes by fly fishing. But, even avid fly fishermen will admit it is difficult. Dry flies will only work, for example, when an insect hatch is taking place. Even then, they may not work because they don't move with the current as they do in streams. Wet flies, streamers, etc., can be used in lakes, and can produce at times, if you're either very skillful or very lucky. Remote, high altitude mountain lakes, when there are hungry trout and little angling pressure, are the best candidates for lake fly fishing success. If you're interested in more information on lake fly fishing, check out several fly fishing books from your local public library.

Trolling for Trout

Trolling is simply pulling an offering at the end of your line, through the water, using a boat. It can and is done with boats ranging from a canoe, to a rowboat, to an inboard/outboard.

There are actually two separate and distinct aspects of trolling for trout. The first is the trolling rig itself, and the second is the tackle/equipment combinations used to troll the rig at a prescribed depth. Let's look at each separately;

Trolling rig – A trolling rig is made up of these components(in order of placement on line);

1. Rudder – A blade to prevent line twist.

2. Flasher – An attractant which imitates a school of bait fish.

3. Swivel – Prevents twist.

4. Snubber – Absorbs shock of a strike. Use is optional, but recommended.

5. Leader – About 18 inches of monofilament.

6. Offering – Spoon, plug or baited hook.

The flasher and rudder are usually sold in a packaged unit. Use larger units for murky water or deep trolling. Then you just attach on the snubber, tie on a leader and attach your offering. See diagram below;

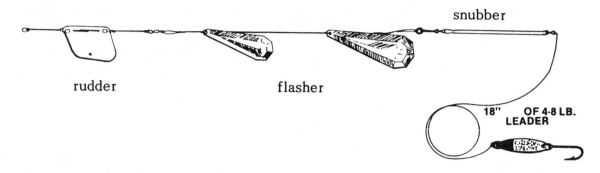

snubber

rudder   flasher

18"   OF 4-8 LB.
       LEADER

Trolling Tackle/Equipment – Unlike the trolling rig, which is quite standard, trolling tackle/equipment provides several options and alternatives.

In the cold months of the year when trout are found near the surface, trolling rigs can be handled with light spinning or baitcasting tackle and about 10-12 pound monofilament line. This is especially true if a flasher is not used. Weight can be added to the rudder(using tied line) to troll 2-10 feet down below the surface.

Unfortunately, many of us do most of our lake trout fishing in the summer when the trout are down deep in the lake. To get a trolling rig down to 30, 60, or more feet you have these choices;

.   Use leadcore trolling line on a good sized conventional reel. Medium Penn freshwater reels with levelwind are popular(e.g. 210 series). With slow trolling speed, leadcore line sinks at about 45°, so, for example, 50 feet of line, will produce a 25 foot trolling depth.

.   Use a downrigger – This is by far the most desirable approach, especially if you need to go down more than 40 feet. A downrigger will take your trolling rig down to a known depth(they're equipped with depth counters) and allow you to play and land the fish on light tackle. See the next page for illustration.

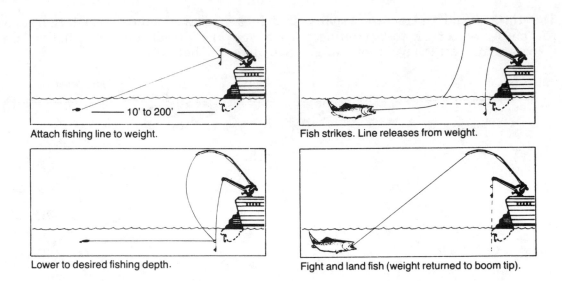

Attach fishing line to weight.

Fish strikes. Line releases from weight.

Lower to desired fishing depth.

Fight and land fish (weight returned to boom tip).

Trolling Tips - No matter what depth you're trolling or what equipment you're using, these tips will help produce fish;

. Troll slowly. The best trolling is slow trolling. Some highly successful trollers, for example, use only oar power.

. Change trolling speed often. Every minute or two isn't too frequent. Sometimes it even helps to speed up for just a few seconds and then slow down. This gives added up-and-down action to the flasher and lure.

. Change depth. If you're not sure of the depth you're trolling at(it can vary depending on boat speed and amount of line out, for all approaches except downrigging) or the depth the trout are at, vary depth until you get a strike. Then stick there.

. Troll an "S" Pattern. Trolling experts suggest this approach, 1)because it covers more territory than straight line trolling and, 2)because it causes speed, direction and depth changes to occur in the flasher and lure. These movements and resulting vibrations attract trout.

Bait Fishing for Trout

Bait fishing can be done from shore or boat. The most common tackle is light spinning equipment.

Despite all the variety in trout bait fishing, the most productive technique is probably the sliding sinker rig. It is most often used from shore, but also is well suited to anchored boat fishing in coves and inlets;

sliding
sinker

$1\frac{1}{2}$–3'

baitholder No 6-12
or, treble No 16

The purpose of the sliding sinker rig is to allow the bait to move freely when a trout picks it up. With a fixed sinker rig, the trout would notice the drag on the offering and drop it.

The process begins by casting out the baited rig to a likely spot. Let it sink all the way to the bottom and then slowly crank in any slack. Now, sit down, get comfortable and open the bail on your spinning reel. Personally, I don't believe in putting a rod down or propping it up on a stick. I believe in holding the rod. Then you can feel the slightest tug on your bait. In fact, I like to have my line, in front of the reel, go between the thumb and index finger of my non-reeling hand. This puts my senses directly in touch with my bait.

When the trout picks up the bait, play off line from the spool, so no resistance is felt by the fish. A pause may be detected after the first movement of line. Wait until it starts moving out again(this means the trout has swallowed the bait, literally swallowed the bait). Close the bail and set the hook. You've got yourself a fish.

A wide variety of baits are used. Salmon eggs, cheese, minnows, shad, worms crickets. A combination of baits is also popular. Some use a small marshmallow/salmon egg/nightcrawler combination. The egg provides visual attraction and the marshmallow provides buoyancy so the whole offering floats slightly off the bottom. Another way to accomplish this buoyant effect using nightcrawlers is to inflate them with air. Crawler inflaters are available to accomplish this task. Many large trout are caught on both combination baits and inflated nightcrawlers.

Bobber fishing can also be quite effective for trout. This is an especially effective method in winter and early spring when lake surface temperatures are cool and trout are often feeding near the surface. Simply tie your hook to the line, put a split shot a foot or so up from the hook, and snap on a bobber up the line. Six feet is a good distance to try first. Cast it out and watch your bobber closely.

Casting for Trout

Casting for trout is a popular shore fishing option, especially among younger anglers. And it can be effective. The most popular tackle is again light spinning or spincasting.

Lures can be tied directly to the end of the main line or attached with a snap swivel. I prefer the snap swivel. It prevents any line twist and provides a way to change lures easily. Most trout lures imitate small bait fish. Silver and gold colors are good in 1/8 to 3/8 ounce sizes;

- Kastmasters

- Roostertails

- Phoebes

- Mepps Spinners

Cast out as far as possible, let lure settle to the desired retrieve depth and return at the speed that provides the most natural action. Slower is probably better. And vary the pace of your retrieve. The small bait you're trying to duplicate don't swim fast and they don't swim at a steady pace. Sometimes it's best to let the lure sink for sometime before starting your retrieve. A problem with this approach is the frequent snags(on sunken branches, etc.) and lost lures. Some anglers minimize this difficulty by replacing the original treble hook with a weedless hook.

Cleaning and Cooking

See Trout(in Streams) for cleaning instructions.

Smaller trout are best when sauteed or oven fried, or when baked, either plain or with a light sauce. The larger, whole trout are excellent when baked or poached. Trout is at its best when prepared simply.

Bay Area Freshwater Hotspots

Almost all Bay Area anglers like getting away for a week-end or week-long fishing trip to one of the many great fishing locales in Northern California. But it's also nice, at times, to take advantage of the great freshwater fishing opportunities close to home.

Seven great "close-to-home" fishing hot spots are featured in the lake section of this book. Anderson, Chabot, Del Valle, Isabel, Merced, Parkway and San Pablo each has a full page write-up and full page fishing map. Look at the map on this page and see how convenient these lakes are to most Bay Area residents. They offer great freshwater fishing only a short drive from home. They're fantastic for day trips, or even half day fishing outings. Read up on these lakes, and then plan a "close-to-home" fishing adventure, with a friend or the family.

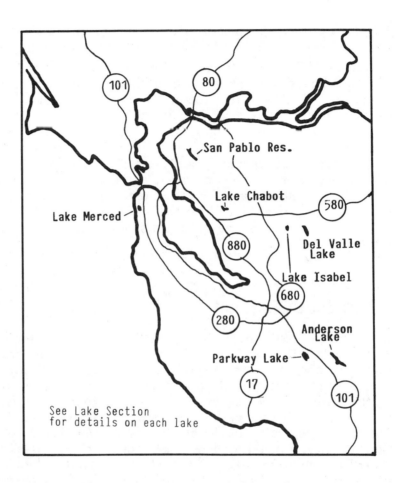

Other North Bay Hotspots

There are seven Marin Water District Lakes in the County. Lagunitas and Bon Tempe Lakes have been planted with trout in recent years. No boats are allowed on any of these lakes. Other fish producing Marin lakes include Alpine, Kent, Soulajule and Nicasio. Anglers hike to Kent and Alpine Lakes for trout, some quite large. Soulajule offers black bass and bluegills, but is not conveniently located. More accessible Nacasio, has an overpopulation of carp, but also bass, panfish and catfish. In winter, the mouths of Lagunitas and Walker Creeks, downstream of the Hwy. 1 bridge, offer steelhead and silver salmon prospects.

Other East Bay Hotspots

Beside Del Valle and Chabot, the East Bay Regional Park District(415)531-9300, also supervises a number of small lakes that offer very fine fishing. Here's a rundown. Shadow Cliffs Reservoir, a 75 acre lake near Pleasanton, has some extremely good trout fishing, including trophy trout. There are also bluegills, some small bass and larger catfish in Shadow Cliffs. Catfish are even more prominent at Cull Canyon Reservoir, a less frequented lake near Castro Valley. Cats are planted regularly and bass and bluegill are also taken. The small Shinn Pond in the Fremont area, at Niles, is a good bass water. At Lake Temescal, in Oakland, catfishing is most popular, but bass and trout are also taken. Don Castro, outside of Hayward, can be good for trout and catfish. The Park District publishes a weekly anglers newsletter, available for a small subscription fee.

Other South Bay Hotspots

Besides Anderson and Parkway Lakes, there are some other good South Bay fishing waters. Coyote Lake, South of Anderson Reservoir, is planted with trout regularly and trout fishing can be good in Coyote Creek below the reservoir. Santa Clara Reservoir System contains eleven lakes in all. One of these, Lexington Reservoir, along Hwy. 17, offers good trout fishing when the water level is adequate. Two smaller reservoirs(Chesbro, Uvas) both West of Morgan Hill, are fished regularly by local anglers for catfish, bass and panfish. In Santa Cruz County, Loch Lomond offers good fishing prospects. This is a beautiful, secluded mountain lake with angling for trout, bass and panfish. Loch Lomond is supervised by the City of Santa Cruz water department.

Party Boat Fishing

Tens of thousands of anglers enjoy ocean fishing on a party boat, or sport fishing boat, each year in Northern California. To say the least, this is a popular and relatively inexpensive way to pursue saltwater fish.

Most party boats take reservations from individuals and operate on a daily schedule. Charter boats are also available for group rental. Party boat anglers range from regulars who go out every week to vacationers from Wyoming who've never even seen the ocean, let alone fished it. One appeal to newcomers is that no equipment or prior knowledge is needed. Rod and reels can be rented(for about $3-5.00 a day). Burlap sacks, to hold the catch are available. Bait is included in the price of the trip and fish filleting services are available at dockside at a modest cost. And there are plenty of helpful people around to explain the best way to catch fish. Observing those that are most successful helps the newcomer with the finer points.

Party boats are large, safe, well-equipped fishing machines. They have wash rooms, lounges and other amenities. But no matter what the season and the shore weather, it's best to bring along warm clothing. It gets cool out on the water. Dress in layers. Then you can build-up or strip down depending on conditions.

Party Boat Particulars

One of the attractive aspects of NorCal party boat angling is the wide variety of fishing experiences that are offered. There are open ocean trips for salmon, albacore, rockfish or lingcod. Then there are what are called "Potluck Trips" in San Francisco Bay for striper and halibut. These trips use the live bait drift fishing technique described in this book, and also, on occasion, take rockfish, lingcod or even salmon. These same live bait boats also offer trips for striper, off Pacifica, when this action is hot. And there are, at times, trips in San Francisco Bay for sturgeon or even sharks. The fishing techniques used on all these trips are those described in the How to Catch . . . Sections of this book. Salmon trips are offered, whenever the fish are hitting between March and October. Albacore trips are usually August-September. Rockfish trips are offered throughout most of the ocean fishing season, while most lingcod trips are fall-early winter. Potluck trips are in summer, as are Pacific striper trips. Sturgeon fishing is best in winter. Trip costs vary depending on travel time to the fishing grounds and the actual fishing time, but most run between $30 and $40, with albacore being higher.

Party boats operate out of several locations(or landings) along the Northern California coast. Here are the major landings; Morro Bay, Monterey, Santa Cruz, Half Moon Bay, San Francisco(Fisherman's Wharf), Emeryville, Richmond, San Rafael, Bodega Bay, Fort Bragg, and Eureka.

Surf Fishing

Surf fishing is man and nature at its best. It's just you, the roaring breakers, the sea birds, salt spray and hopefully the fish. For those who demand more than sea birds and salt spray, there are practical reasons why so many people enjoy surf fishing; there are miles and miles of accessible beaches to fish, it can be done year around, the necessary equipment is inexpensive, bait is often free and the fish can be caught without a great deal of skill.

Bait Fishing Techniques

Northern California anglers catch a good variety of fish. The most common are surf perch(redtail, walleye and barred). But California halibut, flounder, striped bass and even salmon can be taken. The basic approach for taking all these fish is the same. Anglers cast out a rig consisting of a 2-6 ounce pyramid sinker at the end of a leader that has 2 or 3 baited hooks on it. They then set the rod in a sandspike rodholder and wait for the bite. If nothing happens in a few minutes, slowly move the rig in about 3-5 feet and try this new location. Some novices are tempted to run back from the beach, especially when a large fish is hooked. This is not a good idea. Rather, reel the fish in steadily, and move back only if the fish is charging faster than you can take in line. When a large fish is near shore, time your retrieve with the surf so the momentum of a breaker will skid the fish up on the sand. Run and grab him under a gill cover and quickly move back to higher ground.

Tackle and Equipment

As mentioned earlier, tackle and equipment requirements are quite minimal. All you need are;

Rod: 10-12 foot surf spinning rod with 2-handed grip.

Reel: Saltwater spinning reels are most popular. It should hold 200-250 yards of 15-20 pound monofilament line.

Other: Pyramid sinker(assorted 2-6 ounce - use the smallest that tide and wave conditions will allow), surf leaders(available at most tackle counters), hooks(#2, #6), sandspike rodholder, and a big pail(for bait and your catch).

Bait and Rigging:

The basic rig is straightforward;

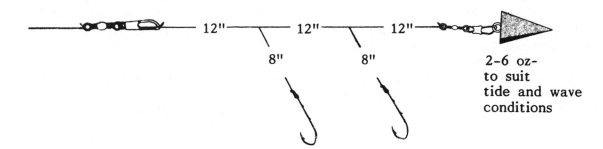

The hook size depends on the fish;

Fish	Typical Catch(pounds)	Hook Size
California halibut	4-8	#2
Striped Bass	4-10	#1/0
Barred Surfperch	1	#6
Walleye surfperch	$\frac{1}{4}$	#6
Redtail	$\frac{1}{2}$	#6

Most anglers prefer frozen anchovies when fishing for halibut and utilize a slow and continuous retrieve through holes and slopes. Perch, both barred and wall-eye, are suckers for bloodworms and sandcrabs. Bloodworms are natives of Maine and are available from bait shops. Soft-shelled sandcrabs and another free bait-mussels, are gathered by anglers themselves. Hook the sandcrab up through the tail end, with the hook tip barely showing. Hook the mussel through the tough grissle-like edge. If possible, it's probably best to be prepared to toss out several of these baits, and let the fish decide. Cut pieces of frozen squid is another good alternative. These strips stay on the hook very well.

Surf Casting

The most aggressive surf anglers are the cast and retrieve people. They cast plugs and spoons that weigh 2-4 ounces into the surf and then retrieve them, alert for a striper or occassional salmon strike. Halibut can also be taken. Surf casters typically use a two-handed grip rod of about 10 feet in length. A shorter rod lacks the needed distance, while a longer one is slower and more difficult to control.

Effective offerings for casters include Pencil-Poppers, Zara Spooks, Hopkins No-Eql,

Krocodiles, Kastmasters and bucktail and bugeye jigs. Plugs are best in rocky areas and spoons are preferred on beaches.

Heavy duty saltwater spinning reels with rear drag are popular. The reel used should hold 200-250 yards of 15-30 test monfilament line. Conventional reels with a free spool and star drag(like the Penn Squidder) are for traditionalists who have mastered the art of thumbing the spool to prevent backlash.

Striper anglers watch for birds like gulls, sheerwaters, pelicans or cormorants diving into the surf in pursuit of bait fish. These bait fish are driven into the beach by stripers feeding. These birds are the casters main clue as to when the stripers are feeding and in which direction they may be moving. The key is to cast the line where the bait fish are and to retrieve it so it duplicates a wounded baitfish. Early mornings and dusk are often the best time to use the birds as trackers.

Where to Fish

Below, some of the best surf fishing spots are listed. But exactly where on a beach to fish is important. It's best, if possible, to scout a beach at low tide. Steeply sloping beach areas are best. Look for holes and channels where the surf is not breaking. When the tide floods in, these become the feeding grounds for fish. The rising tide, up to high tide and an hour or two after are usually the best times to fish. Actually any accessible surf has the potential of being a good surf fishing location. But, some locations are more accessible and have developed a reputation as productive fishing stretches. Starting from the Oregon border and working South, here is a list of some of the best;

North of Humbolt: Prairie Creek Redwood St. Pk., Trinidad St. Beach, Mad River Beach Co. Pk.

Humbolt Bay: No. Spit(take Hwy. 225), So. Spit(take Table Bluff Rd.).

Mendocino County: MacKerricher St. Pk., Manchester St. Beach.

Sonoma County: Coast State beaches North of Bodega Bay.

Marin County: Pt. Reyes Natl. Seashore(No. and So. beaches), Stinson Beach.

San Francisco City and County: Baker, Ocean and Fleishhacker Beaches.

San Mateo County: Thornton St. Beach, Mussel Rock, Sharp Park St. Beach, Rockaway Beach, Linda Mar Beach, Monata St. Beach, Half Moon Bay St. Beaches.

Monterey Bay: Twin Lakes, New Brighton, Seacliff, Sunset and Moss Landing St. beaches. Carmel River St. Beach.

San Luis Obispo County: Hearst Memorial St. Beach and Pismo St. Beach.

Drift Fishing

Here's another instance of a confusing name. As used in San Francisco Bay waters, drift fishing means fishing from a drifting boat over productive areas (reefs, drop-offs). Water movement and wind move the boat with the engine used just to position the boat to start a drift(or correct it).

Drift fishing is included in this section rather than in the Striped Bass Section of this book because this technique is useful for more than stripers. Halibut, rockfish, lingcod, sharks and even salmon, at times, are caught this way.

Tackle and Equipment

Drift fishing tackle is quite basic. Most anglers use a 6-7 foot boat rod with a sensative tip(to detect bites) and a conventional saltwater reel loaded with 25-30 pound test monofilament line. Reel line capacity should be in the 200-300 yard range.

Terminal tackle is also straightforward. Here's the setup;

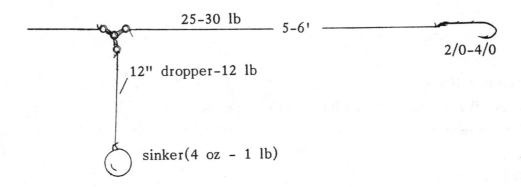

Sinker size depends on current speed. An 8 ounce cannonball sinker is most common but in a fast current, up to a pound is needed to keep the rig in contact with the bottom.

How To

San Francisco Bay drift fishing is actually a second cousin to open ocean bottom fishing. In both instances the idea is to drift over structures, while keeping the rig on the bottom but without getting snagged too frequently. The terminal tackle is different because live anchovies are the bait of choice(most ocean bottom fishing is done with cut pieces of squid or anchovies). Most anglers bait the anchovies up through both lips - not too deep or the bait life and effectiveness will be diminished.

Lower the baited rig until you feel bottom. Then, take up slack and actually lift the weight off the bottom a reel turn or two. Now, by raising and lowering the rod tip, or even by reeling in or letting out a little line, the key is to stay in contact with the bottom without getting hung up. Gently lower the weight to the bottom every few seconds to make sure your offering is still close. Remember, the fish are feeding near structures. You want your bait to be there too. Don't lapse into daydreaming or just drag your weight along the bottom. Rather, try to imagine the shape of the bottom as you drift over it. Try to picture its shape. "Feel" the bottom and its changing depth and adjust your depth accordingly.

Where to Fish

Some of the prime drift fishing locations in San Francisco Bay are listed below(see NOAA Nautical Chart 18652 - which you should have on board for safe boating on San Francisco Bay);

- Alcatraz Island - South side
- Arch Rock
- Blossom Rock
- Buoy #8
- Harding Rock
- Lime Point and Yellow Bluff - off Marin
- Peanut Farm
- Point Bonita
- Raccoon Straits
- Shag Rock
- Sharks Point
- South Tower of Golden Gate Bridge
- Treasure Island and Pier 21 - North and East of island

Pier Fishing

Pier fishing is a special way to fish the Pacific Ocean. Often there is a fellowship and spirit among these anglers that you don't find in other situations. Maybe that's because a number or people share the same experience and the same piece of ocean. Or maybe it's just because there are so many regulars. One fun way to get to know more about this type of fishing is to stroll out onto a pier and observe for an hour or two. You'll see all ages and types of people enjoying picr fishing. And don't hesitate to strike up a conversation or two, especially with anglers who look like regulars. A hint - look for older people with more equipment and more skill. Many anglers are happy to talk. It's part of the whole scene. Slip in the questions that come to mind between their fish stories. Pier and barge anglers do quite well depending on season, locale and conditions. Among the species caught are halibut, rockfish, mackerel, surfperch, and bonito. Often the fish caught are quite large.

Fishing Techniques

There are a number of fishing piers along the NorCal coast. A list is included later in this section and there is additional information in the Ocean Fishing Section of this book. One of the pleasant surprises about pier fishing is that many of them are public. At these facilities, fishing is free and no fishing license is required. Piers offer good facilities including benches, bait(some have live bait), beverages and food, washrooms, fish cleaning tables, etc.

Fishing techniques vary depending on the species being sought. Many times anglers cast out a baited rig(like a surf fishing rig) and wait for a bite. Fishing straight down from the rod tip is also popular. Perch which frequent the pilings are taken this way. Halibut anglers know that they must keep their offerings moving, so they cast out a halibut rig or jig and slowly retrieve it through likely spots, like depressions. Salmon and some other species, can be caught using a bobber and hooked anchovy. Specific questions aimed at seasoned pier anglers are a great way to learn.

Tackle and Equipment

Any type of rod and reel made has been used by pier anglers but since we're talking good-sized fish, tackle should be hefty enough for the fish being sought. For good-sized fish(like striper or halibut) use a heavy freshwater or light-medium saltwater rod(6-8 feet), a reel capable of holding at least 100 yards of 10-25 pound line that has a decent drag system(either spinning or conventional). For bottom fishing you can use a rockfish rig or a striper rig(see these sections for details). Bobbers are also used to drift bait. Popular baits include anchovies, squid, clams, pileworms and bloodworms.

Other things you'll need are a big pail(for your catch), a long piece of clothesline, and a crab net. The net is used to raise-up good-sized fish from the water line to the pier level. Have a fellow angler operate the net and be sure the fish is tired-out before netting and raising it.

When and Where to Fish

Timing is all important to successful pier fishing. Since we can't take the pier to the fish, we've got to go to the pier when the fish are there. And, most fish are not there most of the time. They come and go, often in as little as several days or several weeks. This is where local, timely information is essential. Keep in frequent telephone contact with local bait shops and piers. When fish are there, go after them. As with all ocean fishing, at many piers, tide movements can also effect the bite. A large swing in tides(a large difference between high and low tide) marks a good day to fish and just before, during and after high tide is a good time. A morning incoming tide is good. But, this isn't always so. Some days the fish are just there and biting no matter what, especially if the bait fish are near the pier.

Some of the most popular fishing piers are covered in the Ocean Fishing Section of this book. San Francisco Bay Area fishing piers are listed below;

Antioch - There are 2 fishing piers.

Berkeley Fishing Pier - City of Berkeley.

Point Benecia Fishing Pier - Solano County.

Brisbane Fishing Pier - Off Hwy. 101, 2.5 miles So. of San Francisco city limit.

Candlestick Park Public Pier - San Francisco.

Capitola Fishing Wharf - Take Bay Ave. exit off Hwy. 1 and follow to Capitola Village.

China Camp Pier - China Camp St. Park.

Dumbarton Bridge Fishing Pier - Newark.

Emeryville Fishing Pier - Emeryville.

Fort Mason Piers - Golden Gate National Recreation Area.

Fort Point Pier - Golden Gate National Recreation Area.

Fruitvale Bridge Park - City of Oakland.

Marina Green Jetty - San Francisco.

Martinez Fishing Pier – Martinez Marina.

Middle Harbor Park – City of Oakland.

Missions Rock Pier – San Francisco.

Monterey Municipal Pier – In Monterey at Fisherman's Wharf.

Municipal Pier – City of San Francisco

Pacifica Pier – Pacifica.

Paradise Pier – Marin County Parks.

Point Pinole – East Bay Regional Park District.

Portview Park – City of Oakland.

Pittsburg Pier – Pittsburg.

San Leandro Fishing Pier – San Leandro.

Santa Cruz Municipal Wharf – Located right by the Boardwalk in downtown Santa Cruz.

Seacliff Pier – In Seacliff Beach State Park, just South of Capitola.

Twenty-Fourth Street Pier – San Francisco.

Werder Pier – Foster City.

Rock Fishing and Poke Poling

Rock anglers know, even before going fishing, that they'll catch some fish, that they'll get wet, sooner or later and that the experience at the margins of land and sea will be special. But there are some things they don't know. For instance, they don't know what kinds of fish they will catch and they don't know how many hooks, sinkers, jigs and fish they will lose because of snags and hangups on the rocks. Fortunately the best bait is free, sinkers and hooks are cheap and a dry change of clothing just takes some forethought. So the good side of rockfishing surely outweighs the bad.

But a word of caution is necessary. People die every year walking along slippery, moss-covered ocean front rocks and cliffs. So do exercise caution and wear shoes that provide good traction.

Fishing Techniques

Rockfishing is one of the first ways man took food from the sea. But today rock anglers work both natural rock formations as well as jetties and breakwaters. Rockfish(several varieties), perch, eels and flatfish are all caught. It's not unusual to catch a half dozen varieties on one outing. And the nice thing is that only one basic approach is needed.

Most say that rockfishing is at its best on an incoming morning tide. Anglers sometimes like to arrive before sunrise to gather bait and scout the rock formations before the water covers them over. Fishing is often good up to one hour past high tide. Good spots to fish include deep slots or passageways between rocks and pockets where there is some wave action and surging. Quiet water is usually not productive. Another tip. You usually don't need to cast long distances to find fish. The best spot is often right below where you are standing. The fish you're after have moved in with the tide to feed in and about the rocks. Sometimes anglers drop a jig straight down in water 5 or 10 feet deep.

Another key to successful rockfishing is to keep moving. Try a good looking spot for only a short time and then move to another. If the fish are there they'll hit right away. Speaking of hits, fish in this habitat are aggressive eaters. They hit hard and then shoot for cover, so set the hook immediately and don't give any line. Keep the fish moving in slowly and steadily. Abrupt yanks can tear out the hook. Landing a hooked fish is often a challenge. Smaller ones can be lifted out of the water. If you're lucky, there will be a good miniature bay or shallow where you can guide your catch. Another good approach is to use a surge of water to bring the fish up on a flat that will be aground when the water recedes.

Casting is the basic technique used in rockfishing. A baited hook or jig is cast out to a likely spot and then retrieved. The slowest possible retrieve is usually best. Keep the line taut on the retrieve, always being alert for bites and snags. Maneuvering or speeding up a retrieve for a brief moment will often prevent a snag. If the pool is open, allow the offering to settle a little before retrieving. If you're fortunate enough to be fishing straight down, yo-yo your offering up and down. In some situations, a bobber can be used to help catch fish. Put it about 2 feet above the hook. Now you can bait fish in spots where a sinking rig would result in snags. Kelp-covered areas are one possibility.

Tackle, Bait, Lures and Rigging

Most rock anglers use light tackle. A 6-7 foot medium spinning outfit loaded with 10-15 pound test line is popular. Baitcasting equipment is also used. Heavier rods and reels are used by some. Accurate casts are a must, so use equipment that allows you to accomplish this. A backpack is good for carrying hooks, sinkers, bobbers, pliers, knife, towel, snacks and maybe a second pair of tennis or jogging shoes. A gunny sack is fine for holding your catch. Keep it wet and in the shade, when possible. Some anglers use tidepools, safely above the swells, as a good spot to put fish, once on a stringer.

The most popular rockfishing bait is probably mussels. Pry them off the rocks and open them with a knife. Now use the knife to cut out the strong portion in the middle along with the adjoining more delicate portion. Thread the hook through the tougher section and you're set to fish. Don't forget to check your bait frequently. Other baits that work include cut pieces of frozen squid or anchovy.

Rigging for rockfishing is best when kept simple. This prevents lots of snags. Most anglers use a single hook, often tied directly to the main line. Weight is provided by a sinker up about a foot above the hook. Split shot, rubber core sinkers or clinch-on sinkers are all used. An egg shaped sliding sinker, put on the line before the hook is tied on, is also a workable rig. The cardinal rule for all of these is to use as little weight as possible. Use just enough to make the cast. Then your offering will settle slower, a slower retrieve will be possible and less snags and hang-ups will result. Bait holder hooks in the #1 and #6 size range are best. The bigger hooks(like #1) are best for cabizon and other rockfish. Small hooks(like #6) are good for fish like opaleye. Speaking of hooks, they're the cause of most hangups. It often helps to use a pliers to turn in the tip of the hook(toward the shank) a little ways.

If you're willing to take the risk of loosing more expensive offerings, leadhead jigs are very effective rockfishing lures. Jigs like Scampi, Clouts and Scrounger are popular, for example. Twin tail and curly tail models are both good.

Poke Poling

Poke poling is a variation of rockfishing that goes back a long way, and is becoming more and more popular. Most poke polers use a homemade pole. Start with a fairly stiff bamboo pole about 8-12 feet long. Stiff fiberglass will also work. Tape a 1-2 foot piece of heavy coat hanger wire to the light end of the pole. Loop the end of the wire and tie on a 1-2 foot piece of 30-40 pound monfilament leader and #2 or larger hook.

Opposite from rod and reel rock anglers, poke polers work the rocks around low tide. The lower the low tide the better. A minus 0.5 low tide or more is good. Work the 3 hours before low water. Poke polers roam the rock laid bare by the receding ocean and lower their baited hook into holes and cracks in rocky reefs, sandy bottom tide pools and kelp beds. Fish and eels are lurking in these locations, ready to ambush whatever moves by. Deep probing in cracks and kelp provide instant strikes. Work deep holes even if they are small. These could widen out or even be tops of caves open to the ocean. After a thorough probing, move on to the next likely spot.

The obvious advantage of poke poling over rod and reel fishing is that there are very few hangups. Poke polers most often use mussels, pile worms or cut pieces of squid for bait.

Where to Fish

Many good rock fishing locations(for rod and reel and poke poling) are described in the Ocean Fishing Section of this book.

Introduction to Lake Fishing

In this section, a cross section of some of the best Northern California fishing lakes are profiled. The lakes in this book range from small to very large, from metropolitan to up-in-the-mountains and from "fishing only" to full use facilities. But they all have one thing in common. They all offer outstanding fishing Here they are, in alphabetical order . . .

Almanor	Isabel
Amador	McClure & McSwain
Anderson (and Coyote)	Merced
Berryessa	New Hogan
Camanche	New Melones
Camp Far West	Oroville
Chabot	Pardee
Clear	Parkway
Collins	San Luis
Del Valle	San Pablo
Don Pedro	Shasta
Eagle	Sonoma
Englebright	Tahoe
Folsom	Trinity
Indian Valley	

Almanor Lake

Lake Almanor is one of the best trout and salmon fishing lakes in California. Trout include native rainbow, browns and Eagle Lake rainbow. King(chinook) salmon fishing is excellent. Almanor also provides bass(mostly smallmouth), catfish and panfish angling. This is a large lake(about 13 miles long and 6 miles wide) that has excellent facilities including campgrounds(PG&E), as well as numerous resorts and marinas. Although Almanor is at 4500 feet altitude, the lakes surface temperature in summer is about 70°.

Right next door to Almanor, actually about 4-5 miles South, is another outstanding fishing lake. It's Butt Lake, a 1000 acre gem that offers big brown and rainbow trout, king salmon and lunker smallmouths. Facilities are limited to a single lane launch ramp, two PG&E campgrounds and a picnic area, but don't let this keep you from trying Butt Lake when you're in the Almanor area.

Fishing Seasons   (+=good,   -=fair)

Species	J	F	M	A	M	J	J	A	S	O	N	D
Trout	+	+	+	+	-	-	-	-	-	-	+	+
Salmon	+	+	+	+	-	-	-	-	-	-	+	+
Bass				-	+	+	+	+	+	+	-	
Catfish				-	-	-	-	-	-	-	-	

Fishing Tips

The most productive technique for trout and salmon at Almanor is trolling. During summer when the lake is stratified, trolling is consistently best down 30-35 feet. Favorite trolling lures include solid or jointed Rapalas(gold and red flourescent), Speedy Shiners(silver or gold), Needlefish(bikini or frog pattern) and Flatfish(flourescent orange). Shore fishing is also good. The cove just West of the dam produces trout, salmon and smallmouth bass. The PG&E campground at Rocky Point(about a mile up from the dam) is good for trout and bass. A year round favorite shore fishing location is in Hamilton Branch, where the stream enters the lake. A popular still fishing location, requiring a boat, is Big Spring Cove at Hamilton Branch. Favorite still fishing baits are salmon eggs, nightcrawlers, and salmon roe.

Information/Bait/Tackle

There are numerous sources for fishing information, bait and tackle at Lake Almanor.
Many of the resorts and marinas, as well as several sporting goods stores are anxious to provide information and supplies.

Boating Facilities

Lake Almanor has over a dozen marinas and launch ramps, most located in the Eastern portion and Southern portion of the lake.

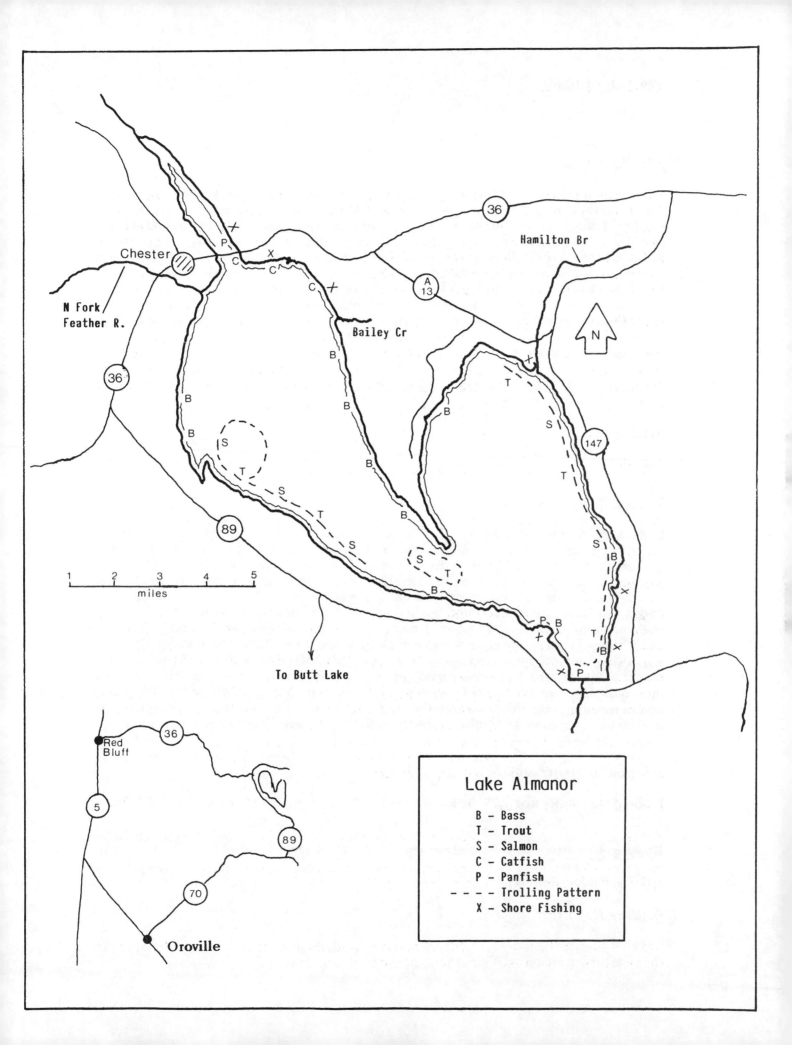

Lake Almanor

B – Bass
T – Trout
S – Salmon
C – Catfish
P – Panfish
- - - - Trolling Pattern
X – Shore Fishing

Amador Lake

Lake Amador is a very small lake, as NorCal lakes go - only about 400 acres. But it offers just about everything any angler could want. First, it is a dedicated fishing lake. No waterskiing is allowed. And the fishing includes trophy size Florida-strain largemouth bass(lake record 15 pounds, 13 ounces), rainbow trout(60-70,000 are planted each year), catfish(up to 20 pounds) and panfish(crappie, redear, sunfish and bluegill). Amador, located about 40 miles East of Stockton, has full facilities including campgrounds, full-service marina, boat rental, cafe, store, water slide, swimming pond, etc. This lake has about 14 miles of shoreline and is open from early February through Thanksgiving.

Fishing	**Seasons**							(+=good,			−=fair)	
Species	J	F	M	A	M	J	J	A	S	O	N	D
Bass		−	+	+	+	−	−	−	−	−	−	
Trout		+	+	+	+	−				−	−	
Catfish				−	−	−	+	+	−	−	−	
Panfish		+	+	+	−	−	−	−	−	−	−	

Fishing Tips

Bass anglers concentrate on Pig 'n Jigs early in the season(through March). Plastic worms come on in March and then take over in April as weed growth makes jigging more difficult. From shore, bass are taken on nightcrawlers and #4 hooks. Work the crawler in slowly. Night angling for bass is productive in summer, under a full moon. Hula Poppers, Rebels, Rapalas and Tiny Torpedos work. Late winter and spring are prime trout times. Fall is fair. Salmon egg / marshmallow combos, Rooster Tails and Mepps work well. Trollers use Triple Teasers, Kastmasters, Needlefish and nightcrawlers behind flashers. Nightcrawlers produce catfish as early as April off the face of the dam. And chicken livers are very effective in the campground coves in the warmer months. Crappie up to 2-3 pounds, are taken in March thru May, using jigs and live minnows. Yellow and red and white mini-jigs are best. Bluegill fishing is best in June and July. Use a bobber and bait like redworms and mealworms.

Information/Bait/Tackle

Lake Amador Resort, 7500 Lake Amador Dr., Ione, CA 95640, (209)274-2625.

Boating Facilities	**Launching**	**Dockage**	**Fuel**	**Boat Rental**
Lake Amador Resort	6	Yes	Yes	Yes

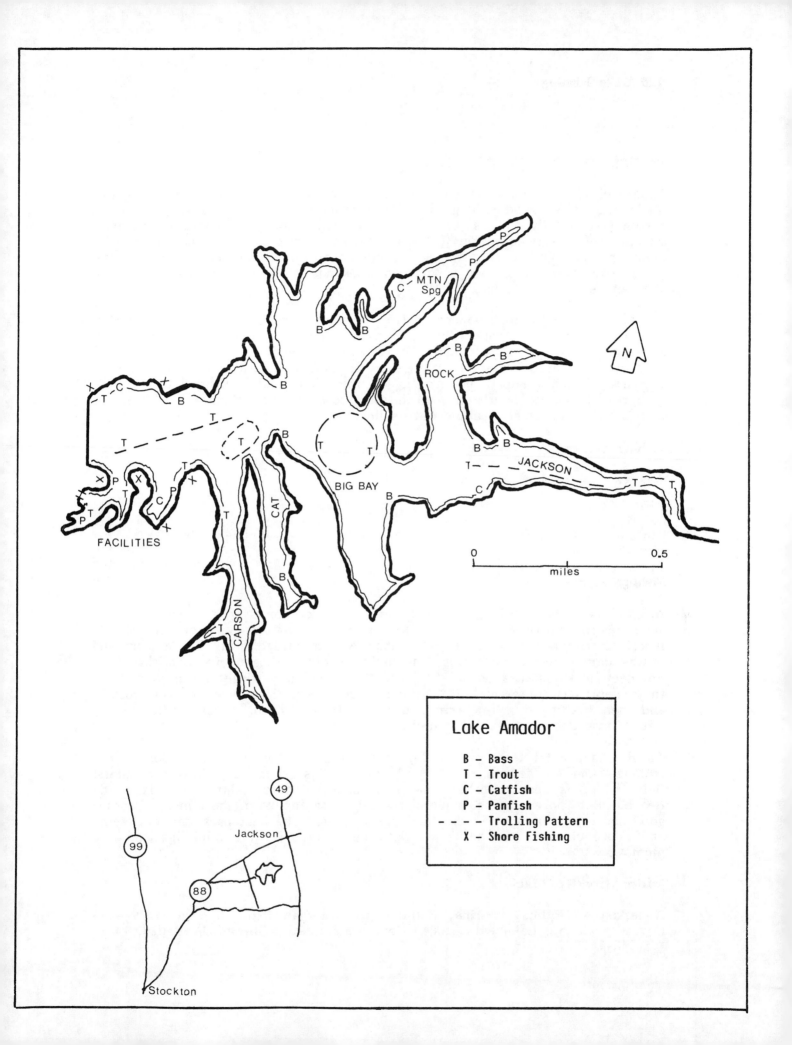

Lake Amador

B – Bass
T – Trout
C – Catfish
P – Panfish
- - - Trolling Pattern
X – Shore Fishing

Anderson(and Coyote) Lakes

Anderson lake is one of a pair of lakes, the other is Coyote(just down the road), that offer good fishing within easy reach of South Bay residents. Anderson is primarily a bass, crappie and bluegill lake. Facilities at Anderson include a full service marina(Holliday Marina), launch ramps and picnicking. Camping and night boating are not permitted at this 7 mile long lake. Powerboating and waterskiing are popular on weekends, so angling is best on weekdays and early in the day.

Coyote Reservoir is located near Gilroy, East of Hwy. 101. Trout are planted here regularly. Best trout fishing months are January through June. Bass, catfish and panfish are also available at Coyote. Bluegills are plentiful for the youngsters. Facilities at Coyote Reservoir include lakeside camping, picnicking and launch ramp. The lake is 4½ miles long and is divided into zones, with the North and South ends of the lake reserved for fishing(a 5 mph speed limit). The center zone allow waterskiing.

Fishing Seasons   (+=good, -=fair)

Species	J	F	M	A	M	J	J	A	S	O	N	D
Bass		-	-	+	+	+	-	-	-	-	-	
Catfish		-	-	-	+	+	+	-	-	-		
Panfish		-	-	-	-	-	-	-	-	-		

Fishing Tips

At Anderson, bass fishing is best near the rocky points by the dam, in the coves on the North shore of the lake and in the narrows at each end of the lake. Catfish are good at the E. Dunne Avenue bridge, near the marina and at the dam. Clams, anchovies and chicken livers work good for catfish. Bass are deep in summer, from 35-50 feet. One good way to get down to bass at these depths is to vertical jig a spoon. Drop it straight down to the bottom and then lift it up a few feet and let it flutter down. Bass strike on the initial drop and on the flutter drop.

Trolling is popular for trout at Coyote when the water is clear. Good areas include from the launch ramp North on the East shore and into the inlets. Bait fishing is best at other times. A popular shore fishing area is Sandy Beach. But shore angling is permitted all along the West shoreline. Another good shore angling spot is the face of the dam. The best bass and catfishing at Coyote come in the fall. At both lakes, crappies hit mini-jigs and live minnows.

Information/Bait/Tackle

Anderson - Holliday Marina, Holliday Dr., Morgan Hill, CA. (408)779-4895
Coyote - Coyote Lake Park, 10840 Coyote Lake Rd., Gilroy, CA 95020, (408) 842-7800.

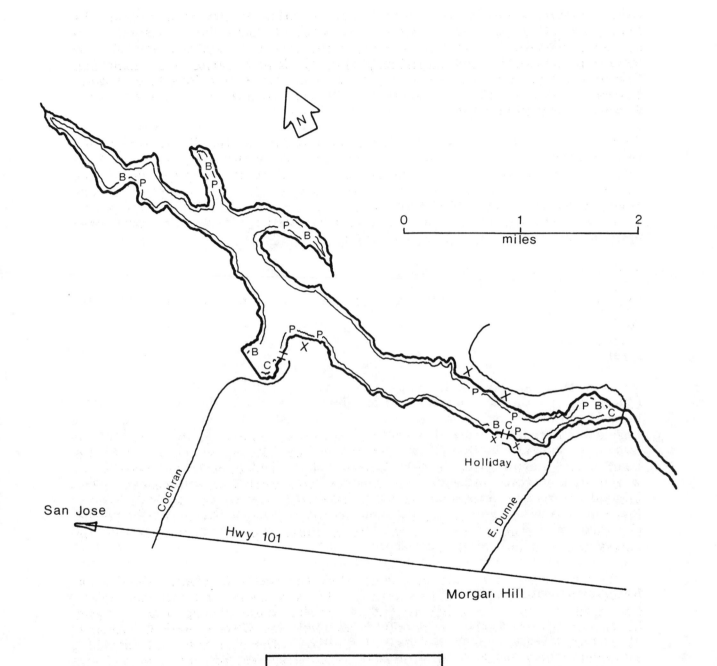

N

0   1   2
miles

Holliday

San Jose

Cochran

Hwy 101

E. Dunne

Morgan Hill

Anderson Lake

B – Bass
C – Catfish
P – Panfish
I – Launch Ramp
X – Shore Fishing

Berryessa Lake

Lake Berryessa is one of Californias premier recreation areas, combining fine fishing with resorts, camping, water and jet skiing and sailing. And it's right near Napa Valley's wine country. Traditionally, trout(rainbow and browns) fishing has been the main draw for anglers at Berryessa. Many trout in the 2-3 pound class are taken, and 5 pounders are not that unusual. But Lake Berryessa, with 165 miles of shoreline and 25 miles of length, also boasts Florida-strain largemouth bass, smallmouth bass, Alabama spotted bass, crappies, catfish and bluegills. There are even a few king salmon that remain from DFG plantings. The lake and its facilities are open all year. In total there are over 1200 campsites in the vicinity and houseboats are available at some resorts.

Fishing Seasons   (+=good, -=fair)

Species	J	F	M	A	M	J	J	A	S	O	N	D
Trout	+	+	+	+	-	-	-	-	-	-	+	+
Salmon	+	+	+	+	-	-	-	-	-	-	+	+
Bass		-	+	+	-	-	-	-	-	+	+	
Catfish		-	-	-	-	-	-	-	-	-	-	
Panfish		-	-	-	-	-	-	-	-	-	-	

Fishing Tips

Rainbow trout and king salmon are taken when the lake is stratified, by deep (30-80 ft.) trolling Kastmasters, Triple Teasers, Mr. Champs and other metal lures that imitate the shad bait fish. Use a flasher. Topline or surface trolling is very productive for these same fish in cooler months, using nightcrawlers or minnows. Trolling is most successful in the Southern portion of the lake, in the narrows all the way to the dam. Catfish can be found in the warm, shallow coves using clams, chicken livers, anchovies, etc. Bass fishing is good off rocky points and in deep coves. When the bass migrate into shallow water, anglers work crankbaits and plastic worms in the brushpiles. Crappies take mini-jigs and minnows. Bluegill fishing is good with redworms and mealworms. Still fishing, from shore or boat, is very productive for trout in the cooler months. Spinners also produce.

Information/Bait/Tackle

There are numerous sources of fishing information, and bait and tackle shops at Lake Berryessa. Many of the resorts and marinas, as well as several sporting goods stores are anxious to provide information and supplies.
Chamber of Commerce, P.O. Box 164, Spanish Flat Station, Napa, CA 94558.

Boating Facilities

There are a number of full service marinas at Lake Berryessa, each with launch ramps, docks, fuel and boat rental. All are located along the Southwest shore of the lake.

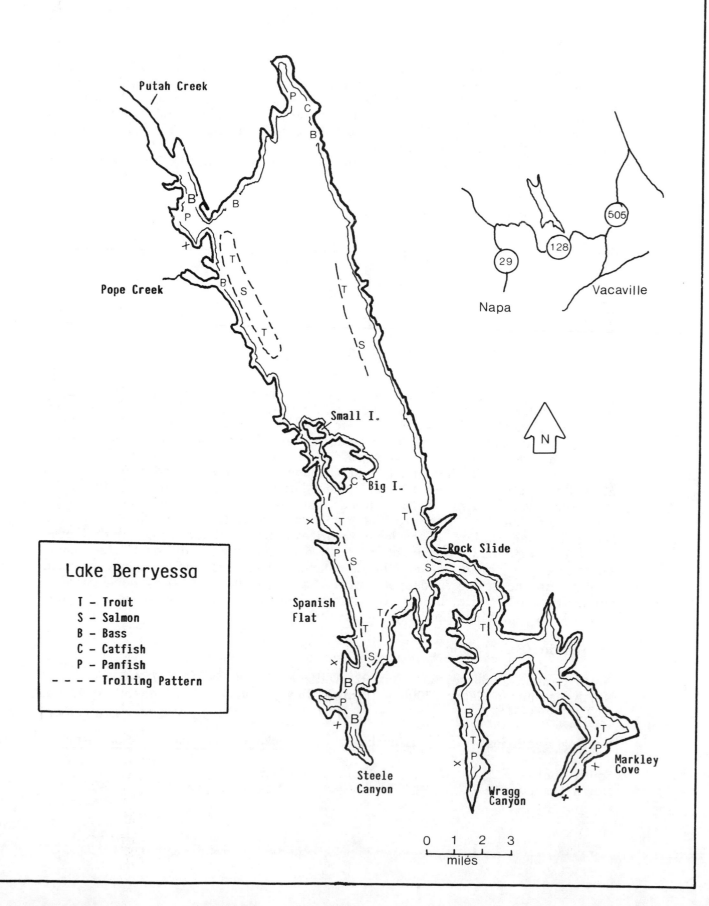

Putah Creek

Pope Creek

P
C
B

B
B
B
P

T
B
S
T

T
S

Small I.

C Big I.

X
T
P
S

Rock Slide

T

S

Spanish
Flat

T
T
X
S

X
B
P
B
X

T

T

B
T
P
X

T

T
P
X

Markley
Cove

Steele
Canyon

Wragg
Canyon

Napa

Vacaville

29
128
505

N

Lake Berryessa

T – Trout
S – Salmon
B – Bass
C – Catfish
P – Panfish
- - - - Trolling Pattern

0 1 2 3
miles

Camanche Lake

Camanche is a large East Bay Municipal Utility District reservoir located in the Mother Lode, about 30 miles East of Stockton. It is a fine fishing lake. Offerings include trout(rainbow and Eagle Lake), bass(including Florida and Alabama spotted), king salmon, catfish(channel and white) and panfish. Camanche is a sizeable lake(53 miles of shoreline) and has camping, recreation and launching facilities on both the South shore and North shore. It is open all year. Facilities include campground, swimming, waterslide, stable and store.

Fishing Seasons   (+=good, -=fair)

Species	J	F	M	A	M	J	J	A	S	O	N	D
Trout	+	+	+	+	-	-	-	-	-	-	+	+
Salmon	+	+	+	+	-	-	-	-	-	-	+	+
Bass		-	+	+	-	-	-	-	+	+		
Catfish	-	+	+	+	+	-	-	-	+	+		
Panfish	-	-	-	-	-	-	-	-	-	-		

Fishing Tips

Trout fishing can be productive all year at Camanche. Trout are down 12-15 feet in cooler months and as much as 30-50 feet in warmer months. Look for them always at 55° water temperature. The night bite for trout is often good. Good trolling lures at Camanche are Krocodile, Needlefish, Triple Teasers and Kastmasters. Nightcrawlers can be trolled or drifted. Bass are caught in spring, summer and fall at Camanche. In fact, some fish are taken in shallow water(less than 10 feet), even during the warm months. But as a rule, the big population in the summer months are down 25-45 feet. Plastic worms and leadhead jigs are the top two offerings. Spinnerbaits and the Bobby Garland Spider Jig are local favorites. King salmon were first planted in 1982. Some now are caught in the 4-6 pound range. Trolling is the ticket. There are also some kokanee in Camanche. Mini-jigs and minnows produce crappies in the spring in deeper coves. Camanche has a healthy population of catfish(channel, white, blue). Good spots include the creek channel and coves and off the dikes and spillways of the main lake.

Information/Bait/Tackle

South Camanche Shore, P.O. Box 92, Wallace, CA 95254, (209)763-5178.
North Camanche Shore, 2000 Jackson Valley-Camanche Rd., Ione, CA 95640, (209)763-5151.

Boating Facilities	Launching	Dockage	Fuel	Boat Rental
South Shore	7	Yes	Yes	Yes
North Shore	5	Yes	Yes	Yes

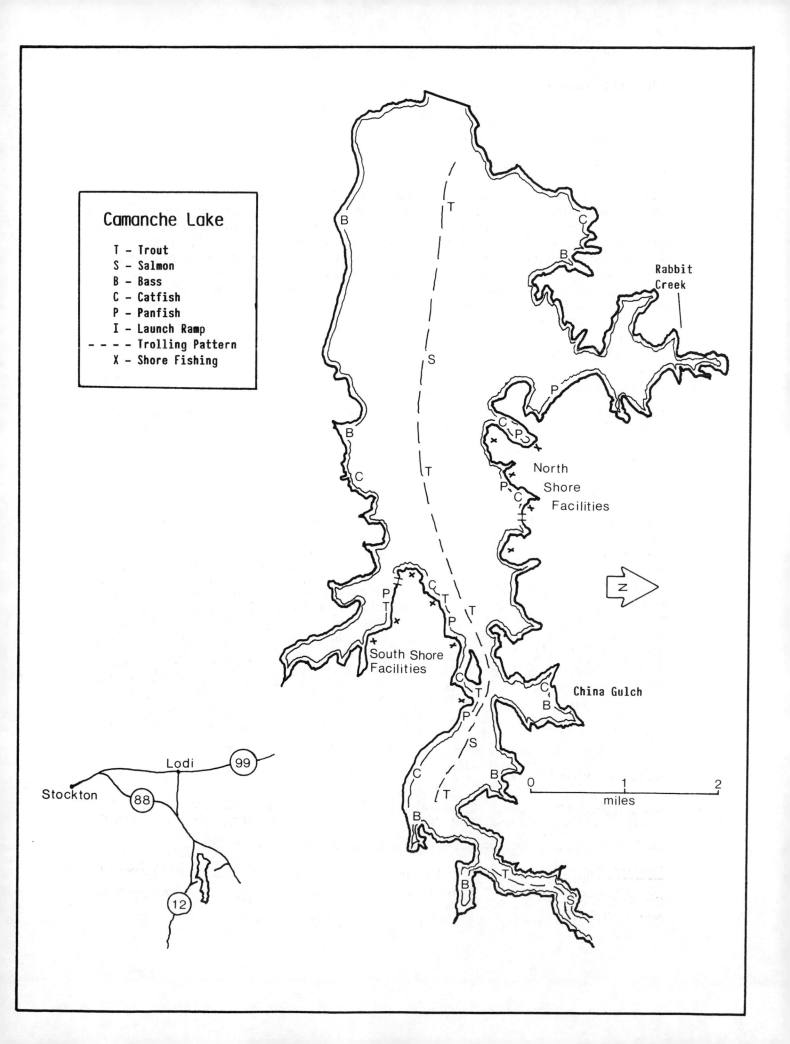

Camp Far West Lake

Camp Far West Lake, located about an hour's drive Northeast of Sacramento, is an excellent all around fishing and recreational lake. An added bonus is its fine striped bass fishery. Camp Far West has been stocked with stripers for over 14 years. 10-12 pound catches are not unusual, and lunkers go up to 20 pounds plus. There are also large and smallmouth bass, catfish, crappies and bluegills. And although this is a warm water lake, it's possible to catch trout up in the extreme ends of both the Rock Creek Arm and the Bear River Arm. Camp Far West covers over 2200 surface acres and has about 30 miles of shoreline. There is camping, picnicking and boat launching at both the North and South facilities. The marina and store are at the South shore. The North shore facility closes in the winter months.

Fishing Seasons   (+=good, -=fair)

Species	J	F	M	A	M	J	J	A	S	O	N	D
Trout	-	-	-	-						-	-	-
Bass		-	+	+	+	-	-	-	-	-		
Striped Bass	+	+	+	-	-				-	+	+	+
Catfish		-	-	-	-	+	+	+	-	-	-	
Panfish		-	+	+	+	-	-	-	-	-	-	

Fishing Tips

Trolling is the prime method of catching striped bass at Camp Far West. Most trollers find success down the middle of the wider part of both the Rock Creek and Bear River Arms. The face of the dam and the deeper cover can also be productive. What varies is proper trolling depth. Twenty feet is a good place to test your luck. Then go deeper, in increments. A faster trolling speed seems to be best. 7 to 10mph is usually best. Two striper plugs are local favorites and seem to be consistently most successful. They are the Rebel and Rapala 7 inchers, in silver with black stripe, or silver with purple stripe. Look for largemouth bass in the shallower areas of both arms - in coves, shaded areas and rocky outcroppings. They average about 2 pounds. Smallmouth are usually down deeper and farther away from cover. February through May is peak crappie time.

Information/Bait/Tackle

Camp Far West Lake, Box 128, Lincoln, CA 95648, (916)645-8069.

Boating Facilities	Launching	Dockage	Fuel	Boat Rental
Camp Far West Marina	2 Ramps	Yes	Yes	Yes

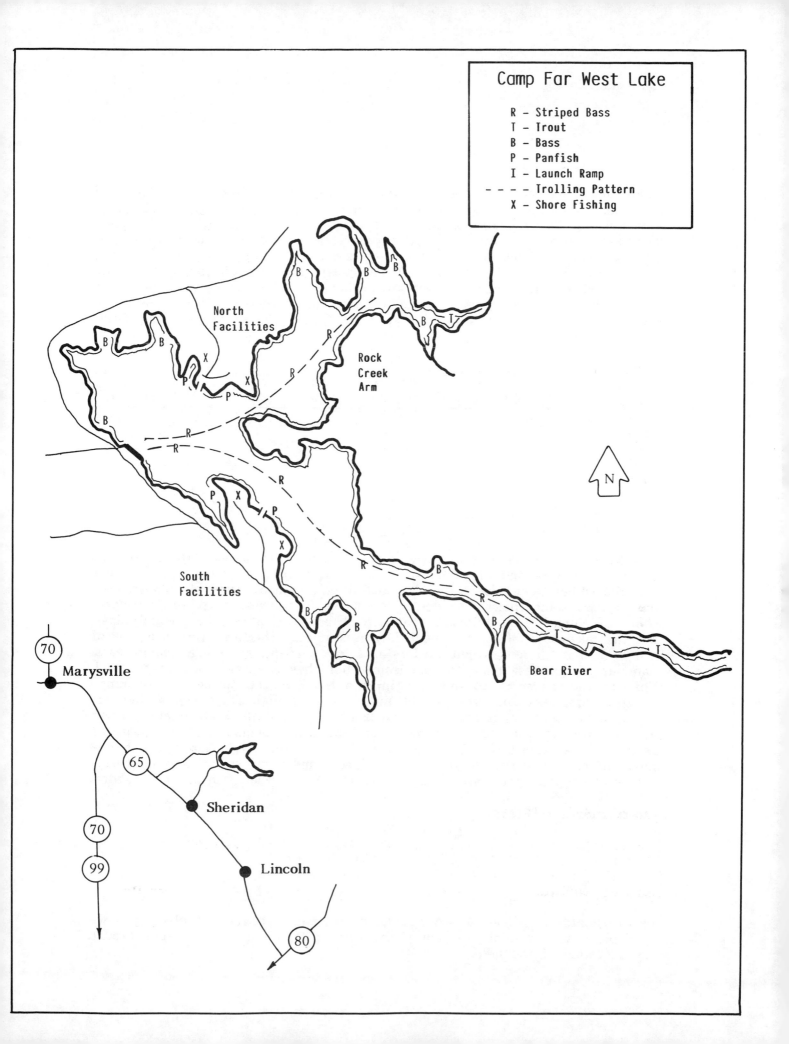

Camp Far West Lake

R – Striped Bass
T – Trout
B – Bass
P – Panfish
I – Launch Ramp
– – – – Trolling Pattern
X – Shore Fishing

North
Facilities

Rock
Creek
Arm

N

South
Facilities

Bear River

70
Marysville

65

70

99

Sheridan

Lincoln

80

Chabot Lake

Lake Chabot rates among the best Northern California urban lakes. This 315 acre lake is in the almost 5000 acre Anthony Chabot Regional Park. Located just East of San Leandro, Chabot boasts big channel cats and Florida-strain largemouth bass, as well as a good and steady supply of stocked rainbow trout. This lake has good stretches of shore fishing access, lots of large fish and a year round schedule. Private boats are not allowed. Rowboats, canoes and electric powered boats are available for rent. The park has horse rentals, hiking, camping, motorcycle hill area, picnicking and fishing piers. To get to Chabot take Lake Chabot Road from Castro Valley or Fairmont Drive East from San Leandro.

Fishing Seasons   (+=good, -=fair)

Species	J	F	M	A	M	J	J	A	S	O	N	D
Trout	+	+	+	+	+	+				-	-	+
Bass	-	-	-	+	+	+	-	-	-	+	-	-
Catfish	-	-	-	-	-	-	+	+	+	-		
Panfish			-	+	+	-	-	-	-	-		

Fishing Tips

Bass fishing is at its best in early spring. Fish up to 5 pounds are not uncommon. Purple and brown plastic worms are local favorites as are plugs like the Rebel Deep Wee R. Rebel and Rapala minnow-type plugs also produce as do spinnerbaits and jigs. Bass Cove is productive as is the North shore of Honker Bay. Channel cats at Chabot are in the 1-4 pound class, but the marina reports some much larger catches. Chicken livers are one of the best baits here. Nightcrawlers produce catfish as well as some bass. Summer is the best time for catfishing, but they are taken all year round. Chabot also has some top-notch crappie activity in the spring. They range up to a foot long and are mostly taken on artificial crappie jigs like Fle Flys. Experienced anglers recommend using the smallest jigs available. Trout are the standby species at Chabot. Trolling is a popular angling technique as is anchored and shore fishing with a sliding sinker rig. Garlic marshmallows and salmon eggs are top baits. Spinners and trout spoons(like Kastmasters in 1/8 ounce gold) are good at lake inflows or when fish are near shore.

Information/Bait/Tackle

East Bay Regional Park District, (415)531-9300.

Boating Facilities

Private boats not allowed. Rowboats, canoes, paddle boats and electric powered boats are available to rent. The Chabot Queen provides a tour around the shoreline of the lake.

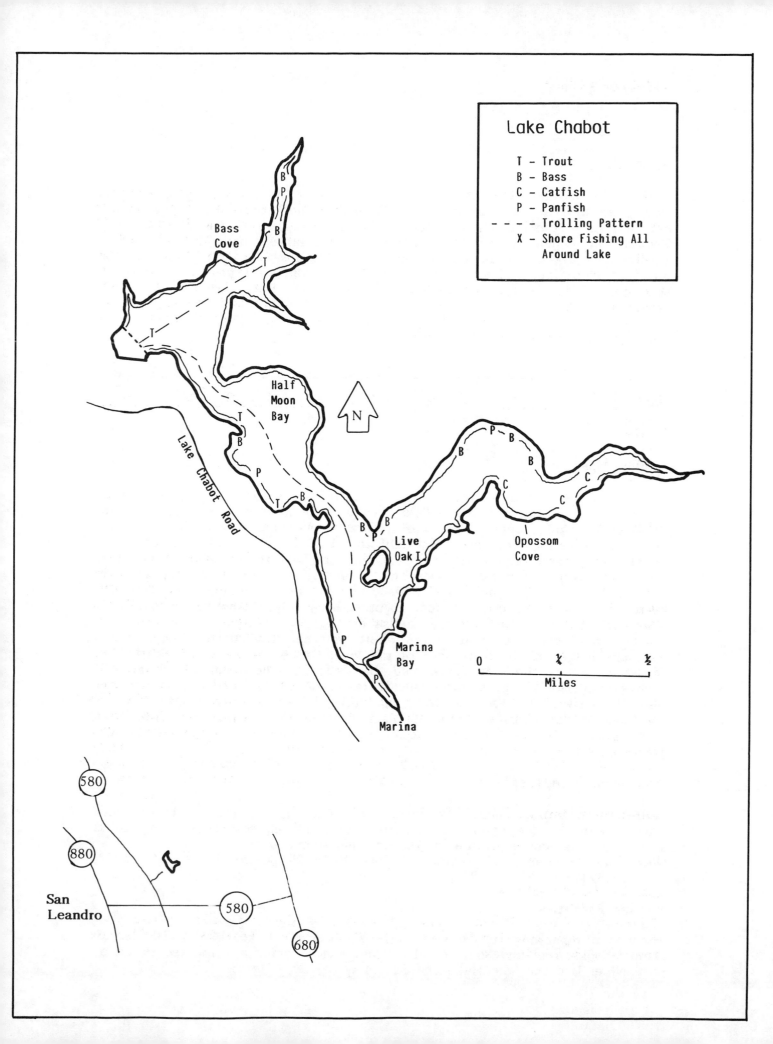

Clear Lake

Clear Lake is an excellent "warm water" fishing lake, offering great bass fishing as well as catfishing and panfishing. Another fishing "opportunity" at Clear Lake, particularly for archers, is the carp. The National Bowfishing Tournament is held there each May. This is the largest natural lake entirely within the state of California. It is about 20 miles long and has about 100 miles of shoreline. Clear Lake has numerous facilities that include resorts, state parks, full service marinas and launch ramps. These are distributed all around the lake.

Fishing Seasons   (+=good, -=fair)

Species	J	F	M	A	M	J	J	A	S	O	N	D
Bass			+	+	+	-	-	-	-	+	+	
Catfish		-	-	-	-	+	+	+	+	-	-	
Panfish		-	-	-	-	-	-	-	-	-	-	

Fishing Tips

Clear Lake bills itself as the "Bass Capitol of the West" and is the host of many black bass tournaments. Tule beds provide cover for the bass and are productive fishing locales. Plastic worms, spinner baits and Pig'n Jigs are productive offerings for bass. As California bass lakes go, Clear Lake has a variety of grasses and cover more similar to Eastern and Southern lakes. There are over 100 miles of shoreline to work. Catfishing is very good in Clear Lake. Catfish ranging from 10-20 pounds are not uncommon. The best catfish bite is in the evening from about 9p.m. to 1a.m. Another good bite is from 4a.m. to 7a.m. The largest catfish are caught at night. The best catfishing areas are near sloughs, or where you can find bottom depressions. Rodman Slough, at the North end of the lake, Cache Creek at the South end, Kelsey Creek at the state park, and the slough at the county park are all good spots. Holes near Monitor Island, Rattlesnake Island and at Jogo Bay are also productive. Clams, anchovies and turkey livers are all good. Recent plantings of the Florida strain of black crappie may revive this fishery at Clear Lake. Waxworms are good offerings for bluegill at boat docks and grassy coves.

Information/Bait/Tackle

There are numerous sources of fishing information, bait and tackle at Clear Lake. Many of the resorts and marinas, as well as several sporting goods stores are anxious to provide information and supplies.
Clear Lake Chamber of Commerce, P.O. Box 629, Clear Lake, CA 95422, (707)994-3600.

Boating Facilities

There are numerous full service marinas on Clear Lake, each with launch ramps, docks, fuel and boat rental. Free launch ramps are located in Lakeport, Nice, Lucerne, Clearlake and Soda Bay.

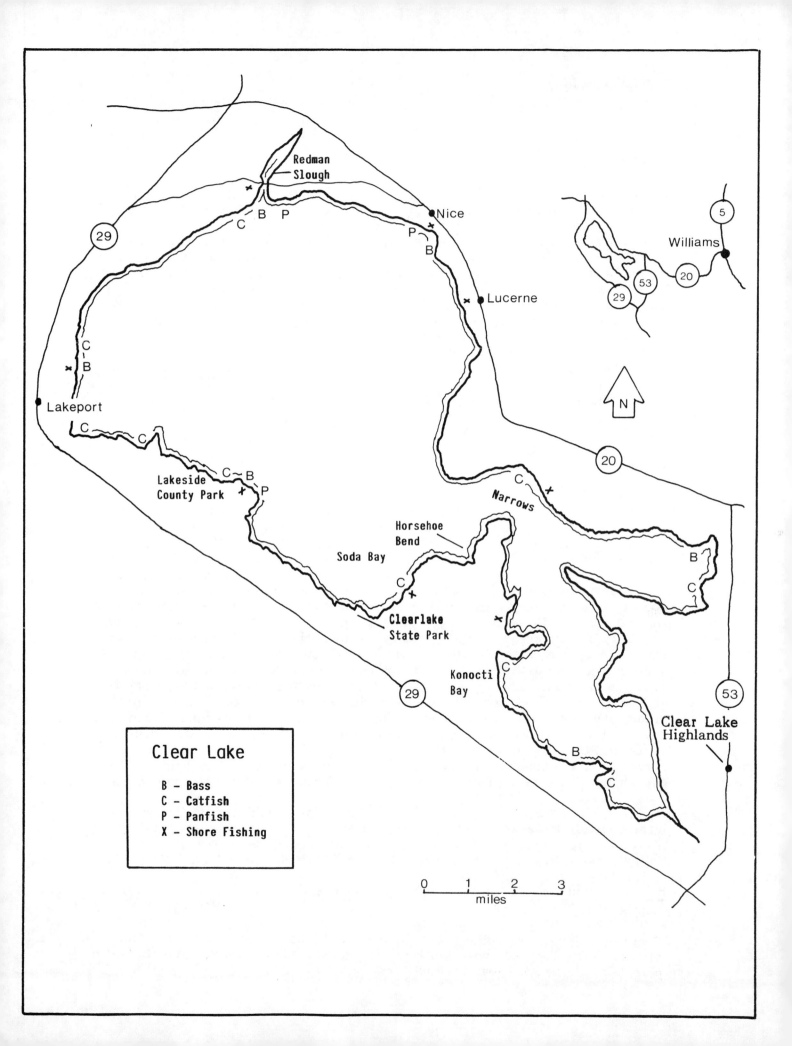

Redman
Slough

C B P

Nice

P
B

Lucerne

29

Williams

5

20

53

29

N

20

C
B

Lakeport

C

C

C B
Lakeside
County Park
P

Narrows
C

Horsehoe
Bend

Soda Bay

C

B
C

Clearlake
State Park

Konocti
Bay

C

C

B

Clear Lake
Highlands

53

C

Clear Lake

B – Bass
C – Catfish
P – Panfish
X – Shore Fishing

0   1   2   3
miles

Collins Lake

Collins Lake has outstanding camping facilities, excellent fishing, all types of water recreation and it's a pleasant 1¼ hour drive Northwest of Sacramento. Don't be confused. Some maps label Collins Lake as "Merle Collins Reservoir" or as "Virginia Ranch Reservoir." By any name it's a worthwhile destination. This 1000 acre lake, in a pretty setting in the foothills, has about 12 miles of shoreline. There are fishing only zones posted on the lake in summer and no waterskiing is permitted from September 15 to May 15. There is an intensive trout planting program from February to May each year, including some big fish. Look to fall for trophy trout action. In addition, there are bass(both largemouth and smallmouth) and very large plentiful catfish(lake record 30 pounds). Facilities include camping, full service marina, store, swimming beach, diving raft, etc.

Fishing Seasons   (+=good, -=fair)

Species	J	F	M	A	M	J	J	A	S	O	N	D
Trout	-	+	+	+	+	-	-	-	-	+	+	-
Bass		+	+	+	-	-	-	-	-	-		
Catfish		-	-	-	-	+	+	+	-	-	-	
Panfish		-	+	+	-	-	-	-	-	-		

Fishing Tips

The best trout action is usually in February and March each year, but is good through May and again in the fall. Shore anglers using a sliding sinker rig and marshmallow/salmon egg combinations or inflated nightcrawlers score on 12-15 inch trout. And lunkers up to the lake record of 9 pounds are caught. A spring surface water temperature of 60° signals peak trout action. Trollers succeed with ¼ ounce gold Kastmasters and #3 or #4 Rebals and Rapalas, in rainbow colors. Bass fishing is good in the coves on the East side and near the Oregon House Bridge. Plastic worms and Bobby Garland jigs(in purple and motor oil) are two good bets. February is the prime month for smallmouths averaging 2 pounds. After storms the catfishing is best in the water inflows at the North end of the lake. Other times, work the East corner of the dam and the submerged treetops along the East bank. Most catfish hit after dark. By the way, fishing is legal at Collins 24 hours a day.

Information/Bait/Tackle

Collins Lake, Oregon House, CA 95962, (916)692-1600.

Boating Facilities	Launching	Dockage	Fuel	Boat Rental
Collins Lake Marina	2 Lanes	Yes	Yes	Yes

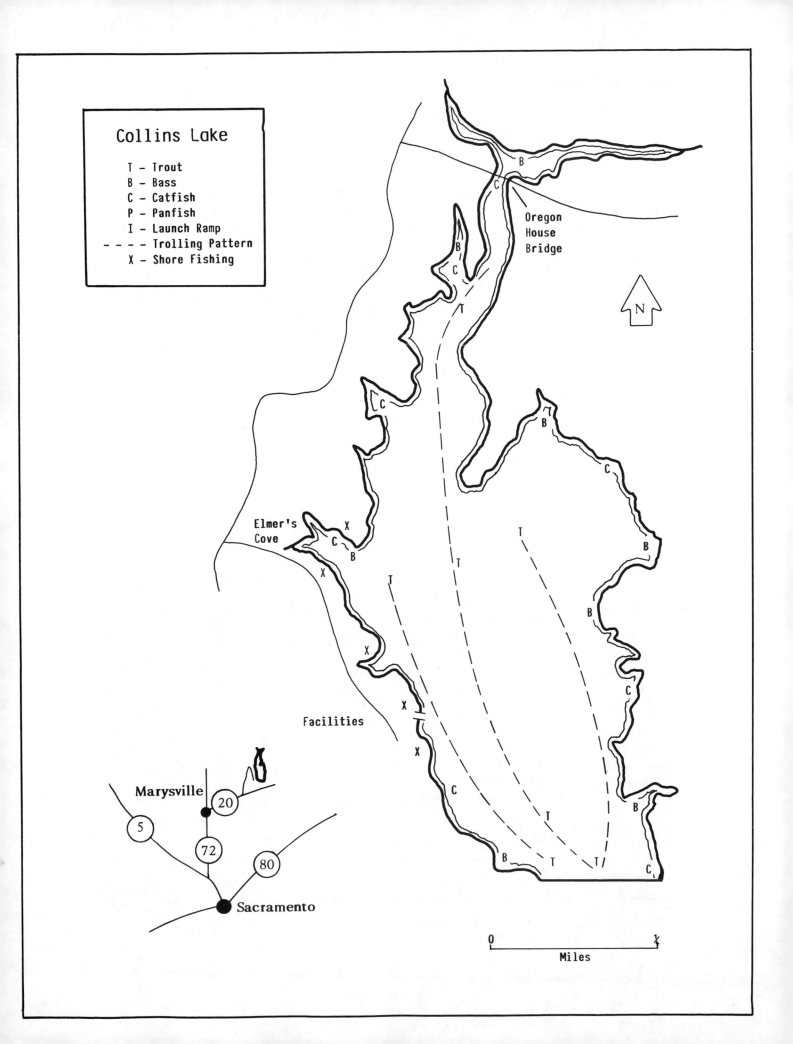

Del Valle Lake

Lake Del Valle is located in Del Valle Regional park in Livermore. This park offers year round camping, fishing and day use. It has 1000 surface acres of water and 16 miles of shoreline. Lake Del Valle provides a varied and exciting fishery. Trout, largemouth and smallmouth bass, catfish, blue-gill and striped bass all provide good action at various times during the year. Del Valle attracts large crowds in the summer but September through May provides plenty of open space for fishing, hiking and boating. Facilities include developed campsites, snack bars, day use areas, complete bait and tackle sales, boat rentals and a 6 lane boat launching ramp. Swimming is allowed and a 10mph speed limit is enforced on the lake. A tour boat operates in the summer as well as scheduled naturalist programs.

Fishing Seasons   (+=good, -=fair)

Species	J	F	M	A	M	J	J	A	S	O	N	D
Trout	+	+	+	+	+	+				-	-	+
Bass	-	-	-	+	+	+	-	-	-	+	-	-
Catfish	-	-	-	-	-	-	+	+	+	-	-	-
Bluegill			-	+	+	+	+	+	-			
Striped Bass	-	-	-	-	-	-	-	-	-	-	-	-

Fishing Tips

Trout provide the most action at this lake. It is planted regularly. Trout ranging from 6 inches to 8 pounds are taken from the lake year round. Anglers working very deep take trout during the summer months. Trout are taken by both bait fishermen and trollers. Favorite baits include salmon eggs, nightcrawlers and cheese. The Dam Area and Creek Channel are the 2 top producers. Where the creek enters the South end of the lake is very productive in April, May and June. Trollers score on a variety of lures including Kastmasters, Panther Martins and Roostertails. Trolling flashers are optional. Bass go for rubber worms, crankbaits and crickets. A Rapala or Rebel is often effective on bass, and sometimes works well on the trout population. Catfish can provide anglers with steady action if you can locate them. Nightcrawlers, red worms, clams and stinkbaits all work well. Usually anglers who locate a school of catfish will catch a stringer full. Big striped bass surprise anglers from time to time. Although not common, they do cruise the Del Valle waters. Stripers are large and difficult to land. A 40 pounder was tops last year. Most are taken by surprised fishermen working for trout or bass.

Information/Bait/Tackle

Del Valle Park Co., 6999 Del Valle Rd., Livermore, CA 94550, (415)449-5201.
E. Bay Regional Pks., 7000 Del Valle Rd., Livermore, CA 94550, (415)443-4110.

Boating Facilities	Launching	Dockage	Fuel	Boat Rental
Del Valle Marina	6 Lanes	No	No	Yes

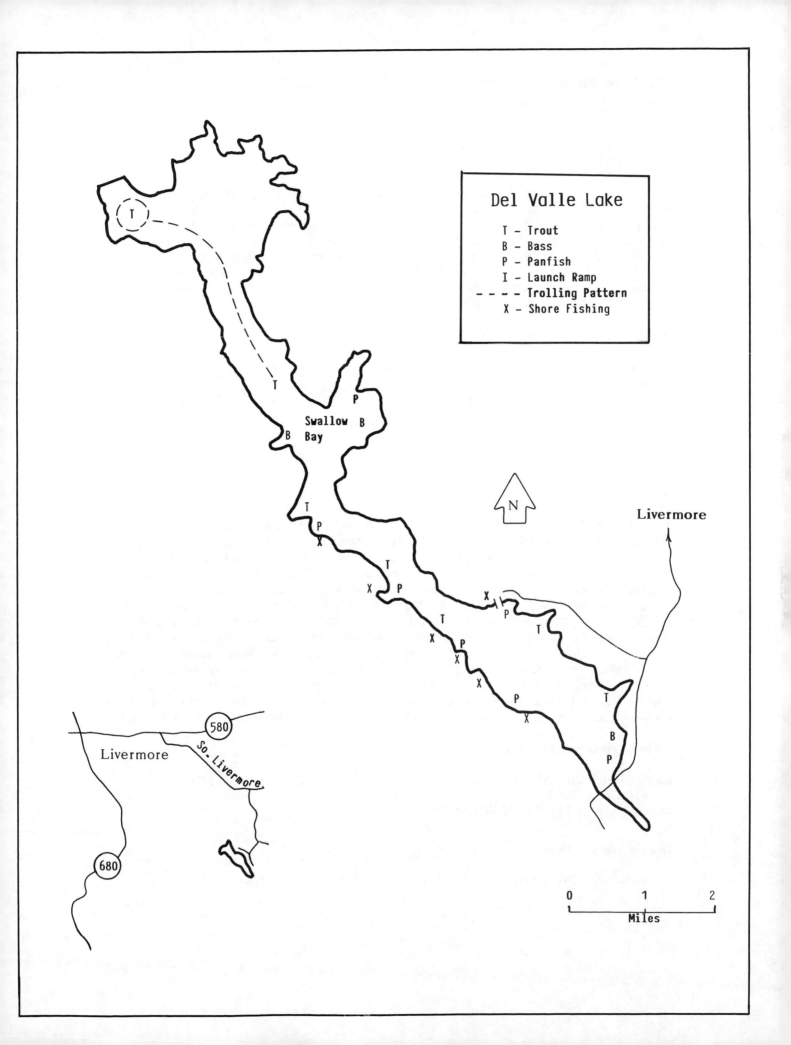

Don Pedro Lake

Don Pedro is an excellent fishing lake, offering a wide variety including rainbow and Eagle lake trout, silver and king salmon, largemouth bass, catfish, crappies and bluegills. It is a large lake, 26 miles long with 160 miles of shoreline. Don Pedro has three major facilities. Each has campsites and launch ramps. Trout range in size up to 6 pounds. Salmon are generally in the 2-4 pound range. Typical bass are 1½ pounds, but range up to 8-10 pounds. The lake has recently been planted with the fast growing Florida largemouth bass. Night fishing is allowed.

Fishing Seasons   (+=good, -=fair)

Species	J	F	M	A	M	J	J	A	S	O	N	D
Trout	+	+	+	+	-	-	-	-	-	-	+	+
Salmon	+	+	+	+	-	-	-	-	-	-	+	+
Bass		-	+	+	-	-	-	-	+	-		
Catfish		-	-	-	-	-	-	-	-			
Panfish		+	+	+	-	-	-	-	-	-	+	

Fishing Tips

Trolling is the most productive method of catching trout and salmon. Silver lures, including Needlefish, Kastmasters, Pheobes, Triple Teasers and Z-Rays, are all winners. Casting spinners like Mepps and Rooster Tails can also be productive in the spring. Still fishing, using a sliding sinker rig and salmon egg/marshmallow combination bait, works well for trout and salmon. Try near or across from Fleming Meadows Marina. Rocky points are a year round hangout for largemouth bass. A sure fire surface plug is the 4 inch gold and black floating Rapala. 4 inch black plastic worms are also top producers. Drag them slowly across the bottom. Chartreuse and white spinnerbaits are local favorites. Crappie anglers score in the back coves where there are tress submerged in 15 feet of water. White mini-jigs and small minnows are the ticket. Use 2 or 4 pound test line. Crappies can be caught in these locales during most of the year. Redworms and mealworms produce bluegills.

Information/Bait/Tackle

Lake Don Pedro Marina, Star Route, Box 81, LaGrange, CA 95329,
    (209)852-2369.
Davis Bait & Tackle, (209)634-0311.

Boating Facilities	Launching	Dockage	Fuel	Boat Rental
Lake Don Pedro Marina	12 lanes	Yes	Yes	Yes

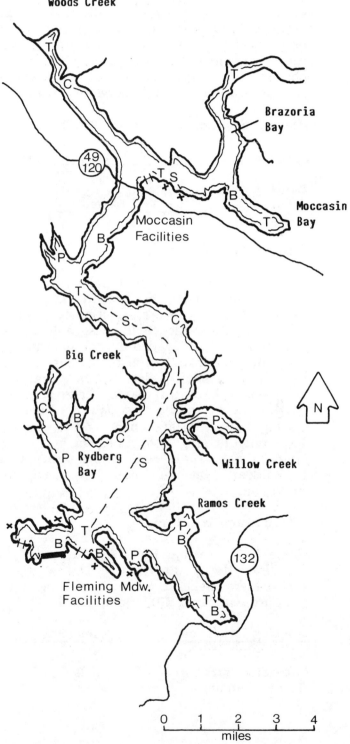

Woods Creek

Brazoria
Bay

Moccasin
Bay

Moccasin
Facilities

Big Creek

Willow Creek

Ramos Creek

Rydberg
Bay

Blue Oaks
Facilities

Fleming Mdw.
Facilities

Lake Don Pedro

- T – Trout
- S – Salmon
- B – Bass
- C – Catfish
- P – Panfish
- I – Launch Ramp
- – – – – Trolling Pattern
- X – Shore Fishing

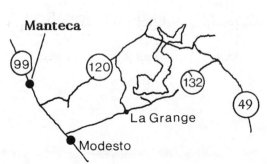

Manteca

La Grange

Modesto

0 1 2 3 4
miles

N

Eagle Lake

Eagle Lake is the home of the famous Eagle Lake rainbow trout. Eagle Lake trout are said by many to fight like steelhead and taste like coho salmon. Eagle Lake is a large(16 miles long), natural body of water located at high altitude(5100 feet) in the Northern Sierras. Its waters are so alkaline that only the Eagle Lake trout and a small minnow called the tui chub can survive there. Eagle Lake trout are good-sized fish. The lake record is almost 11 pounds, 4-6 pounders are frequently caught and 1-2 pound fish are common. Facilities include a full service marina, camping and several resorts.

Fishing Seasons   (+=good, -=fair)

Species	J	F	M	A	M	J	J	A	S	O	N	D
Eagle Lake Trout			closed			+	+	+	+	+	+	

Fishing Tips

As is true in many trout lakes, trolling is the surest way to catch Eagle Lake trout. Offerings(behind flashers) include Speedy Shiners, Needlefish, Z-rays, Triple Teasers, Kastmasters and Rapalas(#5, 7, and 9 sinking Rapalas). When trolling leadcore line use a long leader(30 feet of 6-8 pound) since the fish can see the leadcore. Graph recorders or flashers are helpful in locating the ledges and drop-offs where the trout congregate. Good shore fishing for Eagle rainbow exists. Best locations include Wildcat Point on the West side, Pelican Point(at narrow lake section) and Eagle's Nest(directly in front of the cabins on the East side). Nightcrawlers are the most productive still fishing bait. Inflate them and use a sliding sinker rig. In the fall, many boat anglers still fish, using nightcrawlers, over the springs. Look for the boats, that's where the springs are. One is at Eagle's Nest and another is at Wildcat. One last hint. Fish early in the a.m.; the bite usually ends by 8 or 9 a.m.

Information/Bait/Tackle

Eagle Lake Marina, Box 128, Susanville, CA 96130(Tel: Eagle Lake #2 via
     Susanville operator).
Eagle Lake General Store, Spaulding Tract, Susanville, CA 96103,(916)825-2191.
U.S. Forest Ser., 3015 Johnstonville Rd., Susanville, CA 96103,(916)257-2151.

Boating Facilities	Launching	Dockage	Fuel	Boat Rental
Eagle Lake Marina	3 Lanes	Yes	Yes	Yes
Spaulding Tract	Yes	Yes	Yes	Yes
Stones Landing	Yes			

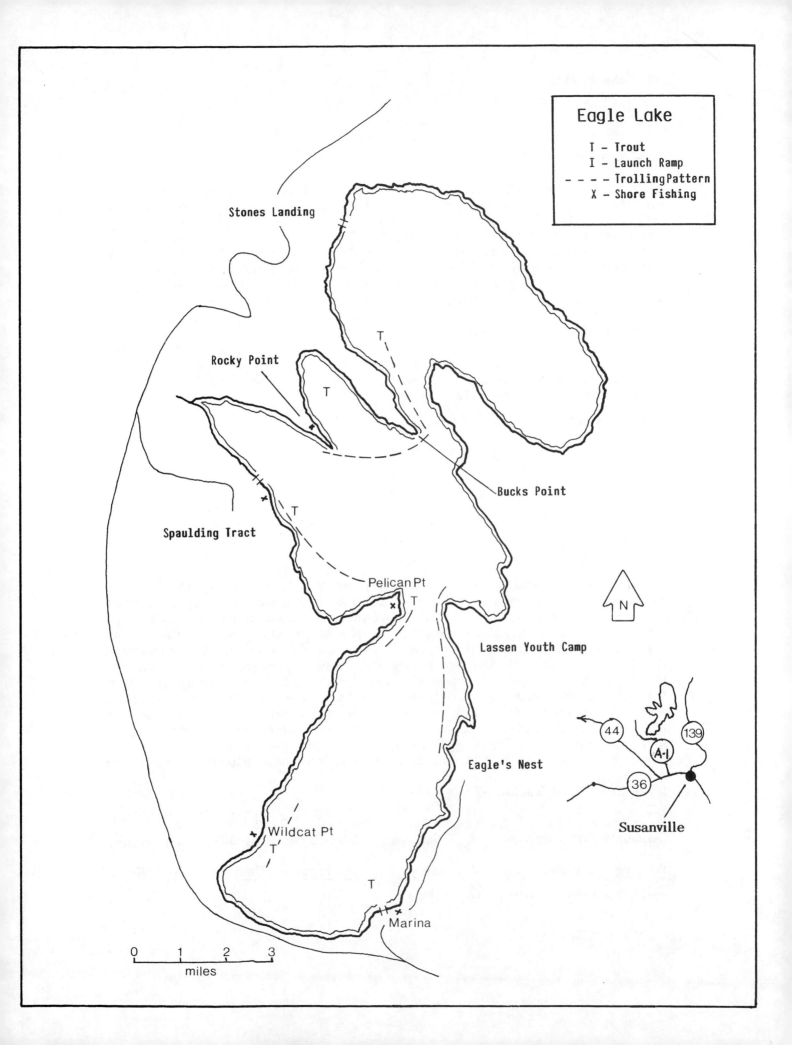

Eagle Lake

T – Trout
I – Launch Ramp
– – – – Trolling Pattern
X – Shore Fishing

Stones Landing

Rocky Point

Bucks Point

Spaulding Tract

Pelican Pt

Lassen Youth Camp

N

Eagle's Nest

Wildcat Pt

Marina

44

A·1

139

36

Susanville

0 1 2 3
miles

Englebright Lake

Englebright Lake offers a special type of camping and fishing experience. All 100 plus campsites are scattered along the 9 mile long, narrow lake, and can only be reached by boat. Granted the campsites are on the primitive side. There are no flush toilets, for example. But in exchange, you get closer to nature. Sites are all near the water, on shelves or sand banks, offering views and bank fishing at your doorstep. An added bonus is that the campsites are free. And in the upper reaches of the lake, waterskiing is not permitted, so noise and wakes are no problem. Surprisingly, for a lake only an hour or so from Sacramento, the facilities are not overrun. Some say its because of its awkward location, off Hwy. 20, between Marysville and Grass Valley. But, rest assured, it's not because of the fishing. Trout and bass fishing is super in this clean, green, winding flooded Yuba River basin. And the water level is usually up near full even in the fall. Facilities include 2 launch ramps, small marina, store and cafe.

Fishing Seasons   (+=good, -=fair)

Species	J	F	M	A	M	J	J	A	S	O	N	D
Trout		+	+	+	+	-	-	-	-	-	-	
Bass		-	+	+	-	-	-	-	-	+	-	
Catfish		-	-	-	-	+	+	+	-	-	-	
Panfish		-	+	+	-	-	-	-	-	-	-	

Fishing Tips

The lake is stocked with rainbow every week or two during the summer. Trolling a small spoon can score both trout and kokanee near the dam. There is good shore fishing for picnickers, between the marina and the dam. The rainbow are not big in Englebright, but there are some large brown trout. Way up the far extreme of the North Fork of the Yuba, at the remains of the Rice's Crossing Bridge, trout action can be very good. Flies, lures, salmon eggs and worms all produce. Bass anglers do best fishing the many flowing stream coves. In the spring there is a large sandbar where the two forks of the lake join. Bass fishing can be good here. Campsites that are farther up in the lake offer better prospects of fishing from shore, or right in the vicinity of the camp. Think about the sun when picking a camp site. Some warm up early in the morning. Others get warm afternoon sun.

Information/Bait/Tackle

U.S. Army Corps of Engineers, Box 6, Smartville, CA 95977, (916)639-2343. Skipper's Cove Marina, Box 5, Smartville, CA 95977, (916)639-2272.

Boating Facilities	Launching	Dockage	Fuel	Boat Rental
Skipper's Cove Marina	2 Ramps	Yes	Yes	Yes

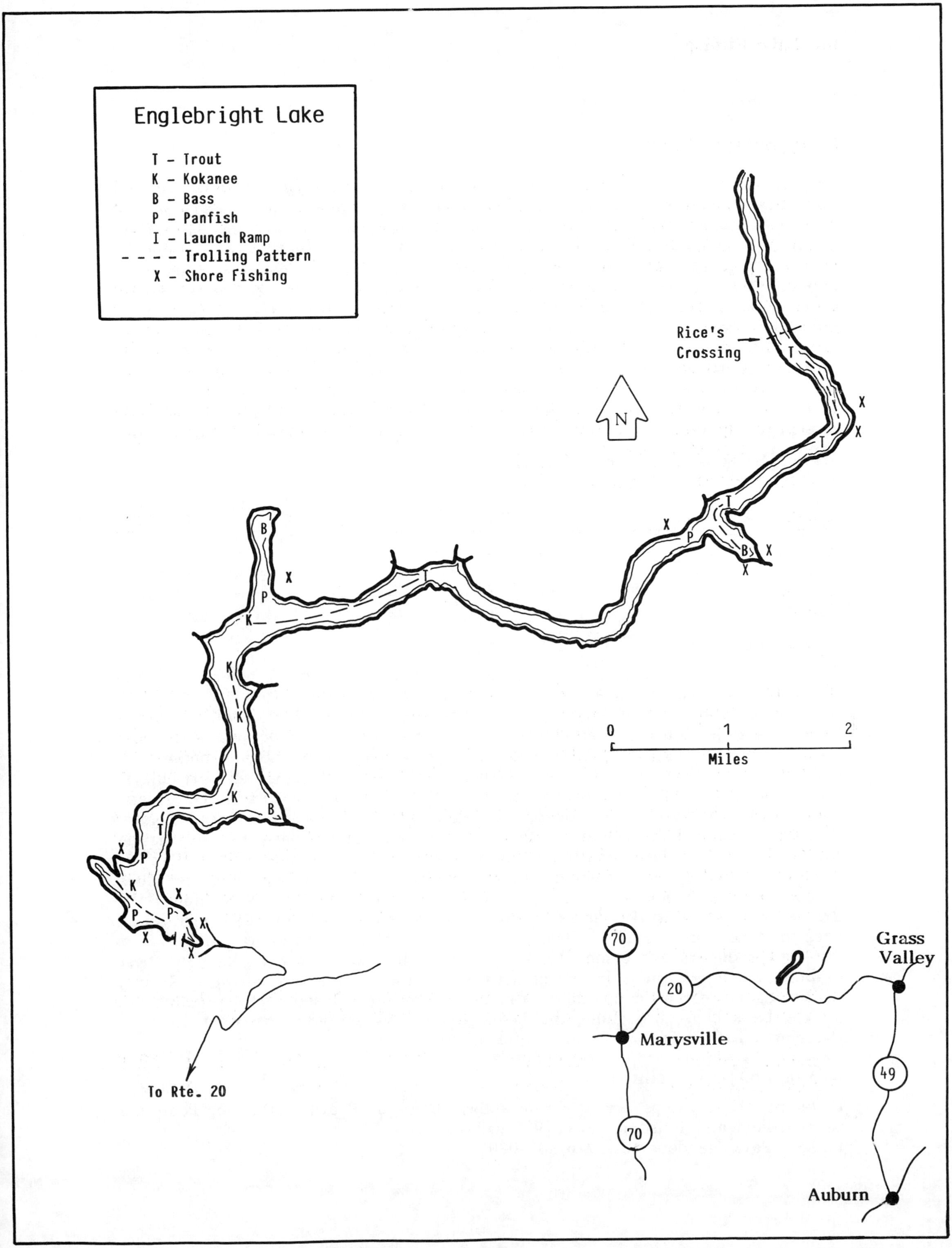

Englebright Lake

T – Trout
K – Kokanee
B – Bass
P – Panfish
I – Launch Ramp
- - - - – Trolling Pattern
X – Shore Fishing

Rice's Crossing

N

0   1   2
Miles

To Rte. 20

70

20

Marysville

70

Grass Valley

49

Auburn

Folsom Lake

Folsom Lake combines excellent fishing with an outstanding full-spectrum recreational facility, all within easy reach of the Sacramento metropolitan area. Planted and holdover rainbow trout are numerous at Folsom. In spring 5,000 half pound or better rainbow per week are put in and trout are caught up to 5 pounds. King salmon in the 16-20 inch range are also a common catch. There are also lots of bass – both largemouths(in the 2-4 pound range, some up to 7 pounds) and smallmouths(just over and under the 12 inch minimum). And for good measure, catfish, crappie and bluegill fishing is also good. This is an urban lake that is heavily used by all types of boaters and other recreational activities, but the fish don't seem to mind. In fact, for the family that doesn't like long drives, and that wants to combine fishing with sailing, waterskiing, or whatever, Folsom is ideal. Facilities include several campgrounds, a large, full-service marina, hiking, boat-in-camping, etc.

Fishing Seasons   (+=good, -=fair)

Species	J	F	M	A	M	J	J	A	S	O	N	D
Trout	+	+	+	+	+	-	-	-	-	-	-	+
Salmon	+	+	+	+	+	-	-	-	-	-	-	+
Bass		-	+	+	+	-	-	-	-	+	+	
Catfish		-	-	-	+	+	+	+	-	-	-	
Panfish		-	-	+	+	-	-	-	-	-	-	

Fishing Tips

Trout and salmon trollers, in spring need only let out 2 or 3 colors of lead-core line. But in the heat of the summer, 15 or more colors are required. Summer trolling with downriggers is increasingly popular. Metallic trolling lures, like Super Dupers, Kastmasters, Triple Teasers and Needlefish are most productive. For example, in Needlfish, a #2 size in rainbow trout, bikini, red and pearl are excellent choices. Spring trout shore anglers do particularly well at Dyke 8, Brown's Ravine and the South end of the peninsula. Many hook a live minnow at the dorsal fin and hang it below a bobber. Note, there are some kokanee at Folsom. Most smallmouths are caught in the North fork, while largemouth are most common in the South fork. Rattlesnake Bar and up in the coves of the Peninsula are two good North fork areas. In the South fork work the coves all the way up to Salmon Falls Bridge. In spring work weedbeds with sandy bottoms. Later concentrate on deeper structures. Platic worms, in purple or black with metal flakes, are the top producers at Folsom. But all popular bass offerings work. The best crappie concentration is in the structure and rocky areas of Brown's Ravine. Catfishing is best at night(note: the park gates are closed in the evening) in all the back bays throughout the lake. Shore anglers like the West bank of the North fork. Try clams and chicken livers.

Information and Facilities

Developed boat ramps are at Granite Bay, Dyke 8, Brown's Ravine, Peninsula Campground and Folsom Marina(916)933-1300.
Folsom Park Headquarters(916)988-0205.

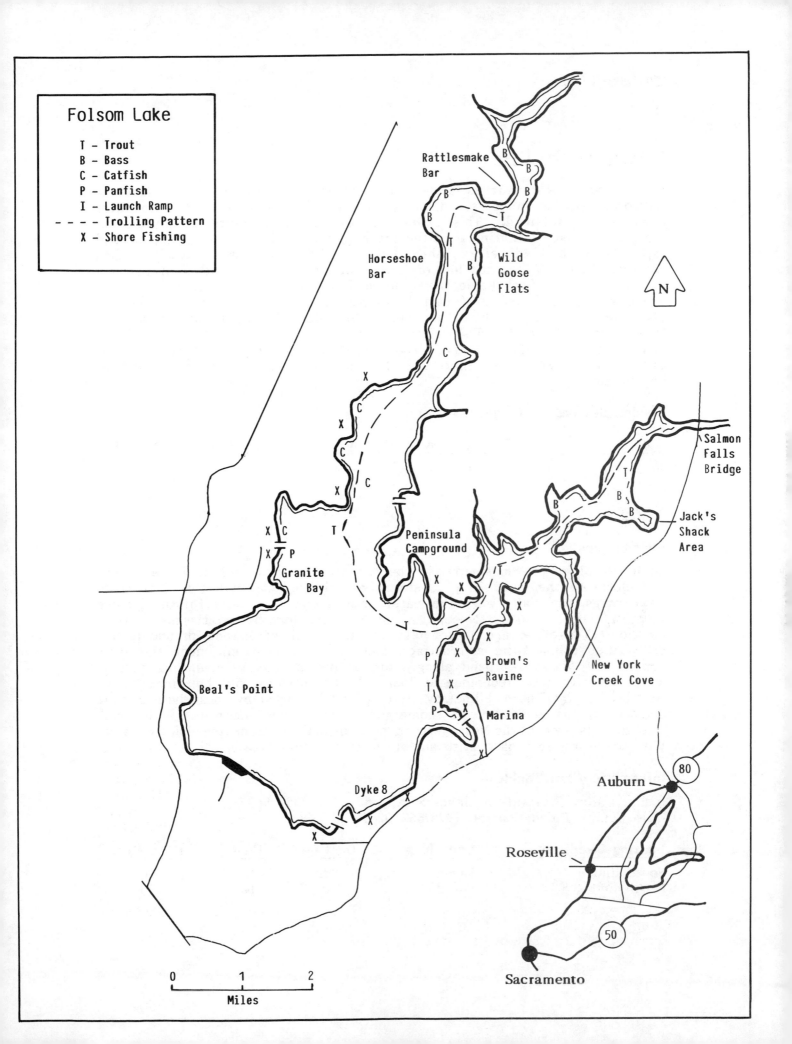

Indian Valley Lake

Indian Valley Reservoir is somewhat different from many other Northern California fishing hotspots. Getting to the lake requires a 9½ mile drive down an unpaved road. This means that the fishing pressure is lighter than most other lakes. And none of the brush and trees in the lake canyons and valleys were cleared before fishing began in 1974; so this is excellent fish habitat. Indian Valley has lots of largemouths(some smallmouths) in the 3-5 pound range, and both Eagle Lake and rainbow trout up to 25 inches. There are also good populations of catfish, crappie and bluegill. Indian Valley has 3800 surface acres of water and about 40 miles of cove-studded shoreline. It is located about 35 miles West of Williams. Located at 1475 feet elevation, most of the lake is about 120 feet deep, and up to 200 feet at the dam. At the South end there is a launch ramp, store, boat rental and 30 campsites.

Fishing Seasons   (+=good, -=fair)

Species	J	F	M	A	M	J	J	A	S	O	N	D
Trout	+	+	+	+	+	-	-	-	-	+	+	+
Bass		-	+	+	+	-	-	-	-	+	+	
Catfish		-	-	-	-	+	+	+	-	-	-	
Panfish		-	-	+	+	-	-	-	-	-	-	

Fishing Tips

Shallow trolling produces trout in the winter. Summer trollers move deeper and closer to the dam. Try to stay above the old Cache Creek Channel to avoid snags, especially when the water level is down. Good offerings include Flatfish, Triple Teasers, Needlefish and nightcrawlers behind flashers. Dark plastic worms(black and motor oil) are the most consistent producers for bass. But spinnerbaits and surface plugs work when used under the right conditions. Bass are found along shore at points and in coves. Flipping is an especially good technique at Indian Valley because of the great cover. And heavier than normal line(say 10-14 pounds) is used by most bass anglers because of the abundance of submerged brush. When the water is up bank catfishing is good at the North end in both directions from the launch ramp. With lower water bank catfish anglers work the dam area.

Information/Bait/Tackle

Indian Valley Store(at the lakes South end), (916)662-9697.
Yolo County Flood Control, (976)662-0265.

Boating Facilities	Launching	Dockage	Fuel	Boat Rental
South End	Paved	Yes	No	Yes
North End	Paved	No	No	No

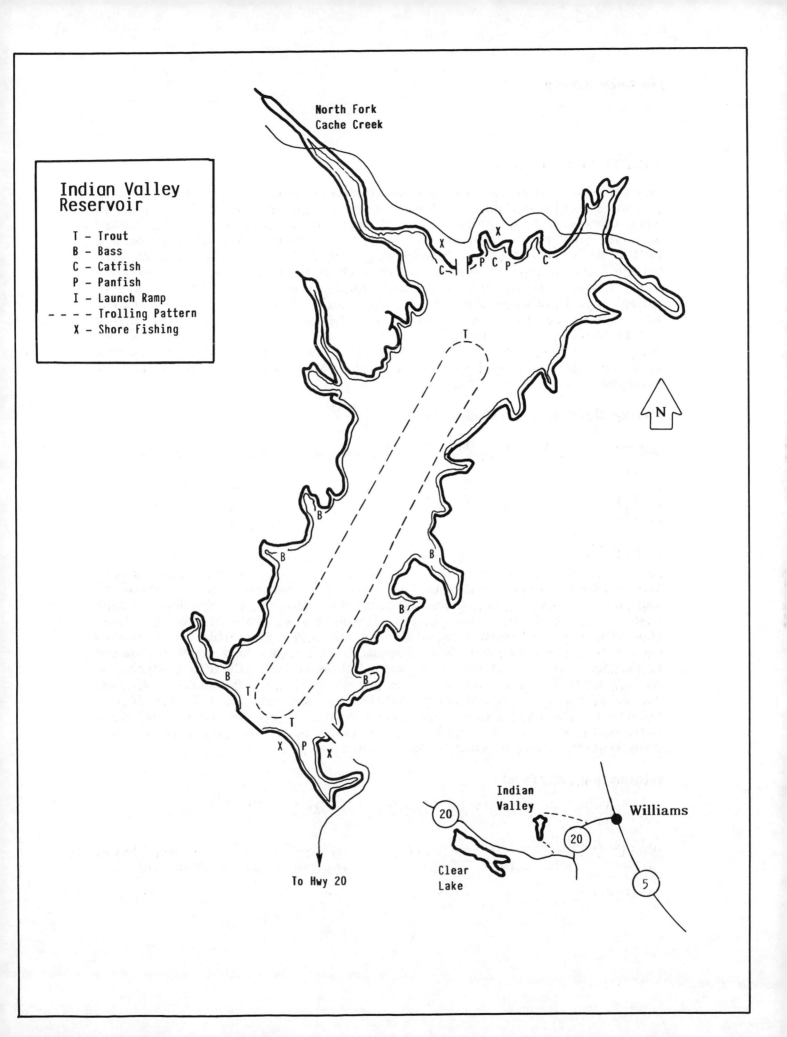

Isabel Lake

Lake Isabel, located near Livermore, offers fine stocked trout fishing, including some trophy-size fish. Isabel also provides good action for largemouth bass, crappie and bluegill. From October through June, trout are stocked weekly. They range in size up to 10 pounds. Often, the average stringer is in the 3/4 pound range. The number of trout in the lake is kept high enough so that it is not difficult to catch your limit(5 for adults, 3 for children). Bass and bluegill provide additional action, especially in the late spring. Catfish are stocked from July through September,and provide excellent night fishing during the summer months. Facilities at Isabel include bait and tackle, snacks and boat rental. Boats with electric trolling motors are available for rent, but no private boats are allowed on the lake. Hours vary by season, so call ahead. No fishing license is required, but there is a moderate per person fishing fee.

Fishing Seasons (+=good, -=fair)

Species	J	F	M	A	M	J	J	A	S	O	N	D
Trout	+	+	+	+	+	+				+	+	+
Bass			+	+	-	-						
Bluegill	-	-	+	+	+	+	+	+	+	-	-	-
Crappie					-	+	+	+	+	+		

Fishing Tips

Trout fishing is good from shore or boat. Bait fishing is best with marshmallows and salmon eggs, nightcrawlers or mealworm combinations. Some anglers use a #16 treble hook(baited with nightcrawler/marshmallow combination) about 3 feet down from a sliding sinker(1/8 oz.). This can be fished on the bottom or below a bobber, using light line(4 pound or even 2 pound test). Cast with Kastmasters, Rebels or Rooster Tails. Clear plastic casting bubbles partially filled with water trailing a dry fly are often successful. Bass go for nightcrawlers or plugs, catfish hit on liver, and bluegills bite on redworms or mealworms. There are several deep holes(up to 40 feet) in Isabel, right out in front of the tackle shop. These holes are probably the most consistent producers of trout in the entire lake.

Information/Bait/Tackle

Lake Isabel, 1421 Isabel Ave., Livermore, CA 94550, (415)462-1281.

Boating Faciltiies

No private boats allowed. Boats with electric motors are available for rent.

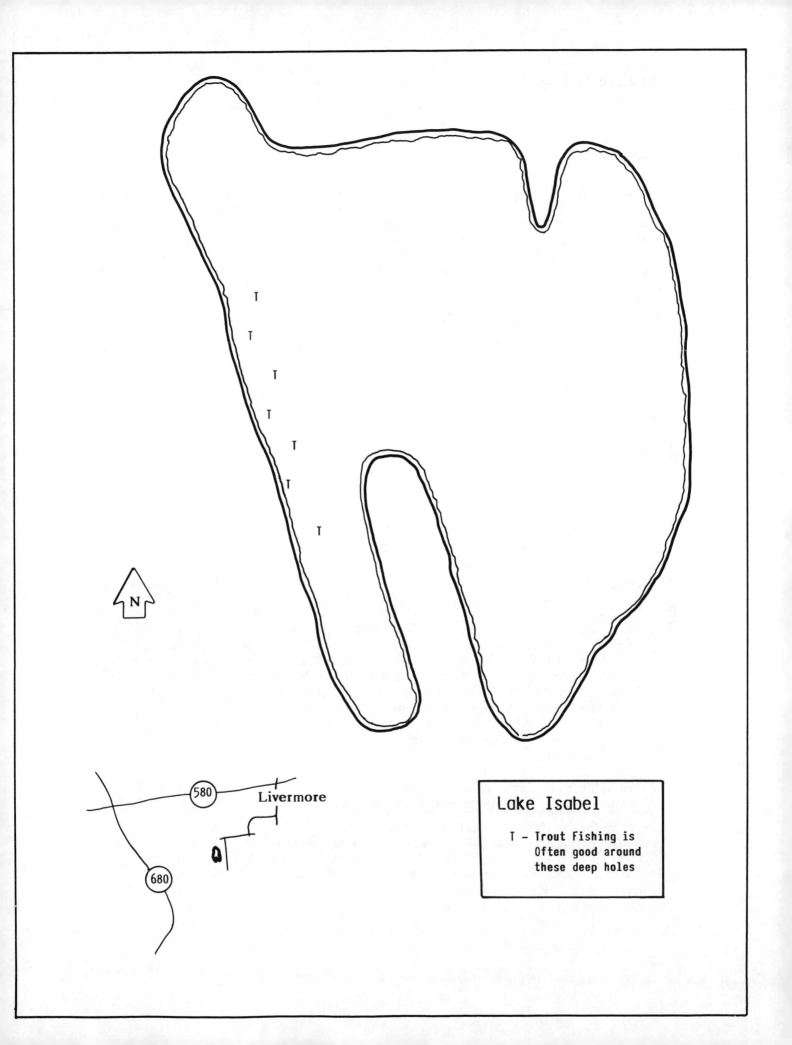

Lake Isabel

T – Trout Fishing is
Often good around
these deep holes

580 Livermore

680

McClure and McSwain Lakes

McClure and McSwain are adjoining reservoirs on the Merced River that are perfect opposites. McClure is a warm water lake(bass, catfish, panfish, trout), is very large(82 miles of shoreline), has numerous coves and inlets, and allows all types of boating(including houseboating and waterskiing). McSwain, on the other hand, is a cold water lake(trout only), is narrow and relatively small, and has no houseboats or waterskiing. What these lakes have in common is fine fishing and outstanding and complete recreational facilities. McClure and McSwain are located in the Sierra foothills East of Modesto(42 miles away) and Merced(27 miles away). There are 5 recreation areas on McClure and one on McSwain. Both lakes have camping(565 sites in all), boat launching, full service marinas, laundromats, fish cleaning facilities, boat rentals, swimming lagoons and stores.

Fishing Seasons   (+=good, -=fair)

Species	J	F	M	A	M	J	J	A	S	O	N	D
Trout	+	+	+	+	-	-	-	-	-	-	+	+
Bass		-	+	+	+	-	-	-	-	+	+	
Catfish		-	-	-	-	+	+	+	-	-	-	
Panfish	+	+	+	-	-	-	-	-	-	-	-	

Fishing Tips

McSwain is a heavily planted trout lake. Holdover fish get large. The lake record is 10¼ pounds and 4 pounders are quite common. Trout fishing is the main on-water activity here. The water is cold, clear and moving through this narrow body of water. Two top trolling lures are the gold-hammered #940 Triple Teaser and the trout-colored Needlefish. A good trolling area is a mile long stretch between the first and second bouy, about a mile up from the marina. Local anglers advise shore anglers to try water shaded by trees on the South or East side of the lake. One accessible spot is off Exchequer Road near the maintenance area at the lakes North end. Another is near McSwain Dam at the South end of the lake. And near the launch ramp after a trout plant should not be overlooked. Bass in McClure are taken in coves and off rocky points. Dark plastic worms are productive. Crappies go for mini-jigs and minnows. Channel catfish go for anchovies, sardines and clams fished on the bottom.

Information/Bait/Tackle/Boating Facilities	Camping Units	Launch Lanes
Lake McSwain Rec. Area(209)378-2521, Marina(209)378-2534	80	2
McClure Pt. Rec. Area(209)378-2521, Marina(209)378-2491	100	5
Barrett Cove Rec. Area(209)378-2711, Marina(209)378-2441	260	4
Horseshoe Bend Rec. Area(209)878-3452, Marina(209)878-3119	85	2
Hunter's Point Rec. Area and Marina	15	1
Bagley Rec. Area and Marina	25	1

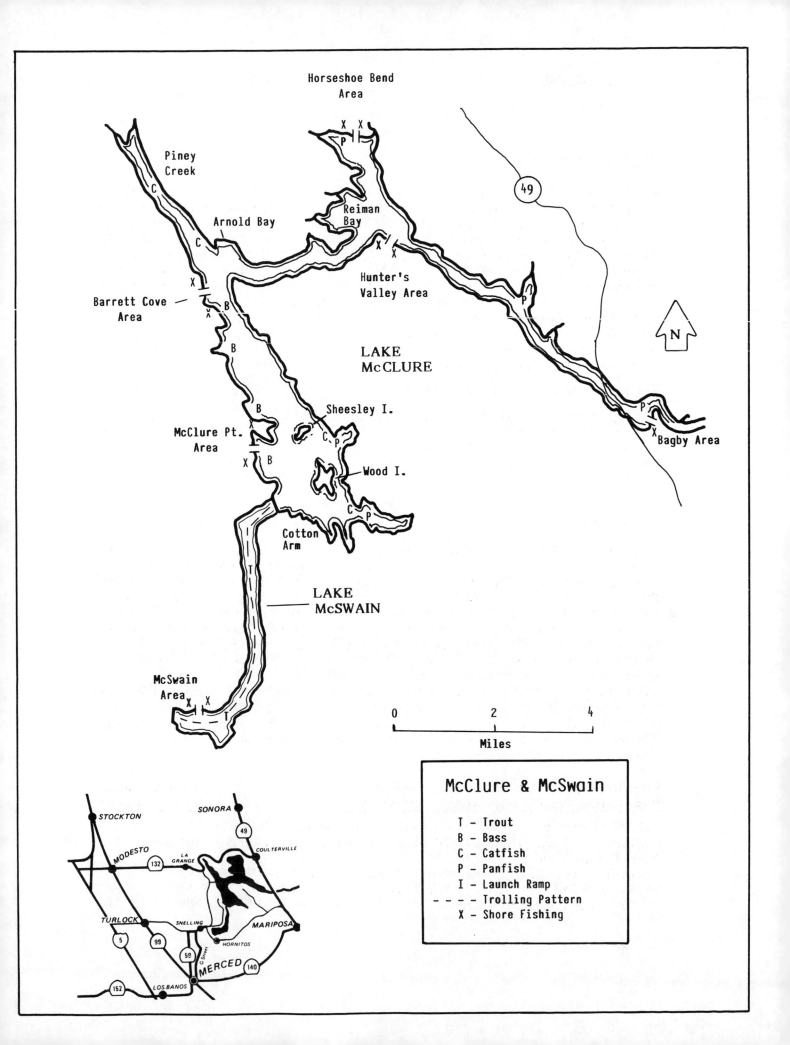

Horseshoe Bend
Area

Piney
Creek

Arnold Bay

Reiman
Bay

Hunter's
Valley Area

Barrett Cove
Area

LAKE
McCLURE

49

N

Sheesley I.

McClure Pt.
Area

Wood I.

Bagby Area

Cotton
Arm

LAKE
McSWAIN

McSwain
Area

0		2		4

Miles

McClure & McSwain

T – Trout
B – Bass
C – Catfish
P – Panfish
I – Launch Ramp
- - - - Trolling Pattern
X – Shore Fishing

STOCKTON
SONORA
MODESTO
49
LA GRANGE
132
COULTERVILLE
TURLOCK
SNELLING
MARIPOSA
5
99
59
G Street
HORNITOS
MERCED
140
152
LOS BANOS

Merced Lake

Both lakes at Merced provide very good trout fishing year round. No need to travel hundreds of miles when this fine fishery is located in San Francisco, in the heart of the Bay Area. Trout fishing tends to be best in the spring and fall but the coastal weather keeps water conditions good throughout the summer. Because of limited run off the water remains clear in the winter providing good fishing conditions. Black bass, catfish and carp also provide action for fishermen. Bass to 8 pounds, carp to 15 pounds and catfish to 3 pounds all provide some action. Rainbow trout remain king, with fish ranging from 6 inches to 10 pounds. 2 pound trout from the North Lake are very common. A state fishing license is required. In addition a $2.50 daily permit is required on the North Lake and a 50¢ permit on the South Lake. The North Lake is planted once a week with trout averaging 3/4 pound to 10 pounds. Calif. Fish and Game plant approximately 7500 fish in each lake monthly. Lake Merced offers Fishing Derbys, trout of the month contest, trout of the day contest, limit buttons and Whopper buttons.

Fishing Seasons   (+=good, -=fair)

Species	J	F	M	A	M	J	J	A	S	O	N	D
Trout	-	-	-	+	+	+	+	+	+	+	+	-
Bass	-	-	-	-	+	+	-	-	-	+	-	-
Catfish/Carp	-	-	-	-	-	-	-	-	-	-	-	-

Fishing Tips

Basic trout fishing methods work here. Bait fishermen score with cheese, nightcrawlers, salmon eggs and marshmallows. Garlic cheese is probably the most popular bait. Fish with as little weight as possible and 4-6 pound test line. Size 6-10 hooks work well. Fish from a boat if possible because it provides better mobility. Move until you find the fish. Shore fishermen do well, but often need to wait the fish out. Try a variety of baits until you score. Trollers and lure casters also take their share of fish. Mepps, Roostertails, Panther Martins and Z-Rays all produce fish. Some trollers often use small flashers in front of nightcrawlers. Black bass fishermen score on spinnerbaits and nightcrawlers. Carp are taken on corn and doughbaits. Merced holds a large population of lunker trout so fishermen need to always be prepared.

Information/Bait/Tackle

Lake Merced Boating & Fishing Co., 1 Harding Rd., San Francisco, CA 94132. (415)753-1101.

Boating Facilities

Power boats and motors are not allowed on either lake. Row boats, canoes and electric motors and boats are available for rent. Private row boats may be launched. No ramps are available.

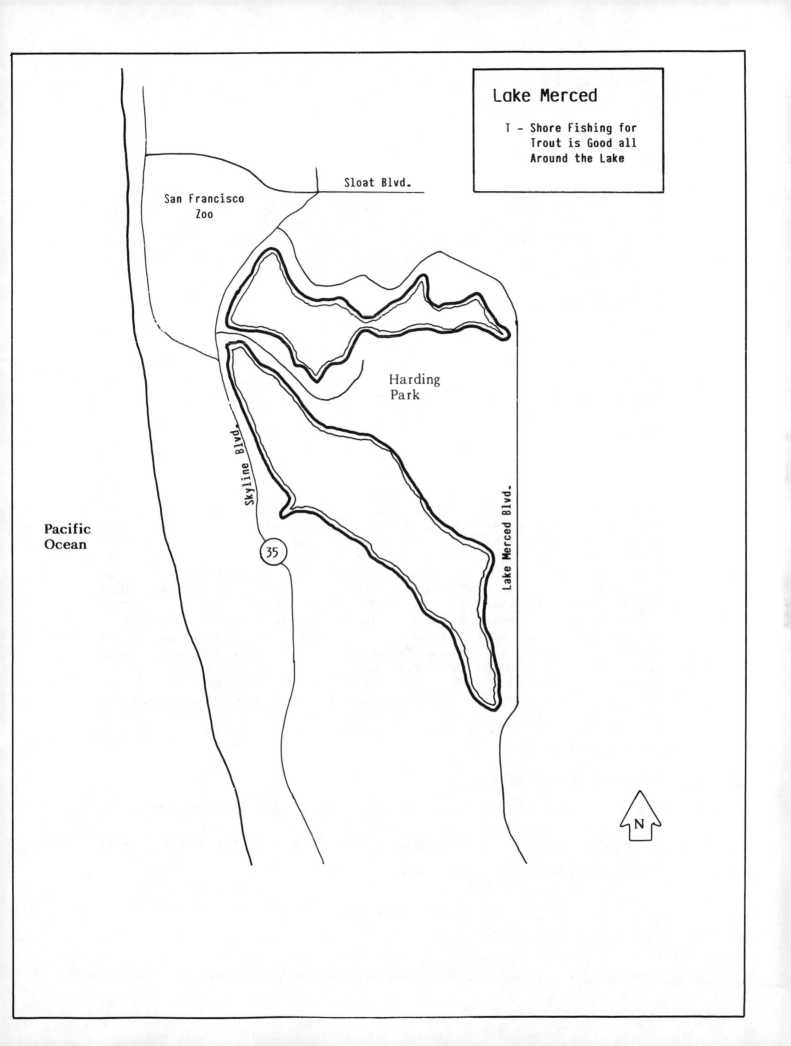

New Hogan Lake

New Hogan is an excellent fishing lake, offering trout, bass, catfish and pan-fish. Also, its striped bass fishing is developing rapidly, with average catches in the 8-10 pound range. The record striper is 18 pounds. Facilities at New Hogan include camping, swimming, marina, store and launch ramps. The lake has 50 miles of shoreline. There is also a boat-in camping area. New Hogan is in the Mother Lode, about 40 miles from Stockton, and is open year round.

Fishing Seasons   (+=good, -=fair)

Species	J	F	M	A	M	J	J	A	S	O	N	D
Trout	-	+	+	+	+	-	-	-	-	-	-	-
Bass		-	+	+	+	-	-	-	-			
Striped Bass	-	-	-	-	-	-	-	+	+	+		
Catfish		-	-	-	-	+	+	+	-			
Panfish		-	-	-	-	-	-	-	-			

Fishing Tips

Trout and salmon catches have dwindled since 1980 when the DFG planted striped bass. Trout plants were discontinued in 1985 when it was evident that the return was very low. Best trout fishing is in the upper stretches of the Calaveras Arm. Small minnows or salmon eggs score on these browns and rainbows up to 14 inches. Bass structure at New Hogan is limited. Haupt Creek Cove on the upper end of the lake and Bear Creek Cove on the South end have good cover. Several small islands and rocky points(like at Coyote Point) provide good bass prospects. Most bass are largemouth. Plastic worms in purple and shad colors are best. The largemouth record is 15 pounds, 8 ounces. Stripers are scattered throughout the lake. And they can be big, the largest caught going 24 pounds. Fairly quick trolling with something flashy, like Kastmasters, Rapalas and Rebels, is a good way to locate fish. Casting minnow-type plugs also works. Striper shore anglers, at hot spots like Wrinkle Cove, the Observation Area and Fiddleneck use anchovies, or cast minnow-type lures. Catfishermen score using chicken livers, anchovies and clams in these same areas. Crappie fishing is not consistent, but can be good using mini-jigs and minnows.

Information/Bait/Tackle

New Hogan Marina, 1955 New Hogan Pkwy., Valley Springs, CA,(209)772-1462.

Boating Facilities	Launching	Dockage	Fuel	Boat Rental
New Hogan Marina	13 Lanes	Yes	Yes	Yes

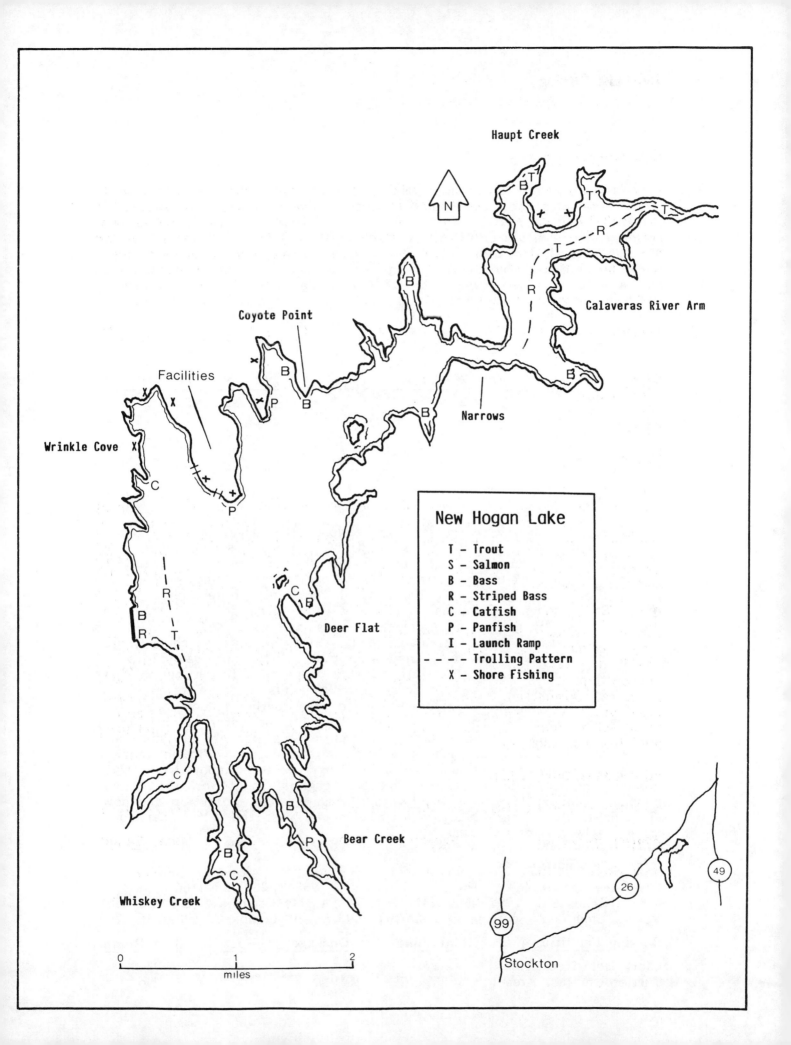

Haupt Creek

N

Calaveras River Arm

Coyote Point

Facilities

Wrinkle Cove X

Narrows

New Hogan Lake

T – Trout
S – Salmon
B – Bass
R – Striped Bass
C – Catfish
P – Panfish
I – Launch Ramp
– – – – Trolling Pattern
X – Shore Fishing

Deer Flat

Bear Creek

Whiskey Creek

0   1   2
miles

Stockton

99   26   49

New Melones Lake

New Melones reservoir is a new reservoir(completed in 1980) that offers excellent fishing. However, shore facilities such as camping, are still under development. Species include trout(rainbow and brown), king salmon, bass(both largemouth and smallmouth), catfish and panfish. This is a large lake(about 8 miles across) that extends up the Stanislaus River canyon over 10 miles. Campsites are available at Glory Hole Recreation Area and picnic facilities are available at Tuttletown. Night fishing is permitted, as are waterskiing and swimming. New Melones is located South of Angels Camp, off Hwy 49, in the Mother lode.

Fishing Seasons   (+=good, -=fair)

Species	J	F	M	A	M	J	J	A	S	O	N	D
Trout	+	+	+	+	-	-	-	-	-	-	-	+
Salmon	+	+	+	+	-	-	-	-	-	-	-	+
Bass		-	+	+	+	-	-	-	-	-	-	
Catfish			-	-	-	-	-	-	-	-		
Panfish			-	-	-	-	-	-	-	-		

Fishing Tips

As is true in other locations, at New Melones the larger fish are usually found in deeper water. This is true for trout, salmon, bass and crappies. So, if you're trolling and catching smallish trout, drop it down 5-10 feet and you're likely to pick up some larger fish. Along the same vane, salmon trollers in the summer go down 75-100 feet, whereas trout trollers hit at 35-60 feet. Still fishing, off the dam and spillway, is often good for trout and salmon, especially during the evenings and night. When New Melones was filling, bass fishing was extremely good. Everyone was catching limits. Things have changed. Now bass anglers must be a little more savvy to score, especially on larger fish. One tip is to work deeper and farther out on whatever structure you're on - be it cover or rocky points. Lure selection is also becoming more critical. Big lures seem to consistently produce bigger bass at New Melones. The Zara Spook can't be beat for top water action. Large plastic worms, up to 6 or 8 inches, as well as big jigs are recommended. Larger crankbaits like the Diving B-3 Bagley are also good. Floating minnow type plugs, about 7 inches long, and colored to look like rainbow trout, often produce big bass. In the summertime bass anglers should work the thermocline at about 35-45 feet down. Work spoons, jigs and worms up and down off ledges, etc. Large bluegills are caught all over the lake, near cover, using mealworms or redworms.

Information/Bait/Tackle

Creekside Sports, 484 E. Hwy. 4, Murphys, CA 95247,(209)728-2166.
New Melones Bait & Tackle, 2245 Hwy. 49, Angels Camp, CA,(209)736-0661.
Vern's Liquors & Sporting Goods, Hwy. 49, Angels Camp, CA,(209)736-2205.

Boating Facilities	Launching	Dockage	Fuel	Boat Rental
Glory Hole Rec. Area	Yes	No	No	No
Tuttletown Rec. Area	Yes	No	No	No

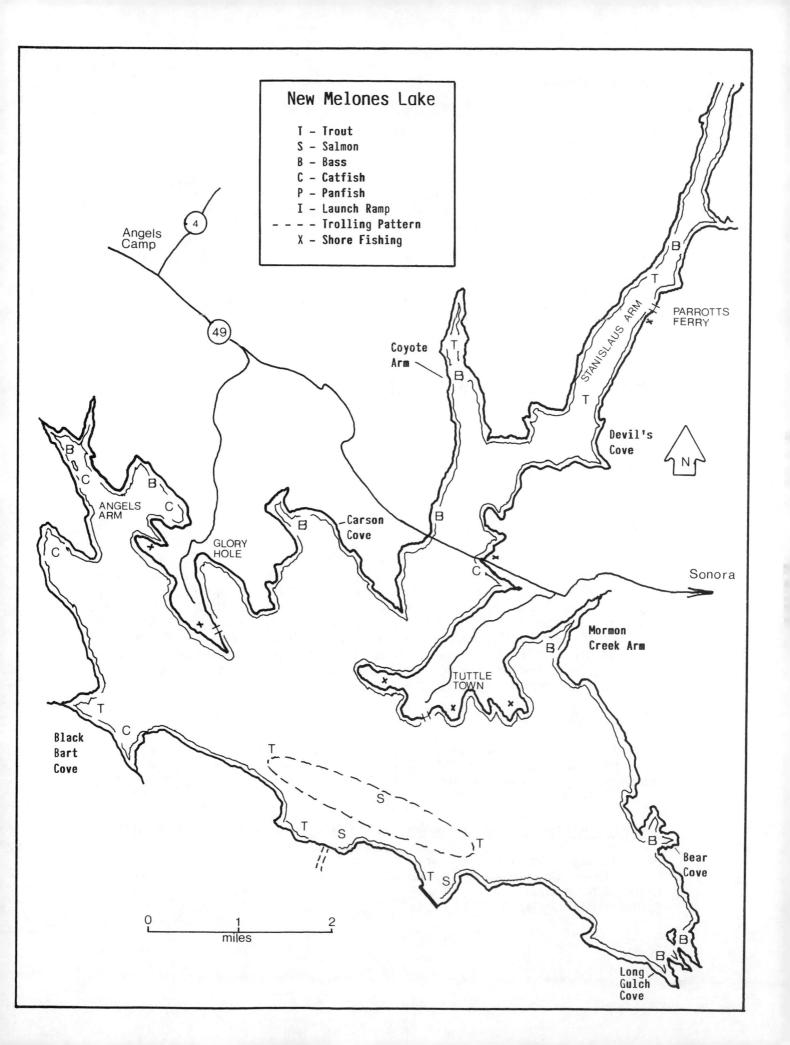

Oroville Lake

Lake Oroville is a very large, beautiful reservoir that offers excellent fishing. Trout, salmon, bass, catfish and panfish are all plentiful. This canyon reservoir is made up of the branches of the Feather River. Camping is concentrated at two locations at the South end of the lake with full service marinas at both the South and North end of the lake. Shore fishing is limited because of the steep shoreline and limited access opportunities. The best shore fishing is at campgrounds and marinas, and in the Diversion Pool, Thermalito Forebay and Afterbay(that surround the city of Oroville). The lake itself has 167 miles of shoreline.

Fishing Seasons   (+=good, -=fair)

Species	J	F	M	A	M	J	J	A	S	O	N	D
Trout	+	+	+	+	-	-	-	-	-	-	+	+
Salmon	+	+	+	+	-	-	-	-	-	-	+	+
Bass		-	+	+	+	-	-	-	-	+	+	
Catfish					-	-	-	-	-			
Panfish		-	-	-	-	-	-	-	-	-		

Fishing Tips

As a maturing canyon lake, Oroville is probably better for smallmouth than for largemouth bass. Oroville is actually 3 separate lakes, from a fishing point of view. The Southern forks warm up first in the spring, so bassing turns on first there. The main body warms next with the North fork warming last. Besides water temperature, keep an eye on your fish locator for the threadfin shad. If they're near the surface, that's where you'll find the bass and trout. If they're down, the gamefish will also be down. Since Oroville is a very deep(over 500 feet) lake, the fish can go very deep to find food and comfortable water temperatures.

Information/Bait/Tackle

Bidwell Canyon Marina, Oroville-Quincy Rd., Oroville, CA,(916)589-3165.
Limesaddle Marina, P.O. Box 1088, Paradise, CA 95969,(916)534-6950.
Huntington's Sportsmans's Store, 601 Oro Dam Blvd., Oroville, CA 95965,
   (916)534-8000.

Boating Facilities	Launching		Dockage	Fuel	Boat Rental
Bidwell Canyon Marina	7	Lanes	Yes	Yes	Yes
Loafer Creek Campgrnd.	7	Lanes	No	No	No
Limesaddle Marina	5	Lanes	Yes	Yes	Yes
Spillway Boat Ramp	13	Lanes	No	No	No

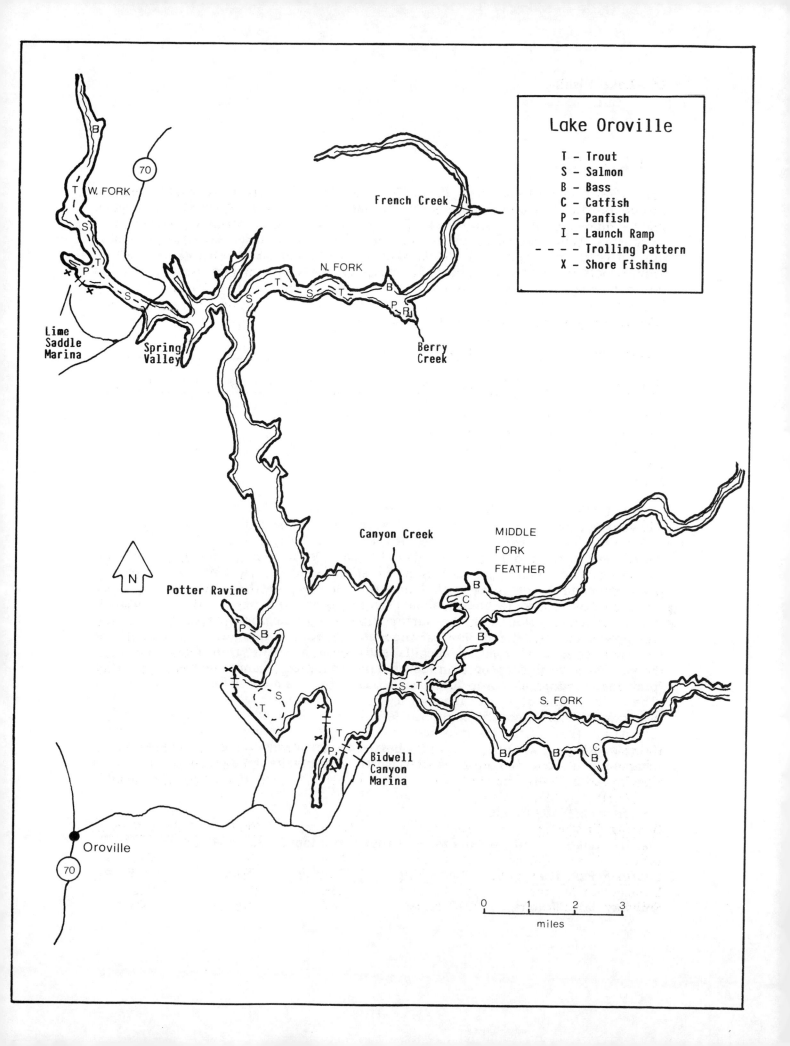

Pardee Lake

Pardee offers well-rounded fishing, but is best known for excellent trout. Trout in the 3-4 pound class are not uncommon. It is a dedicated fishing lake. No waterskiing is allowed. The waters of Pardee are clean and clear. It was built in the 1920's as an East Bay Municipal Utility District reservoir. Facilities include campground, restaurant, store, launch ramp and two swimming pools. Pardee has about 37 miles of shoreline. It is located in the Mother Lode about 40 miles East of Stockton.

Fishing Seasons   (+=good, -=fair)

Species	J	F	M	A	M	J	J	A	S	O	N	D
Trout		+	+	+	+	+	+	+	+	-	-	
Kokanee		-	-	+	+	+	+	-	-	-		
Bass		-	-	+	-	-	-	-	-	-		
Catfish		-	-	-	+	+	+	-	-	-		
Panfish		-	-	-	-	-	-	-	-	-		

Fishing Tips

Trout fishing is good both from shore and boat.   Shore anglers use night-crawlers(inflated) or salmon eggs(floated with marshmallows), or cast Kastmasters, Phoebes and Krocodiles, Roostertails, Mepps, etc.   Lures seem to work best early and late in the day.   Locals recommend a #8 hook, 30 inch leader(4 pound test) and a ¼-½ ounce sliding sinker.   A long leader is also recommended for trolling with leadcore line because the water is so clear. 20 feet of 6 pound leader is about right.   Boat trollers hit with Needlefish, Kokanee King, etc., near the surface in spring and down deeper as surface temperatures rise.   Kokanee are caught by trout trollers.   They school, so repeat a productive troll.   Bluegills and perch hit redworms hung from bobbers.   Bass fishing is best in coves and points on channel arms.   There is practically no brush cover for bass, so look for them at points and drop-offs. The rocky walls of the channel arm are productive.   Best offerings are plastic worms, Pig'n Jigs and nightcrawlers.   Work them deep at the outer edges of structures.   Crickets produce smallmouths in spring.   The lake record largemouth is 12½ pounds.   The best concentrations of catfish are in the channel arm, but the cove at the North end of the lake, at the marina, is good.

Information/Bait/Tackle

Pardee Lake Resort, 4900 Stoney Creek Rd., Ione, CA. 95640,(209)772-1472

Boating Facilities	Launching	Dockage	Fuel	Boat Rental
Pardee Lake Resort	10 Lanes	Yes	Yes	Yes

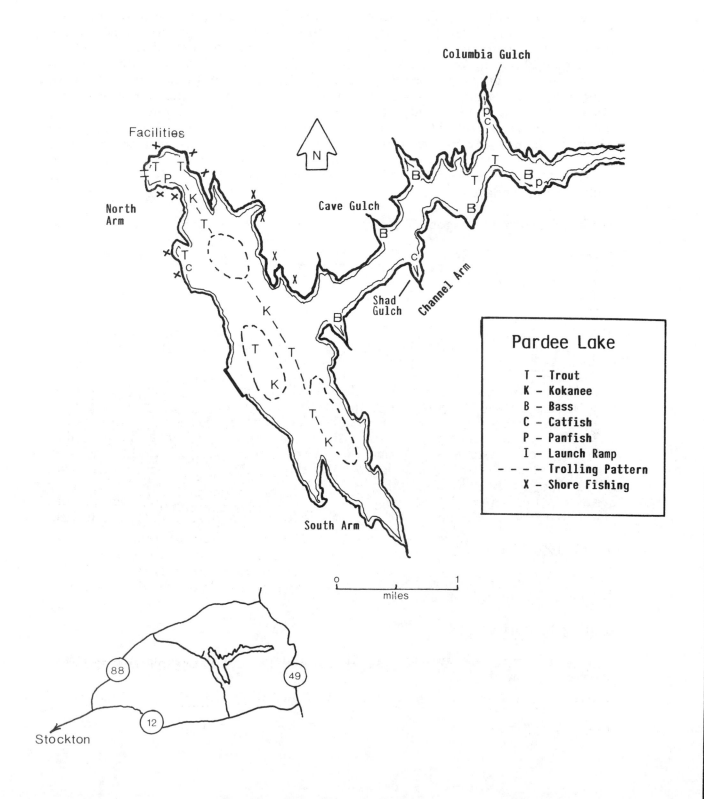

Columbia Gulch

Facilities

North
Arm

Cave Gulch

Shad
Gulch

Channel Arm

South Arm

Pardee Lake

T – Trout
K – Kokanee
B – Bass
C – Catfish
P – Panfish
I – Launch Ramp
- - - - Trolling Pattern
X – Shore Fishing

0   1
miles

88

49

12

Stockton

Parkway Lake

Parkway Lake is a very good, urban trophy trout fishery. During trout season, a dozen or more trout weighing 10 pounds, and up, are caught each month. The average fish caught per rod is better than 3 pounds. And all this fine fishing is only about a 30 minute drive for most anglers in the South Bay. Head South on Hwy. 101 in San Jose. Take Bernal Road to Monterey Road(Rte. 82) South to Metcaff Road and into Parkway Lake. Parkway Lake is small. Only about 35 acres. But it is deep(about 40 feet) and the water is relatively clear. Parkway plants about 15,000 trout per month, including many larger than 8 pounds. In the summer months, there are catfish(also stocked), bass and panfish to pursue. No license is required. A fee of $9.50 per adult, $5.50 for children under 12. 5 fish limit for adults, 3 for children.

Fishing Seasons   (+=good, -=fair)

Species	J	F	M	A	M	J	J	A	S	O	N	D
Trout	+	+	+	+	+	-			-	+	+	+
Bass			-	-	+	+	+	-				
Catfish				-	+	+	+	-				
Panfish				-	+	+	+	-				

Fishing Tips

Bait fishing for trout is popular. Use a sliding sinker rig and bait such as salmon eggs or small garlic marshmallows. Many larger fish are caught on lures like Mepps Lightin', Roostertails and Panther Martins. Wolly worm flies also work. Even though the fish can be big, light tackle is in order. Spinning tackle with 4 or 6 pound line, with patience and skill, will land even a 10 pounder. Trout fishing is good at the Northwest corner of the lake, and at the South end. Catfishing is best on the East shore. Work the brushy areas for Florida-strain largemouth bass. This type of facility is a great place to teach a kid about fishing. Some days it's hard not to catch fish.

Information/Bait/Tackle

Parkway Lake, (408)463-0383.
Coyote Discount Bait & Tackle, (408)463-0711.

Boating Facilities

Row boat rentals are available at $15.00 a day. No private boats or floatables are allowed.

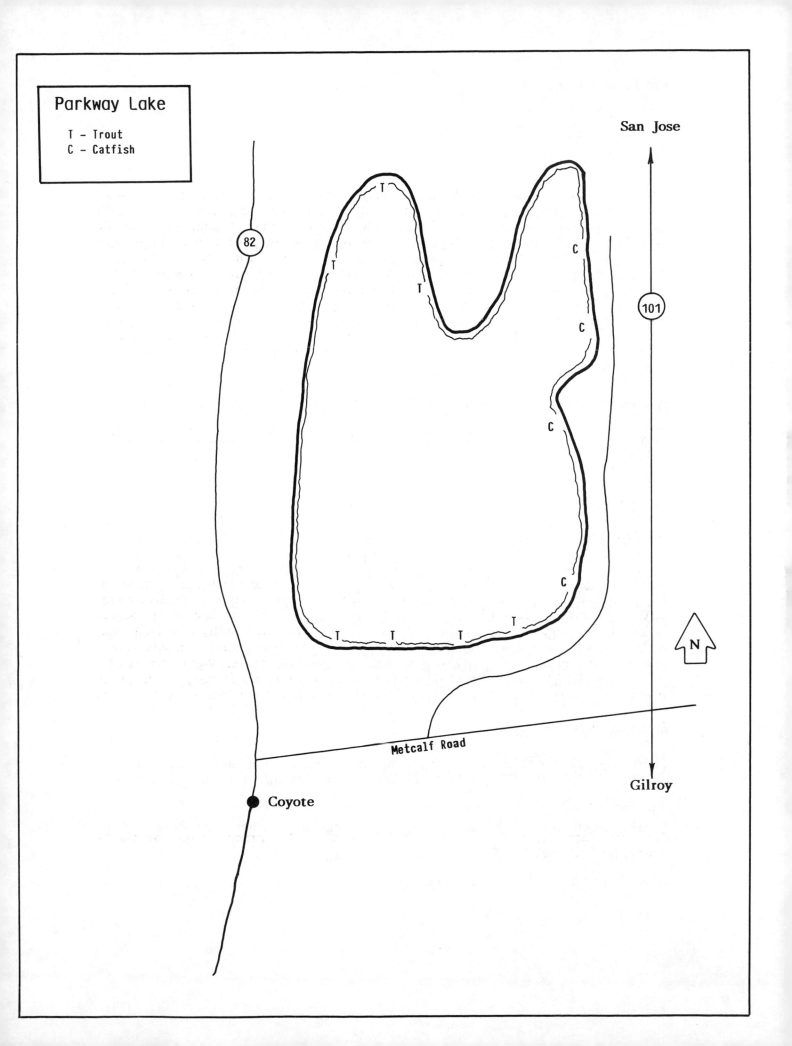

San Luis Lake

San Luis Reservoir and the adjoining O'Neill Forebay offer very good fishing, especially for striped bass. Water(and small fingerling and fry stripers) are pumped into the reservoir from the Sacramento, San Joaquin and the Delta, primarily during the winter and spring. This pumping process and numerous bait fish, produces an abundant supply of striper, most in the 3-8 pound range. But fish over 25 pounds are caught on occasion. Camping and launching facilities are available. But, note that strong winds are common on the reservoir itself. San Luis has 65 miles of shoreline. San Luis is on Pacheco Pass between Gilroy and Los Banos.

Fishing Seasons   (+=good, -=fair)

Species	J	F	M	A	M	J	J	A	S	O	N	D
Striper		-	+	+	+	-			-	+	-	
Catfish		-	-	-	+	+	+	-	-			

Fishing Tips

Stripers feed on threadfin shad. When these bait fish school on the surface, watch for bird action to pinpoint the striper schools feeding on the shad. A popular way to take striper at San Luis is casting from a boat. About ½ oz. Kastmasters, Krocodiles and Hair-raisers(up to 3/8 ounce in yellow or white) are productive. Striper anglers who have a boat, troll at about 3mph to locate fish on this big lake. Large silver Kastmasters and 7 inch deep-diving broken back Rebels(in blue) are popular. After the first hook-up, repeat the troll, or try casting and retrieving. Early morning and late evening are the best times. Shore fishing for stripers, using pileworms and anchovies, is popular at The Dinosaur and Basalt Areas and in the Forebay. Striper limit is 5 fish of any size.

Information/Bait/Tackle

There are numerous sources of fishing information, bait and tackle in the vicinity of San Luis. They are all anxious to provide information and supplies.

Boating Facilities	Launching	Dockage	Fuel	Boat Rental
San Luis Reservoir	2 Ramps	No	No	No
O'Neill Forebay	2 Ramps	No	No	No

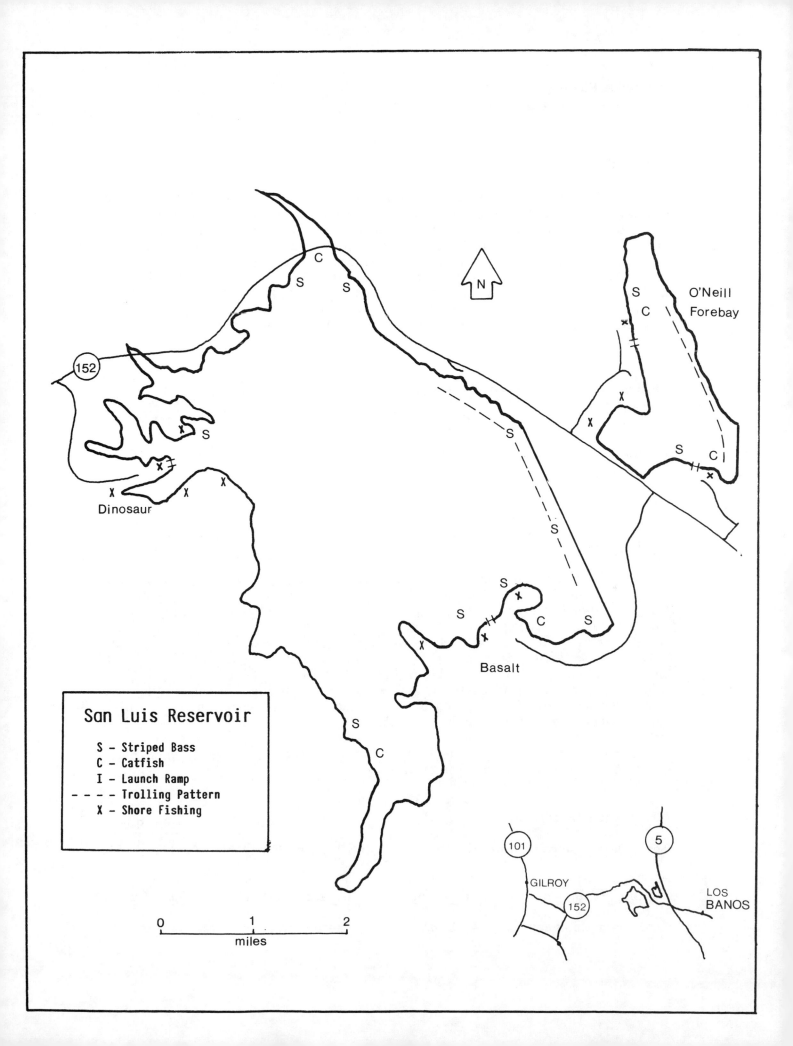

San Luis Reservoir

S – Striped Bass
C – Catfish
I – Launch Ramp
– – – Trolling Pattern
X – Shore Fishing

O'Neill
Forebay

Dinosaur

Basalt

152

101

GILROY

152

5

LOS
BANOS

0   1   2
miles

San Pablo Lake

Excellent fishing is available at this day-use reservoir located just East of the San Francisco Bay near Berkeley. San Pablo Reservoir is a narrow reservoir about 4 miles long. The lakes record rainbow is 9¼ pounds, and many are caught in the 3-6 pound range. Trout plants, done weekly, average about 1 pound per fish. Anglers at San Pablo frequently average 2-3 trout per rod, from both boat and shore. The only live bait allowed at San Pablo is redworms and nightcrawlers. San Pablo offers many good shore fishing locations for trout and catfish. For boaters, a topographical map showing the holes to fish, is for sale at the lake for less than $1.00. The lake is closed from mid-November to mid-February.

Fishing Seasons   (+=good, -=fair)

Species	J	F	M	A	M	J	J	A	S	O	N	D
Trout		+	+	+	+	-	-	-	-	+	+	
Bass		+	+	+	-	-	-	-	-			
Catfish		-	-	-	-	-	-	-	-			
Panfish		-	-	-	-	-	-	-	-			

Fishing Tips

Trout shore fishing at San Pablo is best using a sliding sinker rig and salmon eggs, marshmallows, nightcrawlers and cheese. Inflating nightcrawlers or using marshmallows to float up eggs, nightcrawlers or cheese(to keep bait off the bottom). Casting spinners and spoons also works from shore. Boat trout anglers troll(behind flashers) nightcrawlers, Rooster Tails, Triple Teasers, Needlefish, Kastmasters and Panther Martins. Bass go for 4 inch plastic worms, spinnerbait and Pig'n Jigs. Most of the shoreline on the West side of the reservoir is perfectly suited to shore fishing. Boat fishing hot spots include Scow Canyon, School House Gulch and Sather Canyon. During spring, when the water is high, fish closer to shore for warmer water. Best fishing at this time is from shore to about 30 feet out. In summer, as water warms, try starting from 35 feet out from shore. Look for deep holes close to shore and drop off structures.

Information/Bait/Tackle

That Dam Company, 7301 San Pablo Dr., El Sobrante, CA 94803,(415)223-1661.

Boating Facilities	Launching	Dockage	Fuel	Boat Rental
That Dam Company	4 Lanes	Yes	Yes	Yes

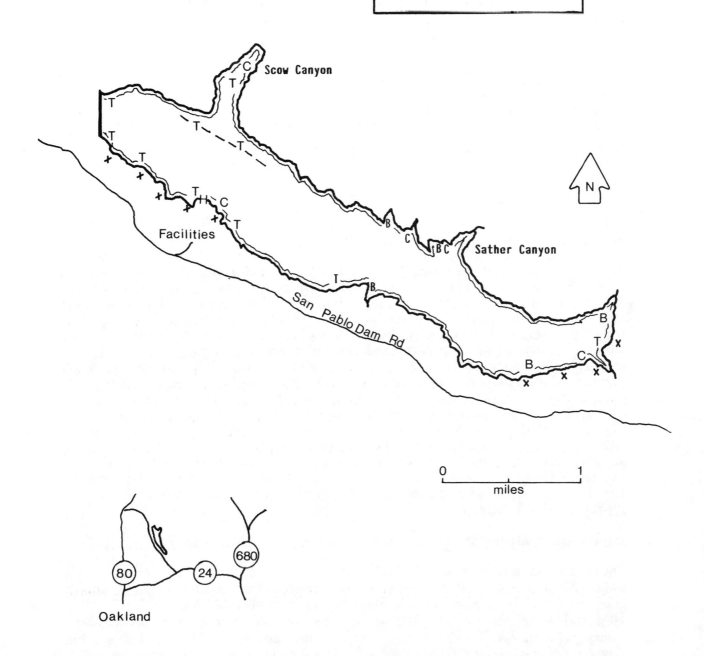

San Pablo Reservoir

T – Trout
B – Bass
C – Catfish
P – Panfish
I – Launch Ramp
- - - - Trolling Pattern
X – Shore Fishing

Scow Canyon

Sather Canyon

Facilities

San Pablo Dam Rd

N

0   1
miles

80   24   680

Oakland

Shasta Lake

Lake Shasta, a large reservoir, provides a wide variety of angling, including rainbow and brown trout, smallmouth and largemouth bass, panfish and king salmon. The lake, which is basically 4 flooded river canyons, is 35 miles long and has about 365 miles of shoreline. Maximum lake depth is slightly over 500 feet. There are a number of full service marinas(many of which rent houseboats) and campgrounds on the lake. Often, one or more families rent a houseboat, and "bring along" their fishing boat for angling and water-skiing.

Fishing Seasons   (+=good, -=fair)

Species	J	F	M	A	M	J	J	A	S	O	N	D
Trout	+	+	+	+	-	-	-	-	-	-	+	+
Salmon	+	+	+	+	-	-	-	-	-	-	+	+
Bass		-	+	+	+	-	-	-	-	+	+	
Catfish						+	+	+	+	-		
Panfish		-	-	-	-	-	-	-		-		

Fishing Tips

Trolling is the most productive trout and salmon approach. Popular offerings include nightcrawlers, Speedy Shiners, Z-Rays and Kastmasters. Trout anglers often use a combination marshmallow/nightcrawler/salmon egg on a sliding sinker rig. The marshmallow "floats" the entire combination. In the cooler months, trout can be caught with bait and a bobber, near the surface. Shasta doesn't have a lot of the cover and structures that typifies many largemouth bass lakes. But smallmouth, and some largemouth bass can be found in coves and near rocky points throughout the lake. Live bait, plastic worms, spinnerbaits, crankbaits and jigs all work depending on the time of day, time of year and location. Try a variety of offerings. Local favorites include white spinnerbaits, Gitzit jigs and Zara Spooks. A good smallmouth area is the Pit River Arm, off rocky walls and points. Live crickets and crawdads are top producers. Work early and late in the day, and in shaded coves. Catfishing peaks in the summer months. Fish over deep holes, or from shore, with clams, chicken livers, etc. Also in summer, fishing around an anchored houseboat with crickets, redworms or small minnows can produce crappie, bluegill or even trout. The shadow of the boat attracts light sensative fish. Shore fishing is good in campgrounds and near marinas throughout the lake.

Information/Bait/Tackle

There are numerous sources of fishing information, and bait and tackle at Lake Shasta. Many of the resorts and marinas, as well as several sporting goods stores, are anxious to provide information and supplies.
Shasta-Cascade Wonderland Assoc., 1250 Parkview Ave., Redding, CA 96001.

Boating Facilities - Lake Shasta has a wide variety of full service marinas and public and private launch ramps. The Chamber of Commerce has information at (916)275-1587.

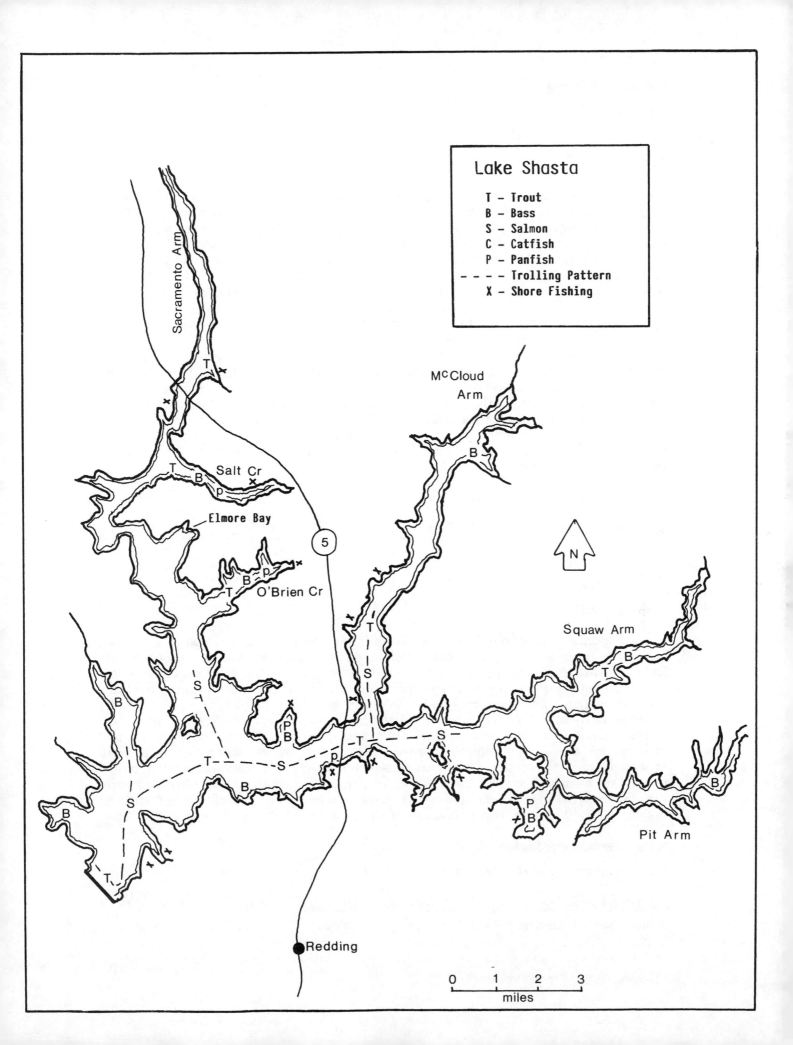

Sonoma Lake

Lake Sonoma(3000 surface acres and 73 miles of shoreline) is the newest major reservoir in Northern California, and it's only a 90 minute drive from the Golden Gate Bridge. On-shore facilities are still being developed, but everything is in place for fishing and boating fun. Sonoma was formed with the construction of Warm Springs Dam at the confluence of Dry Creek and Warm Springs Creek. Filling began in 1982 and finished in 1985. The lake is really divided into two sections. In the main body waterskiing and speed boating are permitted. But up in the Dry Creek Arm and the Warm Springs Creek Arm very little of the brush and trees were cleared, so the bass habitat is ideal. This fact combined with a 10mph boat speed limit makes bass fishing a pleasure. Here the shoreline is thick with submerged and partially submerged vegetation. Sonoma offers largemouth and smallmouth bass, rainbow trout(actually steelhead, both planted and landlocked), catfish, crappie and sunfish. Largemouths are hybrids(Northern strain and Florida), and already fish approaching 10 pounds have been caught. Trout up to 3 pounds are coming out of Sonoma. There are two launch ramps(the one across the bridge is public and free), a marina(with store and boat rental) and a growing number of campsites.

Fishing Seasons   (+=good, -=fair)

Species	J	F	M	A	M	J	J	A	S	O	N	D
Trout	+	+	+	+	-	-	-	-	-	-	+	+
Bass		-	+	+	+	-	-	-	-	+	+	

Fishing Tips

Lake Sonoma is too new to have established much of a pattern for fishing success. Bass anglers work the brush and drop-offs at the numerous points in the two arms. At times, the thick vegetation and wildlife spottings(deer, duck, osprey) may make anglers feel they're in a Southern swamp, but this spell ends for many anglers when they hang up their favorite lure on a submerged branch. So use weedless offerings(plastic worms, Pig'n Jigs, etc.) or cast cautiously. Trout anglers have found most success, so far, in and around the dam. In summer, there is a strong thermocline at around 40 feet, and trolling in the deep water near the dam precludes vegetation hangups. For bass and trout, and the other Sonoma species(e.g. catfish, crappie, redear sunfish) use techniques that have worked for you in other NorCal lakes. You'll be learning how to fish Sonoma along with everybody else.

Information/Bait/Tackle

Lake Sonoma Resort, P.O. Box 1345, Healdsburg, CA 95448, (707)433-2200.

Boating Facilities	Launching	Dockage	Fuel	Boat Rental
Lake Sonoma Marina	2 Ramps	Yes	Yes	Yes

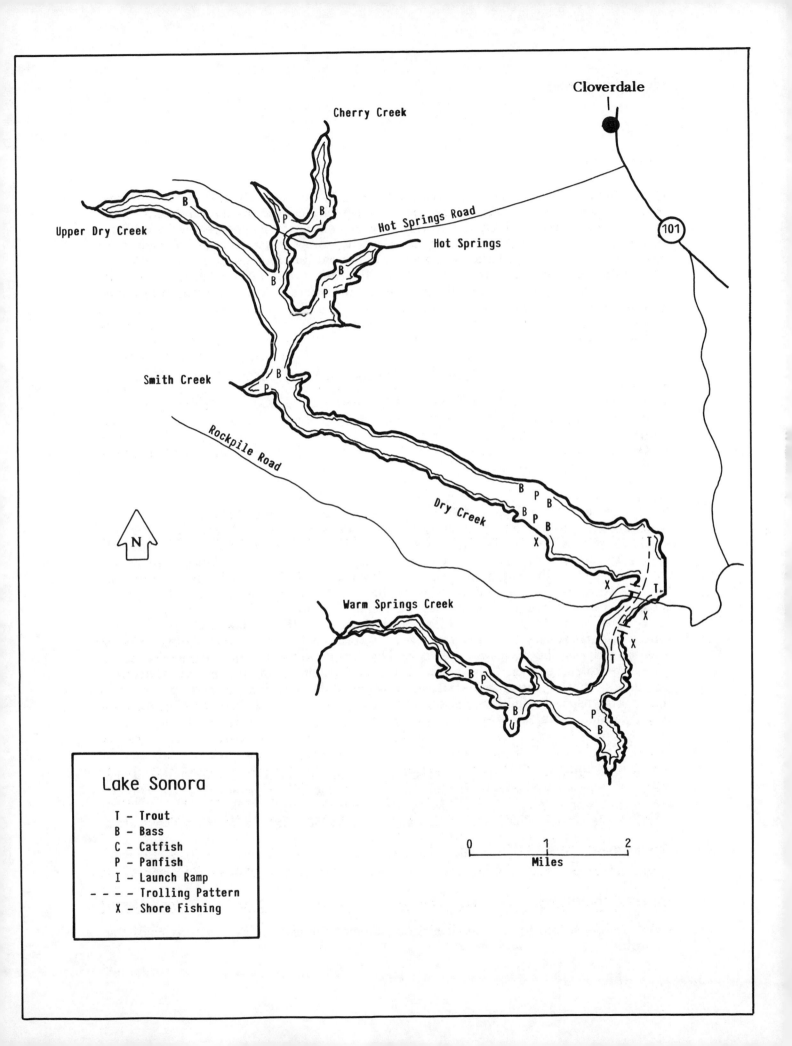

Tahoe Lake

Lake Tahoe is a very good, unique Northern California fishery. It is a large (22 miles by 12 miles, 1650 feet deep), high altitude(6230 feet) natural lake. The dominate native trout(a cutthroat) was commercially netted into extinction years ago. Now Mackinaw Lake trout, rainbow trout and kokanee salmon are the primary fisheries. An occassional brown trout is also caught. Launch ramps, full service marinas and all other types of recreational facilities are widely available in all sections of the lake. A California or Nevada fishing license is required.

Fishing Seasons   (+=good, -=fair)

Species	J	F	M	A	M	J	J	A	S	O	N	D
Mackinaw	+	+	+	+	--	-			-	-	+	+
Browns	-	-	+	+	+	-	-	-	-	+	+	-
Rainbow	+	+	+	+	+	+	+	-	-	+	+	+
Kokanee						-	+	+	+	-		

Fishing Tips

Mackinaw are the prize catch at Tahoe. Rainbow and browns are usually caught by anglers seeking Mackinaw. Mackinaw average 2-6 pounds(about the same as the rainbow) but many are caught in the 6-10 pound range and fish up to 16 pounds aren't that unusual. The state record Mackinaw stands at 37 pounds. Trolling with live minnows(from Lake Tahoe), J-Plugs or Flatfish behind flashers is the established technique. Light-colored plugs(silver or bluish) are preferred. Sometimes Mackinaw trolling is done as deep as 200 feet right near the bottom over structure or a shelf. Mackinaw trolling requires specialized skill and knowledge. Often anglers find that going out on a guide trip is the best way to learn how its done. Kokanee are caught using standard kokanee rigs. Kokanee in the 2-3 pound range are not that uncommon. In the spring and fall, trolling with deep diving minnow plugs produces browns and rainbows up to 5 pounds. Shore fishing for trout is popular using salmon eggs, nightcrawlers and spinners.

Information/Bait/Tackle

There are numerous sources of fishing information, bait and tackle at Lake Tahoe. Many of the resorts and marinas, as well as several sporting goods stores are anxious to provide information and supplies.
North Lake Tahoe Chamber of Commerce, (916)583-2371. South Lake Tahoe Chamber of Commerce, (916)541-5255.
North Shore Visitors Bureau, (800)822-5959. South Shore Visitors Bureau, (800)822-5922.

Boating Facilities

Lake Tahoe has over 20 marinas and launch ramps, located all around the shoreline.

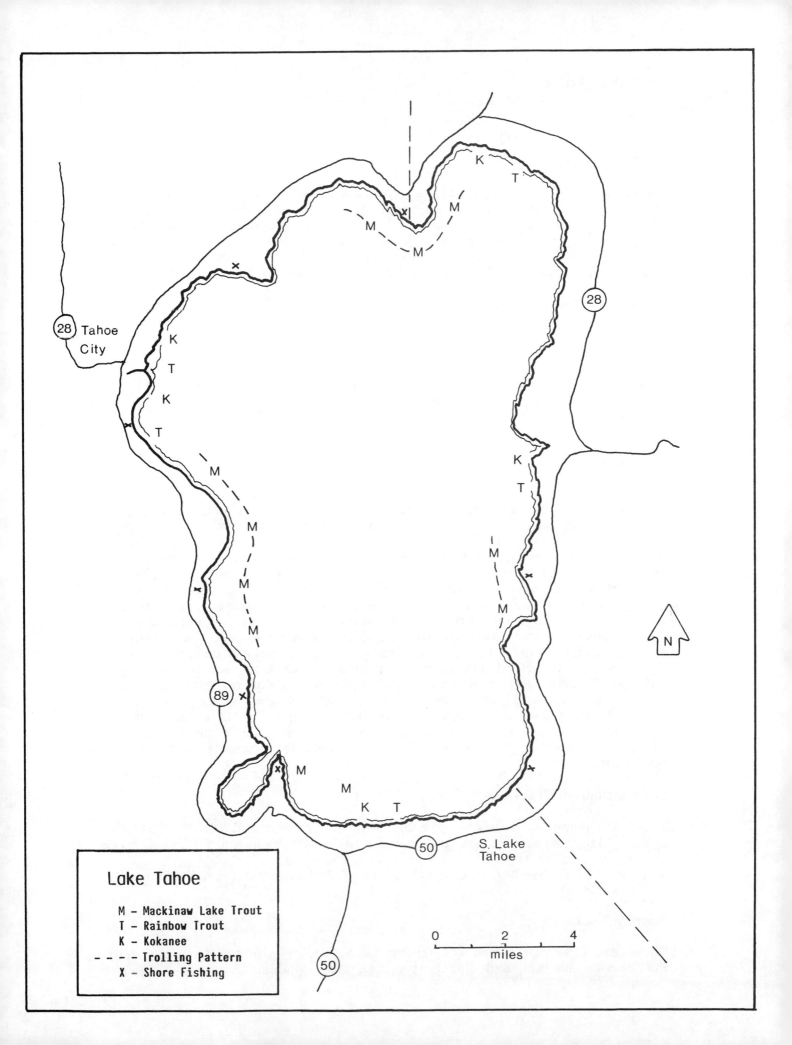

Lake Tahoe

M – Mackinaw Lake Trout
T – Rainbow Trout
K – Kokanee
- - - – Trolling Pattern
X – Shore Fishing

Trinity Lake

Trinity Lake is a beautiful, alpine-type lake, located on the Southern fringe of the Trinity Alps. This is an excellent trout lake. Bass fishing is also very good, particularly for smallmouth bass. But the amount of cover preferred by largemouth is limited. Trinity is a large lake. It is 22 miles long and has about 145 miles of shoreline. The lake has complete resort, boating and camping facilities. It is located about 45 miles West of Redding.

Fishing Seasons   (+=good, -=fair)

Species	J	F	M	A	M	J	J	A	S	O	N	D
Trout		-	-	+	+	+	+	-	-	-	-	
Kokanee		-	-	-	+	+	+	+	+			
Bass		-	-	+	+	-	-	-	+	+		
Salmon		-	-	-	-	+	+	+	+	+	+	
Panfish		-	-	-	-	-	-	-	-	-	-	

Fishing Tips

Smallmouth bass fishing in Trinity is concentrated at rocky points and out-croppings. Another good bass structure to look for is the underwater, shallow water plateaus or shelfs that are most often found off shore of relatively level campgrounds. An example of an area like this is the gentle slope from Wyntoon Camp North, near Tinity Center. This area which goes on for a mile or more, also has some stumps, so it can be productive for largemouth. The state record smallmouth, 9 pounds, 1 ounce, was caught at Trinity, and 4-5 pounders are not unusual. Smaller offerings are better in this lake. Two to 3 inch grubs, 4 inch worms and 1/16 to 1/8 ounce jigs are good choices. Local favorites are the Gitzit, Rebel Wee R and Teeny R, Storm's Wiggle Wart and Rapala's mini Fat Rap. Six pound test line is standard. At the North end good spots are the rock piles near Squirrel Flat and Hay Gulches near Trinity Center. On the South, Chicken Flat and stump beds on the Stuart's Fork Arm are consistent producers. In early spring, trout can be found most often near or in the major feeder streams of the lake. In late spring and early summer, trout are often near the drop-offs of the shallow shelfs. Late summer-early fall trolling is usually productive at 30-40 feet.

Information/Bait/Tackle

There are numerous sources of fishing information, bait and tackle at Trinity Lake. Many of the resorts and marinas, as well as several sporting goods stores are anxious to provide information and supplies.
Trinity County Chamber of Commerce, Box 517, Weaverville, CA 96093,
    (916)623-6101.

Boating Facilities

There are 8 launch ramps on Trinity Lake. Most are on the East shore. Full service marinas, including boat rental, are available.

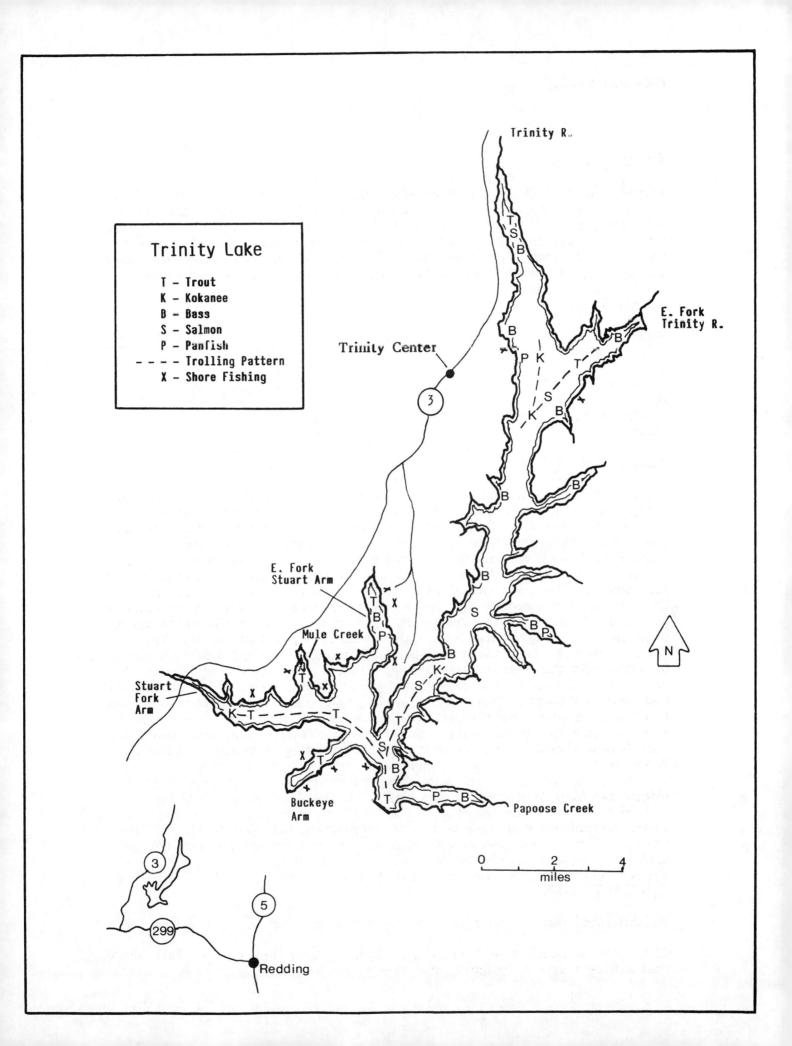

Mountain Trout Fishing

There are a great many excellent mountain trout fishing locales available to Northern California anglers. Some of the best are profiled in this section. These vary from easily accessible streams and lakes to wilderness backpacking experiences.

And they range from as far South as Yosemite to up North near the Oregon border. But all these locales have one thing in common. They take anglers to some of the most beautiful spots in this most beautiful state.

Fishing Tips

The success of a stream fishing experience during this open season depends on many factors including; the amount of snowfall, the runoff, timing of insect hatches, weather patterns, etc. A number of mountain streams and lakes have special regulations, or are closed to fishing altogether, so be aware of current regulations.

Generally, stream trout fishing is better in the spring and fall, than it is in the summer. But summer fishing is often productive. When summer comes on, veteran anglers follow 60-65° water temperature up to higher elevations as backroads become passable. In July and August, a good spot is the cool tailwaters below dams. In the very high mountains, trout fishing is strongly influenced by weather conditions. In some years, ice remains until June and backroads are impassable. In other years, early fall storms cut the season short. And during mid-summer, heavy thunderstorms can interrupt fishing trips. Backpackers should be prepared for all weather conditions.

One approach that always seems to produce more and larger trout is to contradict human nature. Most anglers park at a stream access point, walk to the water and begin to fish. So the pros have found that it's always better to hike for say 15 minutes along a stream before fishing. This will get you beyond the overworked and underpopulated spots into some really good fishing action. Once fishing in a stream, the most productive anglers aren't afraid to get into the water. Don't just wade around the edges and fish from convenient spots. Get in the water with chest waders, if necessary, and move to the spots that provide access to the most likely holes.

SIERRA TROUT

The Northern Sierras encompass an immense area. Take a look at the map on the right of this page. On it are some of the best and most famous lake and stream trout fishing areas in all of California. Let's work our way down the map, starting at the Feather River and you'll see what we're talking about.

Feather River Basin Trout

The branches and tributaries of the Feather River drain a huge triangular section of the Northwestern Sierras between Oroville, Lake Almanor and Portola. Most of this territory is quite rugged and inaccessible, but because the area is so large, there are still miles and miles of rivers and streams that are quite easy to get to. And there are also a number of lakes that offer good trout fishing.

Let's start our tour at Lake Almanor. The lake itself is prime trout and salmon water, and there are two pages devoted to it in the Lake Section of this book. The North Fork of the Feather drains into Almanor at Chester. Starting right in town, the North Fork and its streams (Rice Creek, Warner Creek, Hot Springs Creek, Willow Creek, Brenner Creek, Last Chance Creek) have good access, relatively low fishing pressure and native trout. The North Fork itself, is a fairly large stream, even in autumn. Most of the streams are spring fed, and run clear and cold throughout the summer. Several types of fishing are offered. Willow Creek is very brushy and is best for bait angling. Some others, like Rice Creek are good fly casting waters. There are a number of campgrounds along the creeks providing access and overnighting.

On the Northeast shore of Lake Almanor, the Hamilton Branch flows into the lake. It offers good fishing in a series of big pools, separated by white water riffles flowing through a scenic canyon. The Feather River flows out of Lake Almanor at its South end. Senaca Road parallels the river for about 10 miles and leads to Senaca Resort. Lake Almanor dam provides a regulated flow of very cold water to this stretch of water. The best access is where Senaca Road crosses the North Fork. Fish away from this access, either upstream or downstream, for best results. Butt Valley Reservoir, a fine trout and small-mouth fishery, is also just South of Lake Almanor. For more on Butt Valley see the Lake Almanor Section of this book.

Between Lake Almanor and Lake Oroville, the North Fork of the Feather River flows along Rte. 70 for much of its course through the Feather River Canyon. Where you can get down to it, the main river is good trout water. A good eight mile stretch is from Nelson Creek to Audie Bar. Perennial hot spots include the confluence of the North Fork and the East Branch of the North Fork, and the mouth of Yellow Creek. These are both just above the town of Belden. The lower section of Yellow Creek, near the Feather, is fished heavily, but is still productive. Upper Yellow Creek, accessible from Humbug Road, off Rte. 89 along the West shore of Lake Almanor, is a fine mountain-meadow stream. There is a PG&E campground in the East end of Humbug Valley. The canyon below the valley is also good fishing with flies or bait.

The Middle Fork of the Feather is accessible along Rte. 70/89 between Sloat to Portola. Some of the better areas are Camp Layman, Two Rivers and Carmac Mine. South of the town of Graeagle which is on Rte. 89 there is some fine fishing in Gold Lake Basin. This area of small lakes and streams is about 10 miles out of Graeagle on Gold Lake Road. Some of the good trout lakes in the area include Gold, Big Bear, Cub, Long Silver, Round, Lower Salmon, Snag, Packer and Lower Sardine. Gold Lakes Basin has campgrounds, resorts, hiking, etc. Another way to reach it is from Bassetts Station on Hwy. 49.

The Middle Fork from Graeagle and Red Bridge is good bait territory, although fly anglers also succeed in the shallower parts of the stream. Good tributary streams in this area include Mohawk, Frazier, Gray Eagle, Smith, Eureka, Bear and Dear. Three good trout lakes in this area are Bucks Lake, Southeast of Quincy, Lake Davis North of Protola and Frenchman Lake North of Chilcoot.

For information on the Feather River Basin contact Plumas National Forest, 875 Mitchell, Oroville, CA 95965, (916)534-6500; Almanor Ranger District, Box 767, Chester, CA 96020, (916)258-2141.

Yuba River Region Trout

The Yuba River has three forks – North, Middle and South. The North Fork flows alongside Hwy. 49 from the Sierra summit through Downieville and most of the way to Comptonville. There is good fishing in many places along the

North Fork, especially near Downieville, and in Downie Creek and Salmon Creek.

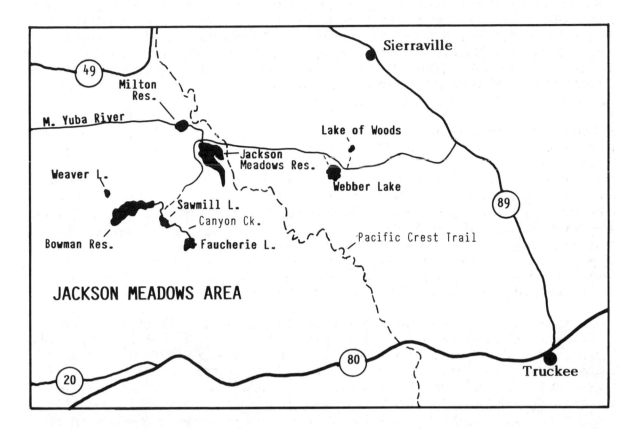

The Middle Yuba is quite inaccessible except where it crosses Hwy. 49 and again at it headwaters below Jackson Meadow Reservoir. The 1.5 mile stretch of the Middle Yuba, below Jackson Meadows, as well as Milton Lake, is a special regulation trophy trout fishery. Only artificial lures with single, barbless hooks may be used and the limit is two fish, both smaller than 12 inches. There are other good fishing opportunities in the Jackson Meadow Area. Jackson Meadow Reservoir, itself, is a full-service recreation lake with 150 campsites, group camping, boat ramp, picnic area, etc. This 1½ square mile lake with 11 miles of shoreline has good brown and rainbow trout fishing. Other good trout lakes in the area include Bowman(brown trout), Lake of the Woods (brook trout), Webber Lake(browns) and Weaver Lake. Bowman has very steep banks necessitating a boat for good fishing. Lake of the Woods is a gorgeous little lake that also is best fished by boat. In the Canyon Creek drainage, there is good fishing in Canyon Creek(several miles of good bait fishing waters), Faucherie Lake(good shore fishing) and Sawmill Lake(launch near the dam or shore fish in selected spots).

Fishing in the South Fork of the Yuba River in its headwaters between Soda

Springs and Lake Spaulding can be good. Here the river switches back and forth with Interstate 80, providing good access. Lake Spaulding can be conveniently reached from I-80, using the Hwy. 20 exit. It has good campgrounds and boat launching. Most anglers troll here. Cooler than expected surface temperatures diminish the need to troll at great depths. The several highway bridges provide good access to the South Fork of the Yuba from Lake Spaulding all the way down to Bridgeport.

For information on the Yuba River region contact the Sierraville Ranger Station, Box 95, Sierraville, CA 96216, (916)994-3401.

North of Lake Tahoe Trout

There is some very good lake and stream mountain trout fishing in the Eastern Sierra, just North of Lake Tahoe. Combine this with quality camping, rafting, Reno and the beauty of this area and it all adds up to one terrific spot for a vacation or weekend get-away.

The Truckee River is the premier stream in the area. It flows along Rte. 89 to the town of Truckee, and then along I-80 all the way to Nevada. There are many good spots in this long and large river. Regulations vary along this river, so be informed. Some of the best fishing is where creeks enter the main river. Especially noteworthy are the mouths of Donner Creek and Prosser Creek. Another fine stretch is from Hirshdale on down to Farrad. Aggressive wading is required in many stretches of the Truckee. Use a wading staff.

Donner Lake, West of Truckee, off I-80

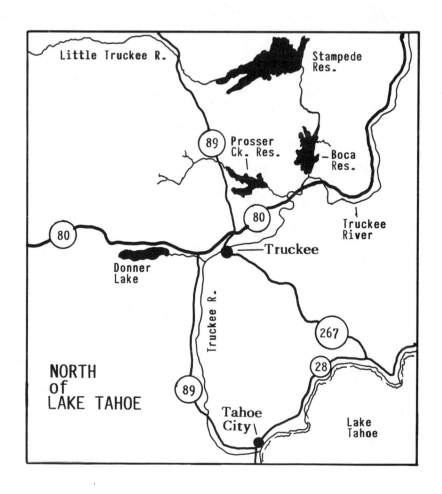

has good fishing for rainbow and brown trout and kokanee. There is also a good fishery for 3-6 pound Makinaw trout. The same approach is used to catch Makinaws in Donner as is used in nearby Lake Tahoe(see Lake Tahoe in Lake Section). Best fishing is in the spring months when the trout are up near the surface. This 3 mile long lake has over 150 developed campsites, boat rental, nature trail, a museum, etc.

Prosser Lake, just about 6 miles North of Truckee, is a fine fishing lake. And the 10 mph boat speed limit makes for serene fishing, even in summer. Both rainbow and brown trout, of good size, are caught in this 750 surface acre mountain lake. The area near the mouth of Prosser Creek is a consistent producer. Late summer deep trolling is good near the dam. There is a good launch ramp, campsites and a picnic area. Prosser Creek, above the lake, is a very good trout stream. The main stream is accessible off Hwy. 89. The North and South forks (near this junction is good fishing) are reached via a Forest Service Road. Prosser Creek flows cold and clear, even in late summer. Small lures and nymph patterns on a light leader are a good bet.

Boca Reservoir, somewhat larger than Prosser Lake, is located about 9 miles Northeast of Truckee. Besides a good trout population, there is also an expanding Kokanee fishery. Anglers troll for Kokanee using a flasher followed by a Kokanee King or Triple Teaser. A white kernel of corn on the hook seems to help. Most Kokanee taken are in the 11-13 inch range. All types of boating are allowed and there is a developed campground.

Stampede is last but not least, in our collection of Truckee area trout lakes. It is by far the largest with 3,500 surface acres of water and 25 miles of shoreline. And, it has some of the best fishing, for brown and rainbow trout, and kokanee salmon. Stampede is relatively shallow in many areas so food production is outstanding. Kokanee go for the same offerings as at Boca, but run 12-15 inches. Trout trollers often do well with nightcrawlers behind flashers. There are excellent camping and launching facilities at the South side of the lake. Good spots include the Little Truckee inflow area and near the dam. Stream trout anglers often find the Little Truckee River to be a good producer. Access is via Rte. 89 and Jackson Meadows Road, which both parallel the stream. Small spinners are effective. The Little Truckee runs above and below Stampede Reservoir.

For information on the area North of Lake Tahoe, contact the Truckee Chamber of Commerce, Box 361, Truckee, CA 95734, (916)587-2757, and the Truckee Ranger District, Box 399, Truckee, CA 95734, (916)587-3558.

Carson Pass Trout

Typical of the scores of mountain trout locales in the Sierras that get little or no publicity, yet offer fine fishing, is the Carson Pass Area of Eldorado National

Forest. Carson Pass, bisected by Rte. 88, is about 35 miles South of Lake Tahoe's South shore, and is best known as home of Kirkwood Ski Resort. But trout fishing, hiking, camping and drinking in the alpine scenery reigns in the summertime. The pass is at 8,573 feet elevation, so the summer season is short. Many visitors come in July and August.

There is a wide variety of trout angling opportunities. The most accessible is the planted waters of the Carson River as it flows alongside Rte. 88. Several small lakes are also easily accessible from the highway, including Red Lake, Round-top Lake, Frog Lake and Winnemucca Lake. Blue Lake Road, off Rte. 88, leads thru Faith Valley to a marvelous collection of small lakes and campgrounds. There are Upper and Lower Blue Lake, Lost Lake, Twin Lake, among others. Blue Creek tumbling down to the Mokelumne from Blue Lake is a rugged but productive stream. And Lost Lake(actually 2 lakes) harbors some large brook trout. Spinners, like the Mepps #2 are good, as are nymphs.

Just West of this collection of lakes is the 50,000 acre Mokelumne Wilderness. One popular destination for backpackers is Fourth of July Lake. The Evergreen Trail to this lake begins on a dirt road North of Upper Blue Lake, near Raymond Peak. The trail starts at Wet Meadow, Near Blue Lake and encompasses part of the Pacific Crest Trail. Raymond Lake offers anglers a chance to catch the fantasically beautiful golden trout. But note, this is a difficult hike. For more information on the Carson Pass area contact Eldorado National Forest, 100 Forni Road, Placerville, CA 95667, (916)622-5061.

Emigrant Wilderness Trout

Emigrant Wilderness, located South of Hwy. 108, the Sonora Pass, in Tuolumne County, is a beautiful and unique area, with breathtaking scenery. It is about 30 miles out of the town of Sonora. There is excellent trout fishing in its many streams and lakes. Terrain is rolling hills, ridges and granite domes with many lakes surrounded by stands of lodgepole pines. High peaks of Sierras border the East side of the Wilderness.

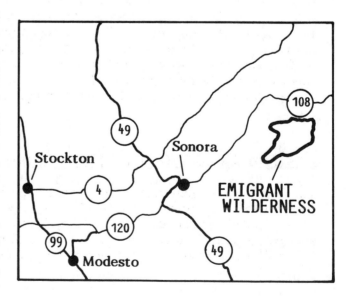

If you and your family or friends like to combine a backpacking trip with trout fishing, this may be the place for you. But don't plan on a late spring trip. Mother nature usually doesn't open these waters until June and it may be July before some trails are clear of snow. Most lakes are ice-free by mid-June.

Access to Emigrant is through the Pinecrest Lake-Dodge Ridge area at Strawberry. There are about 5 different trailheads in this area plus a pack station. Crabtree Trailhead is the most popular. Top streams include Summit Creek above Relief Reservoir, Lily Creek and Horsemeadow Creek. A good pristine lake zone is in the Southwestern portion of the wilderness – Rosasco, Hyatt, Pingree, Big, Yellowhammer and Lord Meadow Lakes. Also the stream between Layton and Yellowhammer Lakes is a good producer.

Emigrant Wilderness is rugged. Only experienced backpackers should explore this area. Information is available from Summit Ranger Station, USFS Star Route, Box 1295, Sonora, CA 95370, (209)965-3434.

Yosemite Trout

Some fine wild trout fishing can be found thousands of feet above Yosemite Valley floor, in Tuolumne Meadows along Hwy. 120. Here above Hetch Hetchy Reservoir, the Tuolumne and its branches, the Dana Fork and the Lyell Fork provide abundant brook, brown and rainbow trout in the 6-18 inch range. The fishing season is short at this 8600 foot elevation. The waters are still high in June. July is usually good fishing and it peaks in August.

The Tuolumne is easily fished in the Meadows itself as it runs along Hwy. 120. A mile or so downstream of the Meadow the Tuolumne quickens its pace as it falls over granite structure. Fish here and about a miles walk up from the Meadows, in Dana Fork, are larger than those caught right in the Meadows. A short drive East on Hwy. 120 from the Meadows provides access at several points to more of the Dana Fork. Follow the John Muir Trail South from the Meadows to fish the Lyell Fork. Tuolumne Meadows is a popular tourist and camping area. August is the busiest month. Here is a good place to combine family sight-seeing, hiking, camping and trout fishing.

EASTERN AND SOUTHERN SIERRA TROUT

There is also a mountain trout fishing section in our **Fishing in Southern California** book. It details trout fishing in the Eastern Sierras, along Rte. 395(the areas around Bridgeport, June Lake, Mammoth Lake, Crowley Lake and Bishop) as well as trout fishing in the Southern Sierras out of Fresno and Bakersfield. See the order page in the front of the book.

REDDING - BURNEY AREA TROUT

Some of the finest trout streams in the Western United States are concentrated in the relatively compact Redding-Burney-Dunsmuir area North and East of Lake Shasta. And, as a matter of fact, Lake Shasta provides some fine trout fishing itself, but that's another story(see Lake Shasta in the Lake Fishing Section of this book).

Take a look at the Redding-Burney Area map, between Dunsmuir and Fall River, a distance of less than fifty miles as the crow flies, there are four outstanding trout streams - Upper Sacramento River, McCloud River, Hat Creek and the Fall River. The features that make each of these so great are presented in the following sections. For information on Redding-Burney trout, contact the Shasta Cascade Wonderland Association, 1250 Parkview Ave., Redding, CA, (916)243-2643.

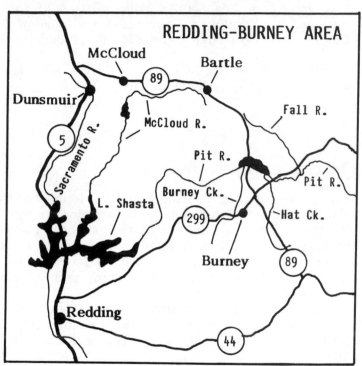

Upper Sacramento River Trout

Many anglers think of the Sacramento River in terms of outstanding salmon, sturgeon, shad and striper fishing. They're correct but they're thinking of the Sacramento from Redding on down to Rio Vista. The Upper Sacramento flows more than 45 miles from Box Canyon Dam at the base of Lake Siskiyou all the way down to Lakehead at the upper end of Lake Shasta. This remarkable, trophy-trout stream just about parallels I-5 from Lake Siskiyou to Lake Shasta. And the major highway, along with accompanying railroad tracks, provides very good access at places like Dunsmuir, Castella, Flume Creek, Sims Campground, Gibson, La Moine, and Delta. But the presence of I-5 doesn't make this an urban river. Anglers often spot wildlife like deer coming down to the water to drink and even cool off on hot summer afternoons. This is a good-sized river with enticing riffles, deep pools, and many trophy-sized rainbow and brown trout. Trout catches up to 18 inches are not all that unusual here. Bait(especially nightcrawlers), spinners and flies are great on the Upper Sacramento. Some fly fishing devotees compare the Upper Sacramento with the prime fly streams of Montana and Wyoming. It has a very diverse hatch of aquatic insects from July to mid-October. One surprising thing about the Upper Sacramento River is that it usually isn't that crowded. And often it's downright barren of anglers. Maybe its just that there is so much access and the river is so long that anglers are spread out. In any case, whatever fishing pressure exists, it doesn't seem to have hurt the fishery. Camping is available at Castle Crags State Park, near Castella, and at Sims Campground.

McCloud River Trout

The McCloud River runs parallel to Hwy. 89 from Bartle toward the town of McCloud and then South to Lake McCloud and finally into Lake Shasta. This is an extremely scenic and prolific trout stream. And variety could be its middle name. It offers every type of water that holds trout. The McCloud is a great stream for the connoisseur angler, and for the youngster or beginner. Flies, bait and hardware(spinners and spoons) all can be effective. There are brook, brown, native rainbow and planted rainbow trout, as well as a few Dolly Varden (which must be released alive. And there is a complete spectrum of regulations, from 10 trout limits in one section of the river to a catch-and-release, barbless flies and lures-only section.

The Upper portions of the McCloud from Bartle down to about a mile below Fowlers Camp is a planted section of stream(10 fish limit) that is easily accessible from campgrounds such as Fowlers, Big Springs, Cattle Camp, Algoma and several others. If you want to get away from other anglers and improve your chances of catching native and hold-over fish, walk the barely hikeable path along the stream to areas between camps. Both spinning and fly fishing is good. Top baits are salmon eggs and worms. Mepps spinners produce. Portions of this stream run through meadow for miles. Flow is gentle and fishermen wade here in summer without waders. Speaking of wading, the McCloud is a waders stream. To fish it properly, in this stretch and also below McCloud Lake, you've got to get wet.

A second alternative is to fish the stretch just South of the McCloud Dam. It can be reached by taking Squaw Valley Road about 12 miles out of the town of Mc Cloud. In this 6.5 mile stretch only artificial lures and flies may be used and the limit is two fish per day. Access is via Ash Campground, about a mile downstream from the dam, on a road on the East side of the river. This is a canyon stream with more flow than in the Upper McCloud.

Finally, there is a catch-and-release stretch of the McCloud that begins at the mouth of Ladybug Creek and extends for about 2 miles. Take the road on the West side of the McCloud Lake Dam that leads to the Ah-Di-Na Campground.

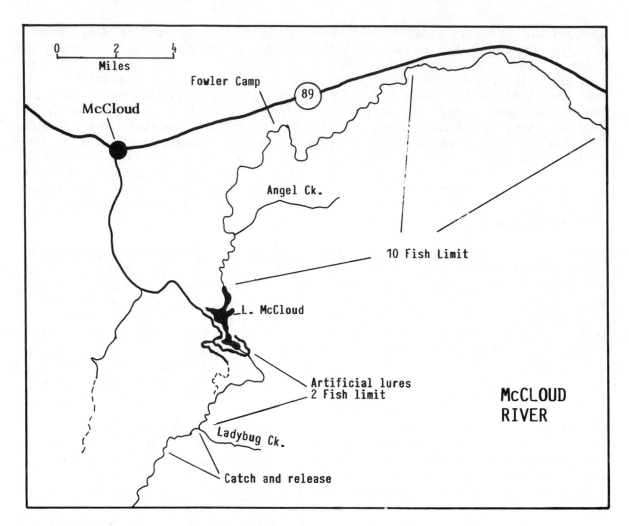

Only artificial lures and flies with barbless, single hooks can be used. Here and in the upper river, the best time for dry fly fishing is from 5:30 p.m. to dark. Adams, Western Coachman, Yellow Cahill and Mosquito are popular. Early morning is weighted wet fly time using a two fly rig of Spent Wing and Burlap, Yellow Jacket or Caddis Larva.

If stream anglers want a change of pace, Lake McCloud(520 surface acres) is a super trout lake. Bank fishing on the lake is best up towards Star City Creek, where the river feeds into the lakes North end. There is also good bank fishing down around the dam and around the ridges that surround the lake.

Hat Creek Trout

Burney Basin, the home of Hat Creek, is located in Shasta County, surrounding the town of Burney, about 50 miles East of Redding on Hwy. 299. Hat Creek and Fall River, in this basin, are considered among the best trout streams in the West.

Hat Creek, which runs through P G & E property, is divided into two portions. The 3.5 miles of Lower Hat Creek(from Power House No. 2 down to Lake Britton) is a designated wild trout stream. Here, only flies and lures with a single barbless hook are allowed, and a two-fish, 18 inch minimum size limit is in effect. Trout hooked here average between 10-16 inches with occassional ones in the 20-24 inch range. There are some lunker browns over 10 pounds! Access is very good. Park where 299 crosses the creek and walk upstream or downstream. Fly fishing is very popular here. This is a broad, meadow stream. Wading is popular, but bank anglers can also do very well.

Upper Hat Creek is well stocked with hatchery fish. Most trout caught are in the 8-11 inch range. This stream from above Baum Lake runs along Hwy. 89 and access is good from the 5 campgrounds along Hwy. 89. Bait fishing(worms, salmon eggs and crickets) is most productive.

Baum Lake is a good, small trout lake. Actually it's just a wide spot in that creek, with a dam at each end, but all types of trout fishing are productive and small, non-powered boats are permitted. There is a campground at the PG & E supervised facility.

Another well-stocked and productive stream in the area is Burney Creek. Best fishing is near Lake Britton, above and below the falls. Camping is available in McArthur-Burney Falls State Park at Lake Britton.

All of the streams in this area, including Fall River, Hat Creek and Burney Creek are actually tributaries of the 200 mile long Pit River. In the Burney Basin, the Pit River above Lake Britton is quite a large, fast river. But it does have a good population of rainbows and browns. Good spots to fish are on either side of the 299 bridge, and at the old Pit

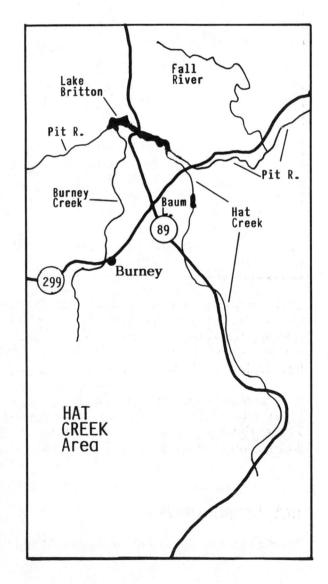

No. 1 powerhouse some four miles from the bridge. More information on this excellent trout fishery is available from the Burney Basin Chamber of Commerce, Box 36, Burney, CA 96013, (916)335-2111, or Vaughn's Sporting Goods, Burney, CA, (916)335-2381.

Fall River Trout

Fall River, like Hat Creek, is a great trout stream. In fact, some experts rank these two Burney Basin streams among the top ten trout streams in America.

This is a deep, 21 mile long stream with widths ranging from 150 feet to 250 yards. It is spring fed, so run-off has little effect on flow.

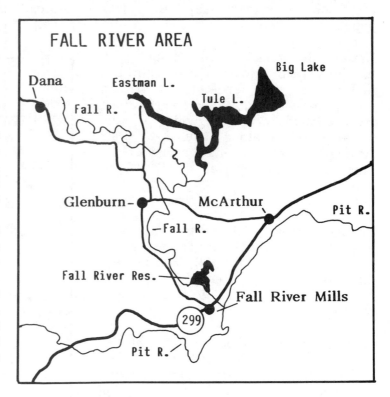

Upper Fall River is a wild trout stream, like Lower Hat Creek. But since it runs mostly through private property, it is fished using float tubes or electric powered small boats. The fish are big here, many weighing from 5-8 pounds. Fly fishing is most popular. There are two lodges that provide access if you stay with them. (Lava Creek Lodge and Rick's Hunting and Fishing Lodge). And there is public access at the Cal Trout Boat Launch at the Island Drive Bridge for cartop boats.

Below, where Tule River meets Fall River, there are no tackle restrictions. There is a put-in for boats off McArthur Road near Glenburn. Good fishing for rainbow, up to 7 pounds can be had on nightcrawlers, Rebels, Kastmasters and Mepps, as well as flies. For information on the Fall River contact Intermountain Fly and Tackle, Fall River Mills, CA, (916)336-6600 and Fall River Chamber of Commerce, (916)336-5840.

WAY UP NORTH TROUT

There is some outstanding mountain trout fishing in the Northwest corner of

California. Of course, there are two big lakes, Trinity and Shasta Two pages are devoted to each in the Lake Fishing Section of this book. But there are two smaller and less publicized lakes that are also outstanding fishing lakes. We're talking about Siskiyou and Shastina. And then there are the two high wilderness areas - the Trinity Alps and the Marble Mountains. Here you can backpack on horse pack into some fine trout lakes and streams. Sources of national forest and wilderness area maps are given in the following sections. For even more detail of a specific area, and a reading of the contours of trails, it's a good idea to have topographic maps. These are available at some sporting goods stores, or you can get them by mail from the U.S. Geological Survey, Denver, CO. 80225. Request an index for California and a price list, and then place **an order for the specific maps.**

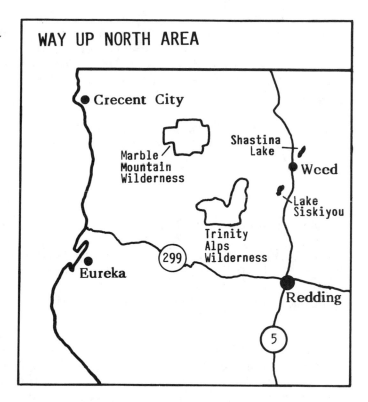

Trinity Alps Trout

Trout fishing is very good in the Trinity Mountains that are North and West of Trinity Lake. Several types of outings are possible here. If you're fishing and camping on Trinity Lake and have a desire to do some stream fishing for trout, then you're in the right place. Here are some choices;

. **Upper Trinity River** - This river runs along Hwy. 3, North of the lake. It and the Little Trinity River, farther upstream, provide good fishing, especially in late spring and fall.

. **Coffee Creek** - This creek is a tributary of the Upper Trinity River. Access is good via Coffee Creek Road which parallels it. Coffee Creek provides some of the best all-season trout fishing in the area.

. **East Fork of Upper Tinity** - This stream runs North out of the Northwest section of Trinity Lake. It has a generous caddis fly hatch. Some of the best fishing is in the riffles and pools downstream of the access where East Side Road crosses the river.

If you'd rather hike than drive to your trout fishing stream, the Salmon-Trinity Alps Wilderness Area is close by. There is some wonderful stream and lake fishing in this area. You'll find 283,000 acres of jagged granite mountains, deep valleys, 400 miles of trails and 45 alpine lakes. Two convenient access points are Stuart Fork near Trinity Alp Resort(Hwy. 3) and Big Flat(end of Coffee Creek Road).

Maps of the wilderness area and of the surrounding national forest are available from Shasta-Trinity National Forest, 2400 Washington Ave., Redding, CA 96001, (916)246-5222.

Siskiyou and Shastina

Lake Siskiyou and Lake Shastina are both within view of magnificent, snow-capped, 14,162 foot Mount Shasta. And they're both magnificent in their own right. They have fine fishing, boat launching, a marina, a fully developed campground and a beautiful setting with crisp mountain air and sparkling blue water.

Lake Siskiyou, the smaller of the two lakes, is located about 2 miles from Mt. Shasta City, off I-5. It is at 3200 feet elevation, has 440 surface acres of water and its shoreline is just over 5 miles long. There is a swimming beach and boat speed limit of 10 mph. Trout fishing is very good at Siskiyou and the lake also has a number of healthy largemouth. Fish for them deep at rocky ledges. Live bait anglers score on crawdads. Trout action is usually best in the Sacramento River Arm. Sliding sinker rigs with bait work good at inlets, early and late in the day. Trolling is also good in the Sacramento Arm. Most rainbows and browns range from 10 inches to 3 pounds, but brood stock from the nearby Mt. Shasta are sometimes "put out to pasture" in Siskiyou, so be prepared. Contact Lake Siskiyou at P.O. Box 276, Mt. Shasta, CA 96067, (916)926-2618.

Lake Shastina, about 5 times larger than Siskiyou, is located about 7 miles North-east of Weed, off I-5. It has 2,700 surface acres of water and even boasts a water slide for the kids and some rental homes for lake visitors. Lake Shastina is well known for its outstanding trout fishery. In fact, big rainbows from 8-10 pounds have come out of the lake. Good catfishing is also a given at Shastina. Hot spots are the East shore and the shoreline South of the boat ramp. And if that's not enough, how about largemouth bass. 2-4 pounders are taken between the islands and at deep dropoffs. Trout fishing is good at the inlets and at the dam. Troll over the old river channel in summer. Shastina Creek between I-5 and Lake Shastina produces many brown trout in the 7-10 inch range, but also has some up to 3 pounds. Use small spinners, dark patterned wet flies or red worms. Access is in Edgewood. Contact Lake Shastina at 6006 Lake Shastina Dr., Weed, CA 96064, (916)938-4385.

Marble Mountain Trout

The Marble Mountain Wilderness(242,000 acres) is within the boundaries of the Klamath National Forest, in Siskiyou County. The area where the Marble Mountains now exist was once part of the flat bottom of an ancient, shallow ocean. Millions of years ago, violent volcanic upheaving and the erosive cutting action of rivers and glaciers combined to form the present day landscape. Almost all of the lakes of the Marble Mountains(there are over 90) were formed by ancient glacial activity. The colors of this wilderness area, from the majestic white of Marble Mountain, to the lush green of Morehouse Meadow, to the deep blue of Cliff Lake, interspersed with various hues of sheer rock cliffs and densely timbered mountainsides, provide a spectacle not soon to be forgotten. These mountains are relatively low - scarcely a peak among them exceeds 7000 feet - but they have an alpine flavor.

Mother nature usually doesn't open the Marble Mountains much before June. Angling for rainbow, brook and brown trout is probably best in September and October, but is rated good earlier in the season. At times, during warm spells in late July and August, fly fishing is apt to be slow as the fish move to the cooler depths. Horse pack trips are popular here, and in the Trinity Alps. This is a popular alternative to backpacking. There are a number of pack guides in the area. Wildlife in the wilderness includes black bear, deer and osprey. The extensive trail system is served by nine trailheads, five of which are open to pack animals. Maps of the wilderness area and of the surrounding national forest are available from the Klamath National Forest, 1312 Fairlane Rd., Yreka, CA 96097, (916)842-6131.

Rainbow Trout—Native of California, found in nearly all lakes and streams where water temperatures do not exceed 70 F for any length of time. Dark, bluish-green back, black spots on back and tail, red stripe on sides, silvery belly. Spawns on gravel bars in fast, clear water. Most suitable of all trout for artificial propagation and highly regarded as a game fish for its fighting qualities.

Brown—A native of Europe, generally the hardest of California inland trouts to catch. Plentiful in many Sierra streams and scattered elsewhere throughout the State. The record fish in California weighed 25 pounds. Dark brown on back with black spots, shading to light brown with red spots on sides. The only trout with both black and red spots on its body.

Golden—State fish of California, the golden trout is native to the high country of the Kern River watershed, and now is found in many lakes and streams in the Sierra from Mt. Whitney north to Alpine County. Medium olive back, shading down the sides to brilliant golden belly and reddish-orange stripes from head to tail, crossed with olive vertical bars. Lower fins golden-orange.

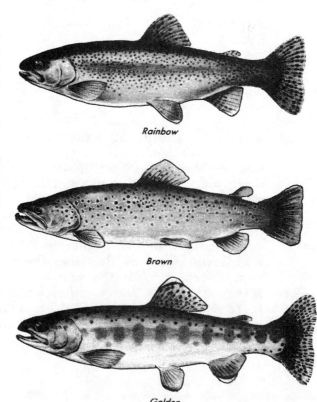

Rainbow

Brown

Golden

Coastal River and Stream Fishing

Northern California coastal rivers and streams offer some of California's most enticing fishing. First there are the fish. The hard to hook, fierce fighting steelhead and salmon. But there is also the environment. Mountains, river canyons, waterfalls, giant redwoods, wildlife and the sounds and smells of the great Pacific Northwest.

California anglers are blessed with some of the best coastal fishing streams in the world. Sure fishing in these waters is not what it was 50 years ago, but, it is still good and improving because of the efforts of a number of agencies, groups and individuals. The Klamath, Trinity, Smith and Eel, as well as a number of lesser-known rivers and streams, from the Oregon border South to San Francisco Bay, provide abundant opportunity for steelhead and salmon fishing. In fact, many of these rivers and streams are synonymous with steelhead fishing. Coastal rivers and streams, and their tributaries, also offer residents wild trout fishing, especially at higher elevations. But in these waters, trout seasons and regulations are special and should be consulted before fishing. These special regulations are designed to protect the young steelhead and salmon.

Fishing Seasons   (+=good,   -=fair)

Species	J	F	M	A	M	J	J	A	S	O	N	D
Steelhead	+	+	+	-				-	-	+	+	+
Salmon							-	+	+	+	+	-

Steelhead and Salmon Fishing Tips

Certain streams(Klamath, Eel, Trinity, for example) have some steelhead in them all year, and summer fishing is permitted(see regulations) in some. But the major run of large fish(steelhead - 8 pounds and up, salmon - average about 20 pounds)takes place in the fall and winter months. This is prime fishing time. Actually migrating fish begin to show in July and August. But good fishing doesn't start in the Trinity and Klamath until September. Fishing in streams with lower summer flow(like the Eel and Russian) doesn't really start until the first heavy rains of the season. Timing is critical to successful steelhead and salmon fishing. The weather, stream flow, volume and clarity, and many other factors can effect the bite. Knowledgeable fishermen use the telephone to gauge conditions on various streams and then, once fishing, they're flexible enough to move around if fish aren't being caught. Some experienced fishermen, if need be, call ahead for fishing reports and then drive. Two hours driving might be more productive than two hours fishing. One rule seems to hold true: The longer the stream, the longer the run; the shorter the stream, the bigger the fish. In smaller rivers, like the Navarro, Garcia and Gualala, the steelhead are able to enter the river only when flows are high. Ideally, fish near the mouth of small rivers some three or four days after a rain, when the river level is raised and a green color is returning to the water. And do it at high tide. Another tip. Many good anglers, new to winter coastal stream fishing or new to a specific river, hire a guide. This is often a good idea. The Shasta Cascade Wonderland Association, in Redding, (916)243-2643, maintains a list of guide services. Ads in fishing newspapers, and in local Yellow Pages, can also be useful.

Eel River

The Eel River is an extremely long coastal stream with several branches. All the opportunities along this river present the same problem; where is the best place to fish at a given time? Steelhead are in the Eel and its branches all fall and winter, but locating them is not always easy in a long river.

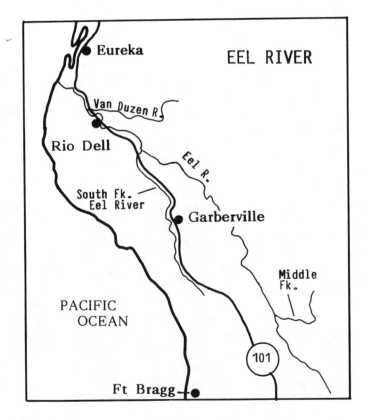

One good spot for a visitor to fish is the tidal area. Steelhead are here as early as Labor Day. The key in this section is to keep moving until you find the fish. Access is good, for boat and by foot. Access is also good all along the main Eel from the ocean up to the South Fork, in Humboldt Redwoods State Park, and there are many fishing opportunities. From this point upriver, the accessibility of the main body of the Eel River is poor. This continues all the way to near its headwaters. But near the headwaters, particularly in the stretch between Thomas Cr. and the Van Arsdale Dam, late season steelhead fishing is accessible and productive. The area is about 5 miles out of Potter Valley. Access is excellent all along the South Fork of the Eel as it passes through Humboldt State Park and farther South, since it continues to parallel Hwy. 101. Finally, the North Fork of the Eel presents serious access problems. The Eel has peek steelhead fishing from December through February. Eel River steelhead are large, averaging 8-14 pounds.

Fishing information is available at Bucksport in Eureka(707)442-1832, Pro-Sports Center in Eureka(707)443-6328, Brown's in Garberville(707)923-2533 and Grundman's in Rio Dell(707)764-5744.

Klamath River

The mighty Klamath River, more than 200 miles long, from the ocean to the Oregon border, provides a wide variety of steelhead and salmon fishing experiences. The lower Klamath, which runs from Weitchpec at the mouth of the Trinity(a tributary of the Klamath) to the ocean is the largest and probably the most heavily fished. The waters here average about 100-200 feet wide. To adequately cover this high, deep stream most anglers use 9 foot rods. Longer surf casting rods are used at the mouth of the river during the salmon run. The bulk of the salmon taken from the Klamath come from the lower Klamath during the fall. Activity begins in July, and is at its peak during August, September and October. Trolling near the deep channels at the mouth of the river is often congested. Farther upstream, salmon are most often taken at tributary inflows. Some of the best are Blue Creek, Trinity River, Bluff Creek, Salmon River, Scott River and Shasta River.

Steelhead anglers crowd the accessible portion of the 40 mile stretch of the Lower Klamath through the fall and winter. Boats are used by many to either backtroll or move to a section of run not accessible by foot, for a less hectic shore fishing experience. The Middle Klamath, between Weitchpec and the mouth of Scott River at Hamburg, provides many foot-accessible areas for shore fishing(from state 96). The water is narrower here and many anglers use light to medium spinner tackle(e.g. a 7 foot rod) normally associated with trout fishing. From Scott River up to Shasta River(near I-5) the Klamath also provides good foot access. From I-5 up to the Oregon border, boat fishing predominates. The river here runs primarily though private property and much of this is posted. Salmon usually reach this stretch of the Klamath in early October, with the steelhead arriving a week or so later. Reliable fishing information is available from sporting goods stores in each town along the river.

Russian River

The Russian River is a good steelhead stream. Sizeable runs of steelhead enter the river from November through February. It flows through more gentle terrain than the streams farther North, and is fished both from shore and by boat. Access is good along most of the river, but private property prevents direct access to some good pools. Early season anglers find good access at the tidal section of the Russian, through Goat Rock State Beach. A good, late season spot is between Cloverdale and Hopland. Here Hwy. 101 crosses the river twice and provides many good pull-off spots. The Squaw Rock stretch is particularly productive. Fish the deep holes.

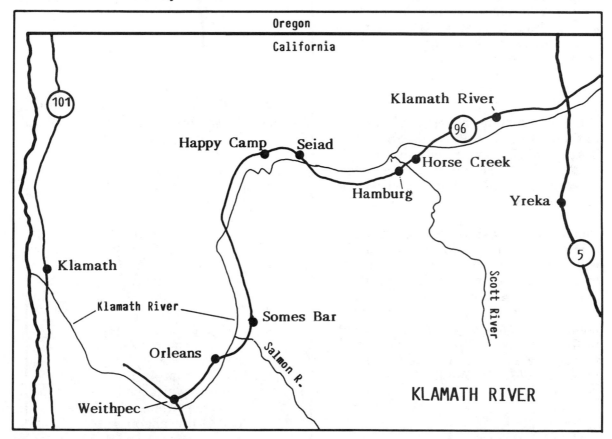

The Russian also has striped bass and shad runs. May is usually prime time for shad. One of the best spots for shad is the pool below the Summer Dam at Healdsburg, especially in the latter weeks of May. Summer anglers take smallmouth bass, primarily on live bait, such as crayfish. A good stretch is between the Monte Rio bridge and Wholler Bridge. Nighttime fishing for catfish is also good in deep holes in the lower Russian in summertime. Use clams, nightcrawlers and sardines. Reliable fishing information is available from King's Western Angler in Santa Rosa(707)542-4432, King's Sports Shop in Guerneville (707)869-2156, Healdsburg Sporting Goods(707)433-4520 and Eagle's Sport World in Cloverdale(707)894-2041.

Smith River

The Smith is the Northernmost of California's major steelhead streams. One desirable feature of the Smith, besides the number and large size of its steelhead, is the quickness with which it clears after a winter storm. Often it is clear and fishable within a few days following most significant storms. Some other streams take up to two weeks to clear. The Smith clears so quickly because most of its streambed is solid rock.

From September on, large salmon run in the Smith. Steelhead usually begin in force in November and run through April. The most productive and legendary portion of the Smith is between the 101 bridge and the 199 bridge. Many large steelhead are taken in this 7-8 mile long stretch. Numerous holes provide excellent holding waters for salmon and steelhead. The Smith is a short river and its access points on the Middle Fork, along Hwy. 199, can be reached quickly. Small boats are launched just below the 101 bridge. One good source of fishing information is Saxton Tackle(707)487-7231.

Trinity River

The Trinity River is an excellent steelhead and salmon stream. The main river, between Weitchpec and Junction City, is noteworthy because of its excellent access, since Hwy. 299 parallels the Trinity along much of its course. And not only is it possible to get to and park near a good location, but the climb down to the river often is comfortable.

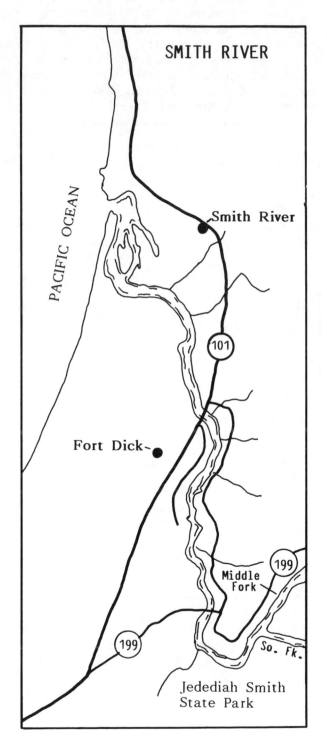

Anglers use 299 to move along the river to find the area where steelhead are being taken. It's possible to cover many promising spots along the river in as little as 2 days. This is a rockhopper's paradise, providing some of the best bankfishing.

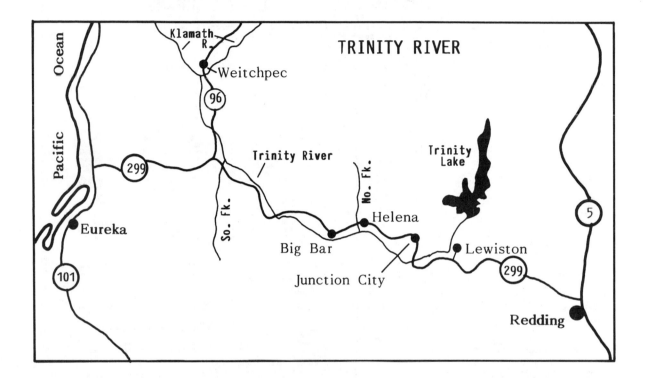

The South Fork of the Trinity offers excellent fishing but access is extremely limited, although there is a road to Hyampon and vicinity. Above the North Fork of the Trinity the main branch changes. It is very brushy, and even the streambed had reeds, willows, etc. This makes fly fishing very difficult. This condition is a result of the dams upstream(at Trinity Lake and Lewiston Lake) which prevent flood level flows from flushing the streambed. Fishing information is available at J & M Tackle in Junction City(916)623-5161 and Brady's Sporting Goods in Weaverville(916)623-3121.

Other Steelhead Streams

Besides the major steelhead and salmon rivers detailed in this section, there are streams that provide good steelhead fishing in the fall-winter months. These are summarized on the next page.

SALMON AND STEELHEAD PORTS AND STREAMS

Coastal Streams and Their Tributaries; Main Streams Listed From North to South, Tributaries Listed From Upstream Down

Stream	Steel-head	Silver Salmon	King Salmon	Time of Salmon and Steelhead Runs and Other Comments
SMITH RIVER	Yes	Yes	Yes	At the mouth and in the lagoon there is a large skiff fishery. King salmon are the biggest attraction. Best fishing for kings is late Sept. through Oct.; silvers run about a month later. Some steelhead are taken in the lagoon. Sea-run cutthroat fishing fall, winter, and spring; best March through May. Above the lagoon fishing for salmon, steelhead, and cutthroat fall and winter. Most of the Smith system is in canyons.
KLAMATH RIVER	Yes	Yes	Yes	At the mouth and in the lagoon there is a large skiff fishery for king salmon, best in Aug. and Sept.; silvers late Sept. through Oct.; sea-run cutthroat fishing Sept. through April; best in March and April. Fall steelhead run is best in the lower river in Aug. and Sept.; about a month later near Copco Dam. Some summer steelhead available. Winter steelhead best in Jan. and Feb.; but high water usually bothers fishermen. Upriver salmon fishing fair in fall.
SCOTT RIVER	Yes	Yes	Yes	Runs through farming country. Much of the bottom has been gold dredged. Salmon and steelhead in fall. Some winter steelhead. Canyon below farming area is best.
SALMON RIVER	Yes	Yes	Yes	Some summer steelhead. Good steelhead and salmon stream in the fall. The mouth of the Salmon River is an especially good spot.
Wooley Creek	Yes		Yes	Spring-run salmon, summer steelhead, no winter fishing, no roads.
TRINITY RIVER	Yes		Yes	Spring-run king salmon available near Lewiston May through summer. Kings also available through most of the river in the fall. Some silver salmon in the lower parts of the Trinity. Some summer steelhead. Best steelhead fishing from the first fall rains through the winter.
SOUTH FORK TRINITY RIVER	Yes	Yes	Yes	Some spring-run king salmon, good fall run of kings. Some silvers in lower part of South Fork. Steelhead in fall and winter.
REDWOOD CREEK	Yes	Yes	Yes	Best in fall and winter. A dry fall may delay the runs. Good sea-run cutthroat fishing in tidewater fall, winter, and early spring.
Little River	Yes	Yes		Fall and winter—runs start after first heavy rains.
MAD RIVER	Yes	Yes	Yes	Fall and winter. A dry fall may delay the runs.
Elk River	Yes	Yes	Few	Fall and winter—runs start after first heavy rains.
EEL RIVER	Yes	Yes	Yes	Trolling for king salmon in tidewater late Aug. through Oct. Kings are caught further upstream fall and winter. Half-pounder fishing below the Van Duzen late summer and early fall. Larger steelhead below the Van Duzen in the fall. Winter fishing for steelhead throughout the river system.
MIDDLE FORK EEL RIVER	Yes		Yes	Salmon and steelhead fishing fall and winter. Some summer steelhead near Covelo and above.
SOUTH FORK EEL RIVER	Yes	Yes	Yes	Fall and winter fishing for steelhead and salmon.
VAN DUZEN RIVER	Yes	Yes	Yes	Fall and winter fishing for steelhead and salmon. Some summer steelhead above Bridgeville.
Bear River	Yes	Yes	Yes	November or later, depending on rains.
MATTOLE RIVER	Yes	Yes	Yes	November or later, depending on rains.
TEN MILE RIVER	Yes	Yes		November or later, depending on rains.
NOYO RIVER	Yes	Yes		November or later, depending on rains.
BIG RIVER	Yes	Yes		November or later, depending on rains.
ALBION RIVER	Yes	Yes		November or later, depending on rains.
NAVARRO RIVER	Yes	Yes		November or later, depending on rains.
Greenwood Creek	Yes			November or later, depending on rains.
Alder Creek	Yes			November or later, depending on rains.
Brush Creek	Yes			November or later, depending on rains.
GARCIA RIVER	Yes	Yes	Few	November or later, depending on rains.
GUALALA RIVER	Yes	Yes		November or later, depending on rains.
RUSSIAN RIVER	Yes	Yes		Fall and winter—runs apt to be delayed by late rains. Silver salmon confined roughly to lower 40 miles of river.
Salmon Creek	Yes	Yes		Fall and winter—depending on rains and water flow.
Walker Creek	Yes	Yes		Fall and winter—depending on rains and water flow.
PAPERMILL CREEK	Yes	Yes		Fall and winter—depending on rains and water flow.
NAPA RIVER	Yes			Fall and winter—runs start after first heavy rains.
Alameda Creek	Yes			Late fall and winter—Recommended only for local people.
San Gregorio Creek	Yes			Late fall and winter—Recommended only for local people.
Pescadero Creek	Yes	Few		Late fall and winter—Recommended only for local people.
Scott Creek	Yes	Few		Late fall and winter—Recommended only for local people.
SAN LORENZO RIVER	Yes	Few		Fall and winter—depending on rains and water flow.
Soquel Creek	Yes	Few		Late fall and winter—Recommended only for local people.
Pajaro River	Yes			Late fall and winter—Recommended only for local people.
CARMEL RIVER	Yes			Fall and winter—depending on rains and water flow.
BIG SUR RIVER	Yes			Fall and winter—depending on rains and water flow.

Central Valley River Fishing

The Central Valley rivers of Northern California offer some of the finest fishing in the entire state. The most productive waters are the Sacramento River and its tributaries(American, Feather, and Yuba Rivers). In these waters fishing is almost a year-round activity. There's steelhead and salmon beginning in late summer and running through winter. Striped bass, strugeon and shad make spawning runs into the Sacramento system in the spring. And if the migratory fish aren't enough, there's still catfishing, smallmouth bass, rainbow and brown trout fishing in these rivers. See the map at the end of this section.

Fishing Seasons   (+=good, -=fair)

Species	J	F	M	A	M	J	J	A	S	O	N	D
Salmon	+	+	+	-	-	-		-	+	+	+	+
Steelhead	+	+	-					-	-	+	+	+
Striper	+	+	+	-	-	-			-	-	+	+
Sturgeon	+	+	-	-	-	-	-	-	-	-	-	+
Shad			-	+	+	-						

Fishing Tips

The key to successful fishing in these rivers is to be there when the action is hot. Salmon, steelhead, striper, sturgeon and shad are migrating through the Central Valley Rivers to get to their spawning grounds. So they're on the move. In addition, most of the best fishing takes place during the rainy season, so stream conditions can change rapidly. Keep in touch with fishing tackle stores, fishing guide services and bait shops, in the stretches of river you want to fish, for up-to-date information. Shore fishing is possible in selected areas, but boats are used by many to increase coverage and to reach spots that flow through the many farms and ranches. But boating these rivers during high water flow months requires experience and skill.

American River

The American offers one of the best metropolitan angling experiences in the entire United States. It flows about 22 miles from the Nimbus Dam in Fair

Oaks to its confluence with the Sacramento River, just North of downtown Sacramento. Salmon, steelhead, striper and shad visit the river, and trout, smallmouth bass and catfish make it their permanent home.

Many anglers use drift boats, putting in near the Nimbus Basin. These boaters fish holes such as Upper Sunrise, Bridge Street, Lower Sunrise, Sacramento Bar, Rossmoor Bar and the mouth at Sacramento. But the American also offers great shore fishing possibilities. Some of the best spots are the Nimbus Basin, Sailor Bar Park, Upper and Lower Sunrise, Rossmoor Bar, Goethe Park, the end of Arden Way, Watt Avenue bridge, Howe Avenue bridge, Paradise Beach, the area behind Cal Expo and the Discovery Park area.

There is a closure on the American River from Nimbus Basin downstream about 8 miles to just below Hoffman Park from November 1st to January 1st. This closure allows salmon and steelhead to spawn in the upper river during these months. Salmon fishing is usually best before the closure and the larger steelhead are usually taken after the closure. A shad and striper hot spot is the Discovery Park Area. Two strains of steelhead use the American. The Coleman strain usually makes its way up the American from September to November. The large Eel River strain is found in the river from December thru March.

Feather and Yuba River

The lower Feather River flows from the Lake Oroville dam in Oroville down to its confluence with the Sacramento at Verona. It offers good salmon, steelhead, striper and shad fishing. The fall salmon run usually begins in early September and lasts for 2-3 months. Due to private property restrictions, most anglers fish with boats from Verona up to Shanghai Bend rapids, South of the

Yuba River confluence. Good boat fishing spots South of Yuba City include deep holes below the rapids of Boyd's Pump, above the rapids, above the mouth of the Yuba River, above and below Star Bend. Above Yuba City two good areas are the Car Body Hole and the Long Hole.

Bank anglers do well just below and above Shanghai Bend. Another good shore fishing area is in the riffles from the Gridley Bridge up to Thermolito Afterbay. Just downstream of the Thermolito outlet is a good spot to cast large, weighted spinners. The Feather is closed to salmon angling from Honicut Creek upstream to the Hwy. 70 bridge in Oroville from mid-October to years end. And the Feather is closed to all fishing from the Hwy. 70 bridge to Table Mountain Blvd. from September to December.

Striper and shad are at their peak in the Feather in May. Shad and steelhead are good in the Yuba River. Good shore access is available from its mouth up to the Hwy. 20 bridge. April and May are prime months for smallmouth bass fishing in the lower Feather. Air temperatures are comfortable, and river flow is low enough that the river forms channels, so that smallmouth are concentrated in the numerous pools and runs. The best fishing takes place when water releases are less than 4,000 cubic feet per second, with about 3,000 being ideal. Anglers fish from shore, use waders, or small drift boats.

Sacramento River

About 60% of all the salmon caught off the coast of Northern California were spawned in the Lower Sacramento River. It runs from Redding to Sacramento. The Sacramento hosts 4 salmon runs each year, and with the right conditions, salmon can be caught here during any season. But the fall-winter run is the biggest. Good fishing can begin in August, with catches of 10-20 pounders. Larger salmon(40 pounders aren't uncommon) are more frequent in the winter months.

The prime salmon fishing in the Sacramento is from Los Molinos North to the cut-off line at the Deschutes Road bridge, near Anderson(just South of Redding). In this section of river, bank access is limited by private property, so most anglers use boats. Public launch ramps are available. Guide services are very active here. A list is available from the Shasta-Cascade Wonderland Association in Redding(916)243-2643. Backtrolling is the most common technique. Salmon and steelhead fishing is also good all the way down the river to the city of Sacramento. Colusa, Meridian, Knight's Landing, Verona are all fishing centers. In the city of Sacramento, two good fishing spots are Miller Park and the Government Docks.

Striper action on the Sacramento extends from Rio Vista all the way up to Colusa-Princeton. Shad fishing on the Sacramento extends from above Freeport to the mouth of the American in Sacramento, to the mouth of the Feather at Verona and all the way up to Los Molinos. Most fishing takes place from bars using waders, or from boats. A winter spawning hot spot for sturgeon is the Princeton/Colusa/Meridian section of the Sacramento. The best shore fishing access points on the Sacramento are at and North of Woodson Bridge State Recreation area near Corning.

Besides striped bass, salmon, steelhead and sturgeon, there is an abundant population of large native rainbow trout in the upper reaches of the lower Sacramento. Prime territory is the stretch of water between Red Bluff and Redding. The average caught fish is 1½ to 3 pounds. Most anglers use drift boats and steelhead type lures like Hot Shots, Wee Warts and Glo Bugs. Low light periods of the day are best, as are river flows of 5-6,000 cubic feet per second.

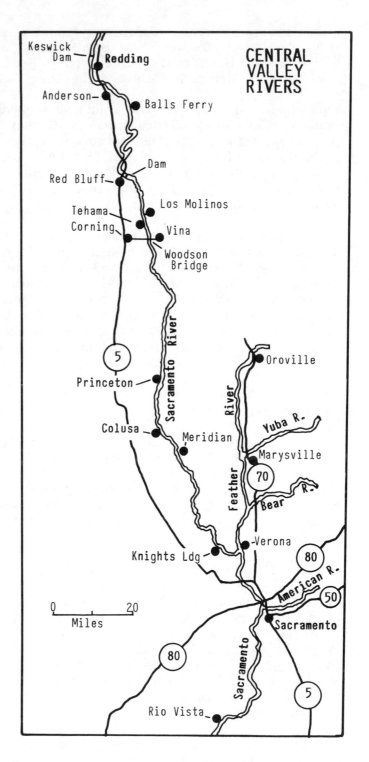

Delta Fishing

The Sacramento-San Joaquin Delta is a 1000 square mile area of diked islands, elevated levee roads and meandering interlocking waterways where the Sacramento and San Joaquin Rivers come together. There are over 1000 miles of navigable waterways. Fishing in these waterways and rivers is excellent. Striped bass(to 30-40 pounds) and sturgeon(to several hundred pounds) are the most prized catches. But the Delta also provides excellent black bass, catfish and panfish, as well as an occassional migrating salmon.

Fishing Seasons   (+=good, -=fair)

Species	J	F	M	A	M	J	J	A	S	O	N	D
Striper	+	+	+	-	-	-			-	-	+	+
Sturgeon	+	+	-	-	-	-	-	-	-	-	-	+
Salmon										-	-	-
Black Bass		-	+	+	+	-	-	-	-	+	+	
Catfish	-	-	-	-	-	-	-	-	-	-	-	-
Panfish	-	-	-	+	+	+	-	-	-	-	-	-

Fishing Tips

Stripers feed most actively on moving water, so it's best to fish when there is a big tide swing. When still fishing for stripers from a boat, fish right where a sandbar drops off. Position your boat(anchored) on the upstream side of the bar on an incoming tide and on the downstream drop off on an outgoing tide. If tide movements are modest, trolling might be a better option. Remember the striper, black bass and catfish are all bottomfeeders, so whether you're fishing with bait or trolling, make sure your offering is near the bottom.

The locations marked for specific species are meant to highlight those specific sloughs that are consistently good producers. But, the sloughs and rivers in the Delta are miles and miles long. So, keep moving in a particular slough until you find fish. Also, the indicated locations are not the only places you can find fish. For example catfish and stripers(especially in late winter-early spring) can be found in many places in the Delta. And any of the back sloughs will produce panfish. The maps in this section are intended only to show choice fishing spots. See Hal Shell's Delta Map for facilities, launch ramps and specific navigational information. Navigational maps, published by the National Oceanic and Atmospheric Administration, are also available for the Delta. Marine supply dealers are a good source.

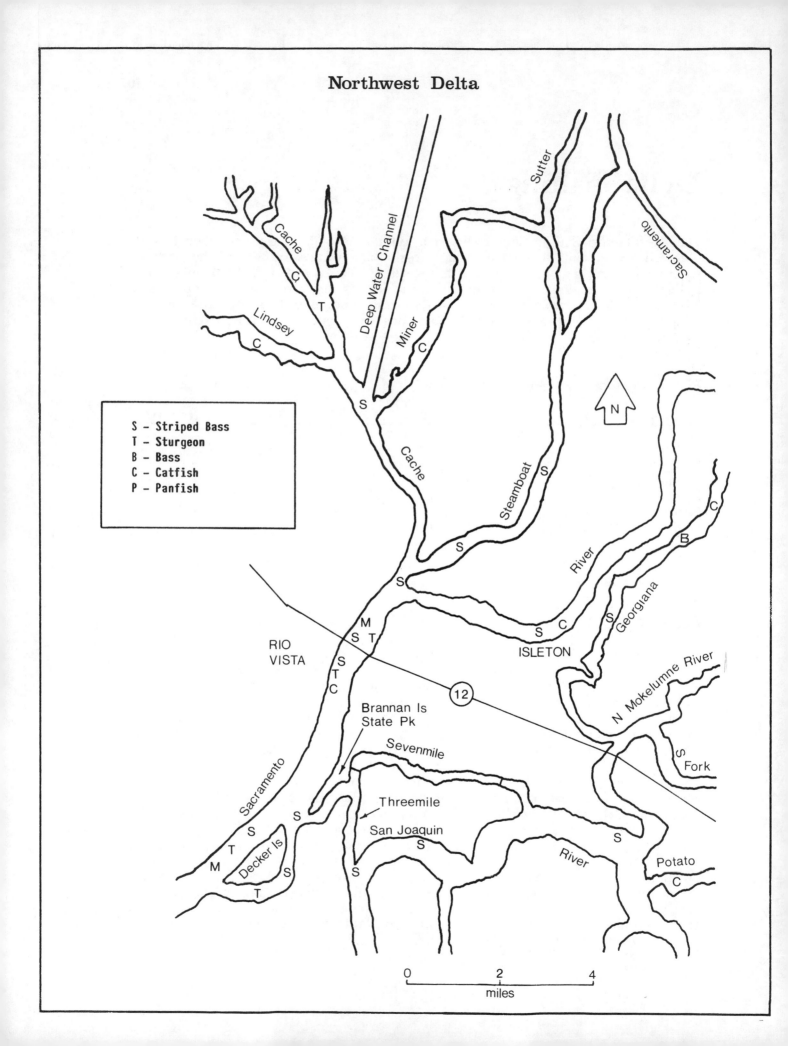

Northwest Delta

S – Striped Bass
T – Sturgeon
B – Bass
C – Catfish
P – Panfish

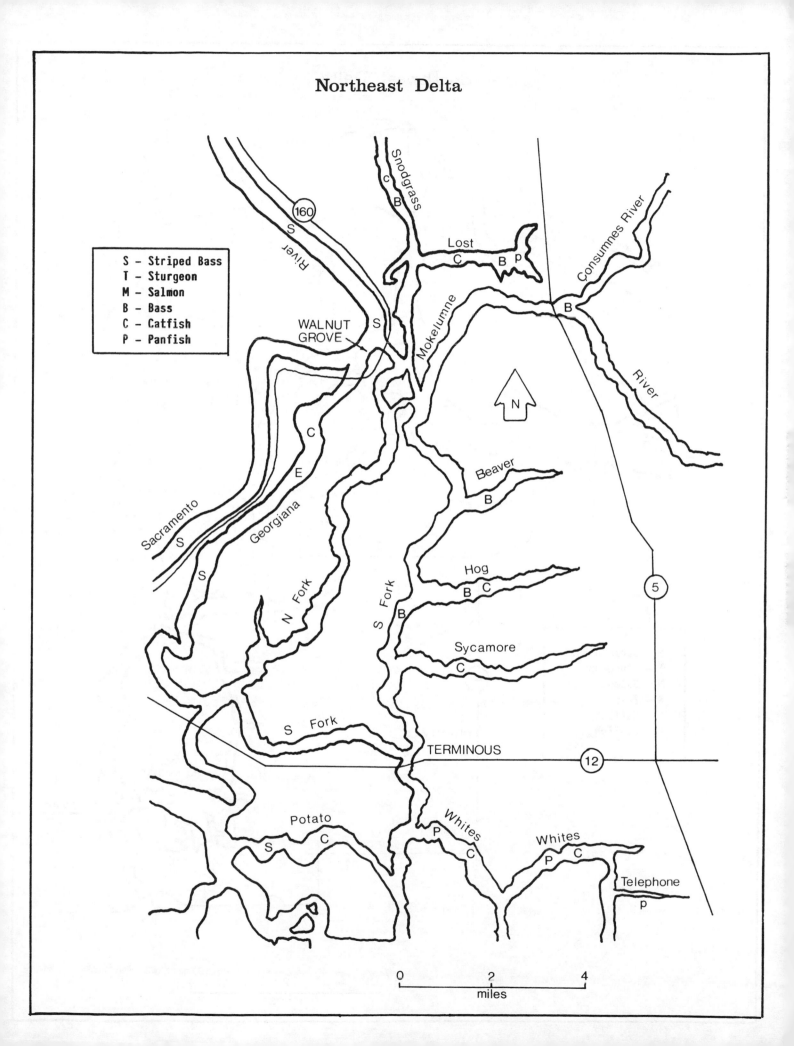

Northeast Delta

S – Striped Bass
T – Sturgeon
M – Salmon
B – Bass
C – Catfish
P – Panfish

WALNUT GROVE

Snodgrass

Lost

Consumnes River

Mokelumne

River

Sacramento

Georgiana

N Fork

S Fork

Beaver

Hog

Sycamore

S Fork

TERMINOUS

Potato

Whites

Whites

Telephone

0   2   4
miles

Southwest Delta

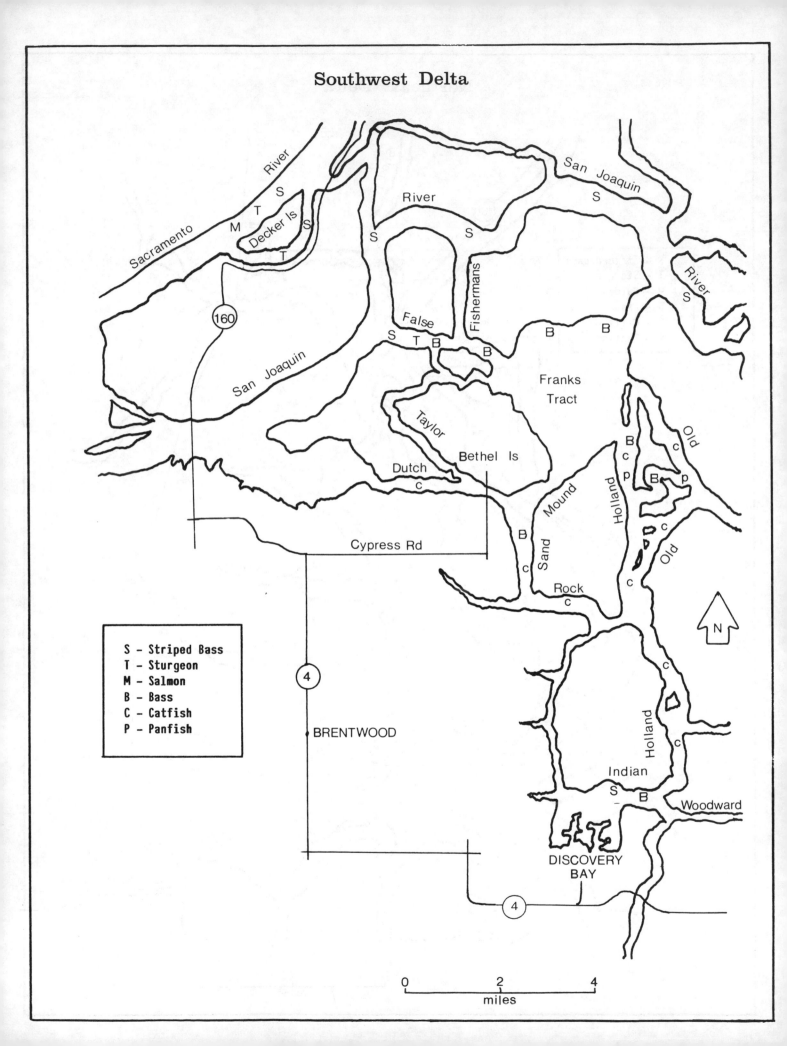

S – Striped Bass
T – Sturgeon
M – Salmon
B – Bass
C – Catfish
P – Panfish

0   2   4
miles

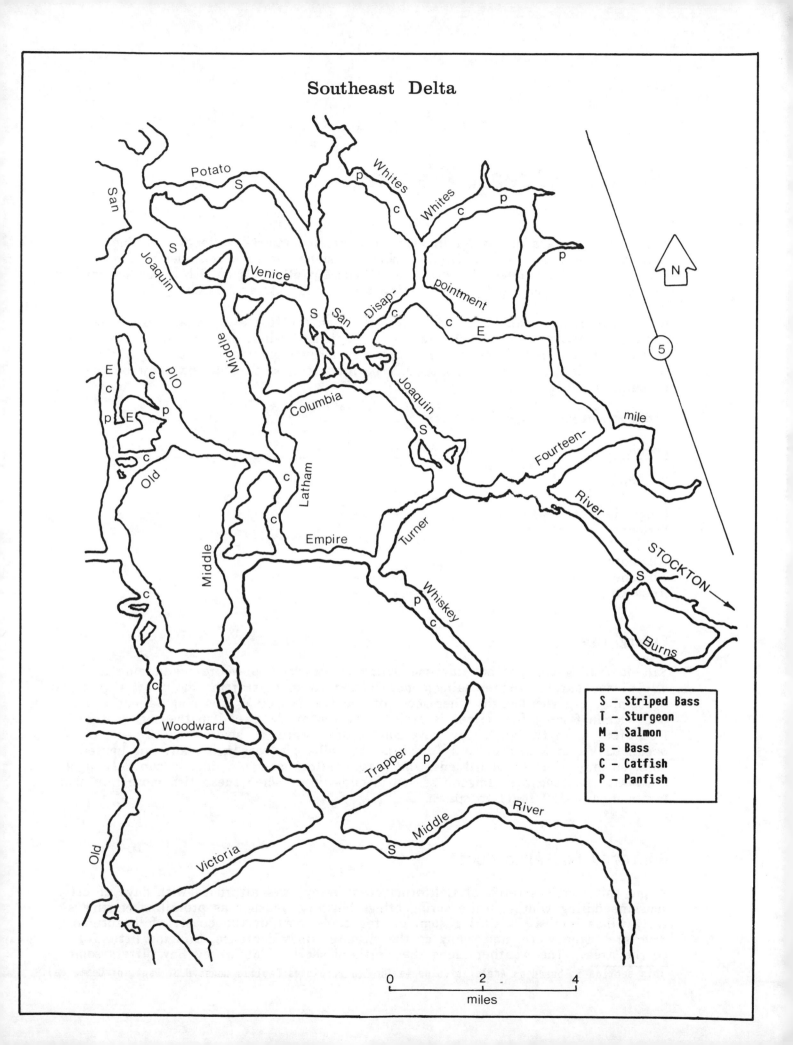

Southeast Delta

N

5

S - Striped Bass
T - Sturgeon
M - Salmon
B - Bass
C - Catfish
P - Panfish

0   2   4
miles

Pacific Ocean Fishing

The coastal waters of the Pacific Ocean offer an immense variety of fishing opportunities. There are salmon trolling, bottom fishing for rock cod and lingcod, albacore fishing 20-30 miles offshore, pier fishing for all kinds of fish depending on location and season and finally, surf fishing for striped bass and perch.

But, ocean fishing can be dangerous. Fishermen are lost every year. Breakers wash anglers off rocks. People fall overboard. Increased winds are foolishly ignored. Equipment fails. But don't let this scare you away from fishing. Do enjoy the marvelous experience of ocean fishing, but be prepared, be careful and error on the side of caution.

Fishing Seasons (+=good, -=fair)

Species	J	F	M	A	M	J	J	A	S	O	N	D
Salmon		-	-	-	+	+	-	-	-	-		
Rock Cod	-	-	-	-	-	-	-	-	-	-	-	-
Lingcod	+	+	-	-	-	-	-	-	-	+	+	+
Striper						-	+	+	-			
Halibut						-	+	+	-			
Albacore								-	+	-		
Abalone				-	-	-	+	+	-	-		
Rock Crab	-	-	-	-	-	-	-	-	-	-	-	-

Fishing Tips

Salmon fishing can get hot anytime during the season, but more predictable is the size of the catch. Bigger salmon move closer to shore starting in July. August and September are the months when most of the twenty pound plus king salmon are taken. Ocean fishing for striper is probably best near shore and in the surf in the Pacifica area, when the anchovies move into shallow water(as shallow as 10 feet) of ocean bays like Monterey and Tomales. The albacore season is short and unpredictable, so stay alert or you'll miss the season. Rock cod and lingcod can be caught all year. But the best lingcod season is mid-winter when these fish move into shallow water(50-150 feet) to spawn.

Monterey Bay Area Coast

Along this scenic stretch of California coast rainy days alternate with days of crisp sunshine during winter, while spring brings blustery weather as prevailing Northwesterly winds intensify. During summer, fog cools most of the coast, while autumn days are often warm and sunny as the onshore winds decrease, bringing little fog to the area. The weather along the Northern shore of Monterey Bay differs some-

This section is based on Angler's Guide To The United States Pacific Coast(U.S. Dept. of Commerce).

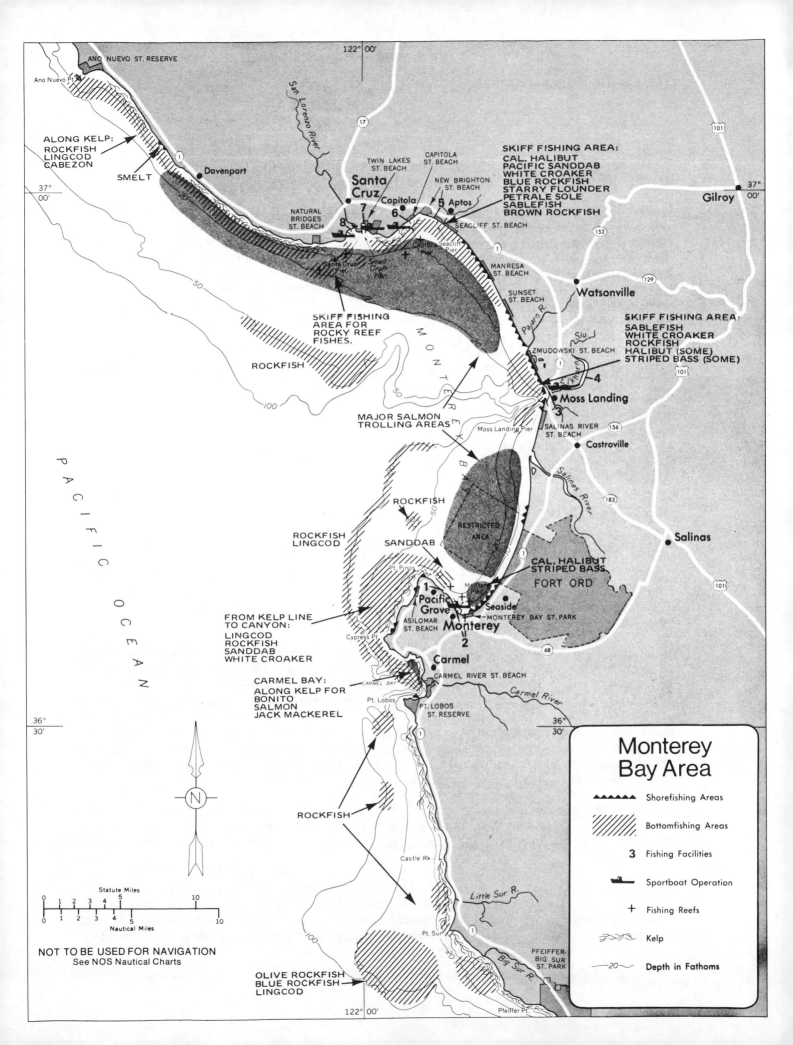

ANO NUEVO ST. RESERVE

Ano Nuevo Pt.

ALONG KELP:
ROCKFISH
LINGCOD
CABEZON

SMELT

Davenport

37°
00'

PACIFIC OCEAN

ROCKFISH

ROCKFISH

ROCKFISH
LINGCOD

FROM KELP LINE
TO CANYON:
LINGCOD
ROCKFISH
SANDDAB
WHITE CROAKER

CARMEL BAY:
ALONG KELP FOR
BONITO
SALMON
JACK MACKEREL

ROCKFISH

36°
30'

Statute Miles
0 1 2 3 4 5   10
0 1 2 3 4 5   10
Nautical Miles

NOT TO BE USED FOR NAVIGATION
See NOS Nautical Charts

OLIVE ROCKFISH
BLUE ROCKFISH
LINGCOD

San Lorenzo River

122° 00'

17

TWIN LAKES
ST. BEACH

CAPITOLA
ST. BEACH

NEW BRIGHTON
ST. BEACH

Santa
Cruz

Capitola

7   6   5 Aptos

NATURAL
BRIDGES
ST. BEACH

8

SEACLIFF ST. BEACH

Capitola Pier

Seacliff Pier

Santa Cruz Pier

Small Craft Hbr.

SKIFF FISHING
AREA FOR
ROCKY REEF
FISHES.

MONTEREY

50

100

MAJOR SALMON
TROLLING AREAS

Moss Landing Pier

BAY

ROCKFISH

50

SANDDAB

RESTRICTED
AREA

Pt. Pinos

Pt. Pinos

1

Pacific
Grove

ASILOMAR
ST. BEACH

Monterey

2

Cypress Pt.

Pt. Lobos

CARMEL BAY

Carmel

CARMEL RIVER ST. BEACH

PT. LOBOS
ST. RESERVE

1

Castle Rk

Little Sur R.

Pt. Sur

122° 00'

SKIFF FISHING AREA:
CAL. HALIBUT
PACIFIC SANDDAB
WHITE CROAKER
BLUE ROCKFISH
STARRY FLOUNDER
PETRALE SOLE
SABLEFISH
BROWN ROCKFISH

37°
00'

Gilroy

152

MANRESA
ST. BEACH

1

SUNSET
ST. BEACH

Pajaro R.

Watsonville

129

SKIFF FISHING AREA:
SABLEFISH
WHITE CROAKER
ROCKFISH
HALIBUT (SOME)
STRIPED BASS (SOME)

ZMUDOWSKI ST. BEACH

1

Elkhorn Slu.

4

3

Moss Landing

SALINAS RIVER
ST. BEACH

156

Castroville

Salinas River

183

CAL. HALIBUT
STRIPED BASS
FORT ORD

Salinas

101

Monterey Pier

Seaside

MONTEREY BAY ST. PARK

68

Carmel River

36°
30'

PFEIFFER-
BIG SUR
ST. PARK

Big Sur R.

Pfeiffer Pt.

Monterey Bay Area

▲▲▲ Shorefishing Areas

▨ Bottomfishing Areas

3 Fishing Facilities

⛵ Sportboat Operation

+ Fishing Reefs

〰 Kelp

―20〜 Depth in Fathoms

what, particularly around Santa Cruz, which is protected from the prevailing winds by the curve of the land. This area is almost fog-free during summer.

Monterey Bay is an important recreational fishing area, and an impressive number and variety of marine game fish are taken here. Most sport fishing from party boats is for bottomfish(particularly rockfishes) although albacore, bonito and chinook salmon also are landed in season. In some years salmon are abundant in the bay in spring and good fishing many last till late summer. In general, the major marine sport fishes caught from boats and from shore are rockfishes, chinook salmon, California halibut, Pacific sanddab, surfperches, lingcod, kelp greenling, white croaker and albacore.

Location	Sport Fishing Boats	Pier Fishing	Boat Rental	Launch Ramp	Jetty Fishing
Pacific Grove(1)			+		
Monterey Harbor(2)	+	+	+	+	
Moss Landing Harbor(3)	+		+	+	+
Kirby Pk., Elkhorn Sl(4)				+	
Seacliff Pier(5)		+			
Capitola Pier(6)	+	+	+	+	
Santa Cruz Harbor (7)	+		+	+	+
Santa Cruz Pier(8)	+	+	+		

Shore and Pier Fishing: As one approaches the Monterey Bay area from the South there is little access to shore along this rugged section of the coast as State Hwy. 1 makes a gradual descent out of the mountainous Big Sur country and then passes through rolling coastal hills before dropping down to sea level about a mile South of Carmel. Where the shoreline can be reached there is excellent rocky-shore fishing for lingcod, kelp greenling, cabezon, striped surfperch and rockfishes.

Shore fishermen can reach the beaches of the Monterey Peninsula from the South by way of 17-Mile Drive(toll road), which has a South entrance at Carmel, or by approaching from the Northeast through the town of Monterey. Along scenic 17-Mile Drive, shore fishing is allowed at Fanshell Beach just North of Cypress Point, in Pacific Grove at Asilomar State Beach and between Point Pinos and Lover's Point. Some of the more common species taken by shore anglers at these locations are striped surfperch, kelp greenling, cabezon and blue rockfish. Sometimes steelhead are caught around the mouth of the Carmel River in fall after heavy rains, but fishing even at its best, is considered spotty.

The town of Monterey has 2 public piers, but most fishing takes place from Municipal Pier #2 at the Eastern end of the harbor. Here the catch is young bocaccio, blue rockfish, surfperches, jacksmelt, white croaker, and some years, jack mackerel in summer.

Broad sandy beaches rim the coast from the Monterey Peninsula North along the inner curve of the bay all the way to Seacliff State Beach. Most beaches offer excellent fishing for a variety of sandy-shore fishes. Striped bass sometimes are taken by surf casters during the summer along beaches from Monterey North to the Salinas River(check locally about fishing the Fort Ord area - beachfront restrictions change from day to day). All beaches North of the Salinas River offer excellent surf fishing for sand sole, jacksmelt and surfperches. There also is surf netting for night smelt in summer along beaches adjacent to Moss Landing.

At the entrance to Moss Landing harbor, anglers fish from the jetty for surfperches, starry flounder and occasionally California halibut and striped bass. There is also fishing from shore inside Elkhorn Slough for surfperches plus sharks, rays, sand sole and starry flounder.

The Northern end of Seacliff State Beach, near Aptos, has a fishing pier(actually a cement ship) from which anglers catch Pacific sanddab, surfperches, white croaker, jacksmelt, small bocaccio, jack mackerel(during some summers), and an occasional California halibut, starry flounder, lingcod, salmon and steelhead.

Rocky outcroppings and low bluffs begin to interrupt sandy beaches North of Aptos, and rocky-shore fishes start to appear in the angler's catch, finally replacing sandy-shore fishes in importance as one proceeds Westward. At the Capitola pier, which is mostly over sandy bottom, the usual fare is white croaker, jacksmelt, small bocaccio, walleye and shiner surfperches, cabezon, staghorn sculpin and an occasional barred surfperch.

To the West of the Santa Cruz pier, anglers catch both rocky and sandy shore fishes such as surfperches, lingcod, cabezon, young bocaccio, kelp rockfish, topsmelt, jacksmelt, staghorn sculpin, skates, Pacific sanddab, sand sole, starry flounder and white croaker. Rockfishes are taken from Santa Cruz Small-Craft Harbor jetties, and in some years coho salmon and steelhead are taken around the mouth of the San Lorenzo River.

From Natural Bridges State Beach North to Ano Nuevo Point the shoreline changes rather abruptly to a predominently rocky coastline, and fog and blustery Northwest winds once again sweep the coast. This rocky shoreline offers excellent shore fishing for kelp greenling, cabezon, grass rockfish and surfperches. Where the rocky shoreline is broken occasionally by short stretches of sandy beach, netters work the surf from Scott Creek Northward for surf and night smelts from March to October.

Party Boat Fishing: Commercial sport fishing boats operate year-round out of Monterey and Santa Cruz and intermittently out of Capitola and Moss Landing.

The fleet based at Monterey, which fishes mainly for rockfishes, has expanded its range over the past 10 years. Blue, yellowtail and olive rockfishes dominate the party boat landings although an assortment of other rockfish species also contribute to the catch. Those taken in the shallower nearshore areas along the kelp are blue, olive, black, copper, starry and rosy rockfishes. In deeper water spots in Monterey Bay and off Point Sur, the yellowtail, blue, and bocaccio predominate. Monterey party boat anglers also take lingcod, Pacific sanddab, Pacific bonito(in summer, September best), sablefish and albacore(late summer). In most years, albacore schools appear about 10-15 miles offshore, usually in water about 61° to 64°F.

Along the North shore of Monterey Bay, Santa Cruz and Capitola party boats fish over the rocky reefs from Point Santa Cruz North to Ano Nuevo Point for rockfishes, lingcod and cabezon. The Ano Nuevo gounds are exceptionally good for lingcod and blue and black rockfishes. Other rockfishes entering the party boat catch along the Northern section of the coast include copper, olive, brown, yellowtail, widow, green-spotted, bocaccio and chilipepper - the last five in deepwater areas. Party boats also go after chinook salmon during the season when good runs develop(best catches usually in May and June). Along the North shore, the party boats catch other fishes such as bonito, sablefish, petrale sole, rock sole, Pacific sanddab and kelp greenling.

Skiff Fishing: Most of the Monterey Bay area skiff catch is made up of several species of rockfishes, Pacific sanddab, chinook salmon and lingcod. Most small-boat fishing takes place inside Monterey Bay, although on calm days Monterey skiff anglers occasionally venture out around the peninsula between Point Pinos and Cypress Point to fish for lingcod and some of the nearshore rockfishes, or try their luck in Carmel Bay.

Inside Carmel Bay, skiffs work along the edge of the kelp for lingcod and rockfishes; sometimes in summer, jack mackerel and bonito make a showing in the bay. occasionally, salmon are taken when a good run develops. Skiff anglers making the trip around the Monterey Peninsula to Carmel Bay are warned that the return trip can be extremely rough, if not impossible, on all but the calmest days.

Within Monterey Bay, from early spring to late summer, skiff anglers troll for chinook salmon in areas shown on the map. Pacific sanddabs are plentiful over sandy bottom, and California halibut are taken trolling just beyond the surf line during summer and fall. The area South of the Salinas River is closed by the military when Fort Ord target ranges are in use, so check locally before fishing this section of the bay. Warning flags are flown from the Coast Guard breakwater in Monterey when this area is restricted.

Skiff anglers out of Moss Landing on Elkhorn Slough fish both the tidewater section of the slough and outside in Monterey Bay. The area around the entrance is particularly good for Pacific sanddab, sablefish, white croaker and occasionally California halibut. Salmon trolling is very popular with Moss Landing skiff anglers, who actively fish in the bay for chinook salmon during the season(June and July considered best). Surfperches are particularly abundant inside the slough. Jacksmelt, sand sole, staghorn sculpin, starry flounder and sharks and rays also are common in the estuary. A shark derby is held in Moss Landing each year.

To the North and West, skiff anglers who fish off Capitola bring in a mixed catch of blue rockfish, white croaker, Pacific sanddab, jacksmelt, and California halibut. Boats also work the area off the Seacliff pier and to the South for California halibut, starry flounder, white croaker, petrale sole and sablefish. To the West, Santa Cruz small-boat anglers fish mainly the reef and kelp areas for rockfishes(blue, grass and brown), lingcod and cabezon or troll along the sandy beaches to the East for halibut in summer. During the salmon season boats work the area between Sunset Beach and Davenport.

San Francisco Area Coast

The climate along this coast is cool and temperate with little seasonal variation in air temperature. During summer, San Francisco's famous fog funnels in through the Golden Gate mornings and evenings, drawn inland by the warmings of the Central Valley.

Most offshore recreational fishing is for chinook salmon from spring through fall, although bottomfish tend to dominate the sport catch in areas South of San Pedro Point where salmon runs occur less predictably. In most years, migrating albacore are taken around the Farallon Islands in fall.

Location	Sport Fishing Boats	Pier Fishing	Boat Rental	Launch Ramp	Jetty Fishing
Princeton, Half Moon Bay(1)	+	+	+	+	+
San Pedro Point(2)			+	+	
Pacifica Pier(3)		+			

Pigeon Point to Half Moon Bay: The main angling activities from Pigeon Point to Bean Hollow State Park are rock fishing and poke poling from shore. From Bean Hollow State Park North to Pillar Point the shore is alternately sandy beach and rocky outcroppings. Along this coast, striped bass begin to enter the shore angler's catch during summer and early fall; some of the better locations are Pescadero State Beach, San Gregorio State Beach, Martins Beach and Half Moon Bay State Beaches. These are also good areas for surfperches and for netting surf and night smelts (March to October).

Pillar Point Harbor on Half Moon Bay is the major recreational fishing port along this section of coast, and party boats based at the harbor fish over nearshore and offshore reefs for lingcod, cabezon and rockfishes(blue, copper, olive and yellowtail). Occasional bottomfish trips are made to the Farallon Islands and albacore are sometimes taken West of the Farallons from August to October. Small-boat anglers actively fish for salmon when the fish make a showing nearshore, or fish on the bottom around the entrance to the harbor and North along Pillar Point for rockfishes, lingcod, cabezon and white croaker.

Inside Pillar Point Harbor, anglers fish from the Princeton Pier for Pacific sanddab, white croaker, surfperches, jacksmelt, topsmelt, brown smoothhound shark, skates, staghorn sculpin and rockfishes. Anglers also fish from the East and West jetties that partially enclose the harbor. At the West jetty the catch consists mainly of striped surfperch, kelp greenling, cabezon, grass rockfish, and occasionally lingcod. From the East jetty they catch sandy bottom species such as white croaker, starry flounder, sand sole and rubberlip surfperch.

Pillar Point North to the Golden Gate: North of Pillar Point the coast becomes rocky once again until you reach Montara State Beach - a narrow, coarse-sand beach backed by sandstone bluffs. Here surf casters take surfperches and catch striped bass during the summer.

North of the State Park, Hwy. 1 is above steep sandstone cliffs and access to shore is difficult, if not dangerous, especially around the Devils Slide area.

At Point San Pedro on Shelter Cove, skiffs can be rented and launched when weather permits. The area off the Point is especially good for rockfishes, lingcod and white croaker. During good salmon years, chinook are landed off the Point in spring and summer; striped bass are taken from boats and from shore during late summer and fall.

The coast North of Point San Pedro has no party boat operations, skiff rentals or launching facilities; all these facilities are in San Francisco Bay. However, a public fishing pier has been constructed at Pacifica. From Pacifica North to the Golden Gate the coast is mostly sandy beach, and it is along these beaches that the heaviest runs of striped bass occur in the surf. The map shows some of the more popular fishing spots, although this entire coast is good for striped bass when they are running. One of the most heavily fished places is Bakers Beach near the Golden Gate Bridge. These ocean beaches are also good bait-casting areas for redtail surfperch during winter and spring, and at times, for jacksmelt and other surfperches.

The Gulf of the Farallons is fished primarily by San Francisco Bay party boats and occasionally boats from Half Moon Bay. This area produces the most consistent ocean sport fishing for salmon in the state. Most fishing is for chinook salmon, although some coho also are landed. The season extends from mid-February through mid-November(check state regulations), and there are two major chinook runs – one in the spring and one in the fall. During the height of the spring run from about March to June, most fishing occurs offshore between Duxbury Reef and the Farallon Islands, while from July to mid-October the fish are taken closer to shore. The most productive area for large fall-run chinook extends from the San Francisco light buoy, or "light bucket," former site of the San Francisco lightship, to the Marin County beaches and North to Duxbury Reef, where fishing is best from July through September. The Golden Gate area, especially around Mile Rock and the South tower of the bridge, is also a good fishing spot in midsummer and fall for striped bass and occasionally salmon.

When salmon are not running, boats may fish for rockfishes and lingcod around the Farallon Islands, and occasionally travel as far West as Cordell Bank about 20 miles West of Point Reyes.

There is some skiff fishing for chinook salmon off Muir and Stinson Beaches in late summer, but weather and sea often restrict small-boat fishing in the ocean. Fourfathom Bank(also called Potato Patch Shoal) can get particularly rough on windy days, but in calm weather this sandy shoal area is a good fishing spot for California halibut and striped bass. California halibut are also taken around Seal Rocks and to the South(July and August best).

Shore Fishing North of the Golden Gate: Only a limited amount of shore fishing takes place along the rugged rocky coast from the Golden Gate Bridge North to Stinson Beach. Access is difficult in most places. Striped bass occasionally are

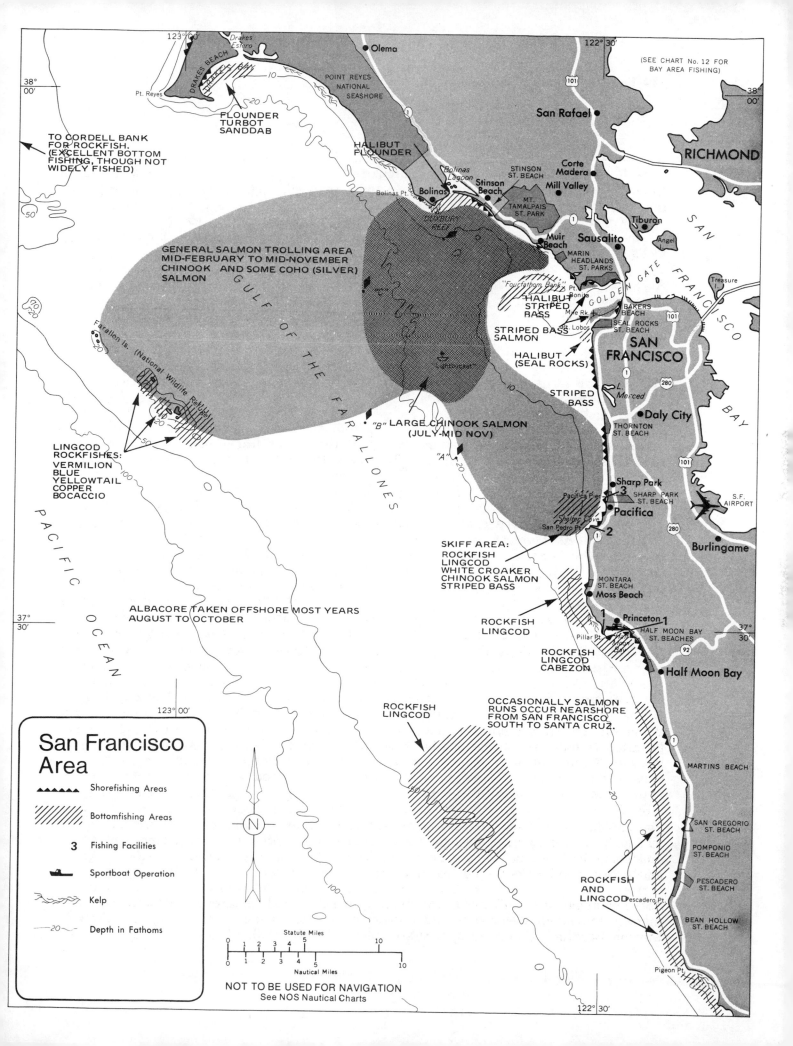

San Francisco Area

TO CORDELL BANK FOR ROCKFISH. (EXCELLENT BOTTOM FISHING, THOUGH NOT WIDELY FISHED)

(SEE CHART NO. 12 FOR BAY AREA FISHING)

FLOUNDER TURBOT SANDDAB

POINT REYES NATIONAL SEASHORE

HALIBUT FLOUNDER

RICHMOND

San Rafael

Corte Madera
Mill Valley

STINSON ST. BEACH

MT. TAMALPAIS ST. PARK

Tiburon

Angel I.

Olema

Bolinas Lagoon
Bolinas
Stinson Beach
Bolinas Pt.

DUXBURY REEF

Muir Beach

MARIN HEADLANDS ST. PARKS

Sausalito

Treasure I.

GENERAL SALMON TROLLING AREA MID-FEBRUARY TO MID-NOVEMBER CHINOOK AND SOME COHO (SILVER) SALMON

GULF OF THE FARALLONES

"Fourfathom Bank"
Pt. Bonita

GOLDEN GATE

BAKERS BEACH
SEAL ROCKS ST. BEACH

SAN FRANCISCO

HALIBUT STRIPED BASS
Mile Rk.
Pt. Lobos

STRIPED BASS SALMON

HALIBUT (SEAL ROCKS)

Farallon Is. (National Wildlife Refuge)

Lighthouse

STRIPED BASS

L. Merced

Daly City

THORNTON ST. BEACH

LINGCOD ROCKFISHES: VERMILION BLUE YELLOWTAIL COPPER BOCACCIO

"B" LARGE CHINOOK SALMON (JULY-MID NOV)

"A"

S.F. AIRPORT

Sharp Park
SHARP PARK ST. BEACH
Pacifica Pier
Pacifica

Burlingame

SKIFF AREA: ROCKFISH LINGCOD WHITE CROAKER CHINOOK SALMON STRIPED BASS

Shelter Cove
San Pedro Pt.

ALBACORE TAKEN OFFSHORE MOST YEARS AUGUST TO OCTOBER

ROCKFISH LINGCOD

MONTARA ST. BEACH
Moss Beach

Princeton
HALF MOON BAY ST. BEACHES

PACIFIC OCEAN

ROCKFISH LINGCOD CABEZON

Pillar Pt.

Half Moon Bay

ROCKFISH LINGCOD

OCCASIONALLY SALMON RUNS OCCUR NEARSHORE FROM SAN FRANCISCO SOUTH TO SANTA CRUZ.

MARTINS BEACH

ROCKFISH AND LINGCOD

Pescadero Pt.

SAN GREGORIO ST. BEACH

POMPONIO ST. BEACH

PESCADERO ST. BEACH

BEAN HOLLOW ST. BEACH

Pigeon Pt.

Legend

San Francisco Area

- ▲▲▲ Shorefishing Areas
- ▨ Bottomfishing Areas
- **3** Fishing Facilities
- 🚤 Sportboat Operation
- 〜 Kelp
- —20— Depth in Fathoms

Statute Miles
0 1 2 3 4 5 ... 10

Nautical Miles
0 1 2 3 4 5 ... 10

NOT TO BE USED FOR NAVIGATION
See NOS Nautical Charts

caught from shore in summer and fall along isolated sandy coves near the Golden Gate(Fort Baker, Fort Barry, Fort Cronkite and at Muir Beach). From Muir Beach to Stinson Beach, where rocky shores can be reached, anglers fish for blue rockfish, lingcod, cabezon, kelp greenling and surfperches, or poke-pole for monkeyface eels at low tide. This stretch of coastline can be dangerous during rough weather; it is advisable to fish here only on calm days and always keep an eye out for changing sea conditions.

At Stinson Beach State Park, rocky shores abruptly give way to a long and wide expanse of sandy beach where surf anglers cast for surfperches. To the North along the sandy shores of the point Reyes Peninsula, there is bait casting for surfperches.

Point Reyes to Fort Ross

Along this rural and often wind-swept part of the coast party boats operate year-round, weather permitting, out of Bodega Harbor and Dillon Beach. Most offshore fishing is for bottomfish - particularly rockfishes or "rock cod." Some boats also fish for chinook salmon when the fish are running, but, in general, salmon appear less predictably here than off San Francisco and areas to the North.

The range of the party boat fleet extends South to off Point Reyes and North to Fort Ross. Areas most frequented by the fleet are Tomales Point, the 27-fathom reefs off the Western shore of Point Reyes Peninsula, and areas North along the coast from Bodega Head to Fort Ross. Occasionally, special trips are made to Cordell Bank, about 23 miles Southwest of the Bodega Harbor entrance. Most of the party boat catch is made up of rockfishes. Other rocky-bottom fishes such as cabezon and lingcod also are caught along with an occasional chinook. Lingcod appear to be more plentiful in the Northern areas off Fort Ross than in areas to the South, and flatfish are sometimes taken incidentally as boats drift over from rocky to sand bottom.

Skiff Fishing: Skiff fishing is generally limited to the confines of Tomales Bay and around the entrance to Bodega Harbor. Experienced boat anglers familiar with the area sometimes venture farther out to fish for salmon or bottomfish, but this practice is not without its risks. Many people(up to 13 in 1 year) have lost their lives at the entrance to Tomales Bay, where huge waves are known to appear and capsize boats with little warning. Strangers to the area would do well to stay within the protection of the bay.

Inside Tomales Bay, small-boat anglers fish for sharks and rays, California halibut(June to October), sand sole, turbot, jacksmelt(September to November best) and an assortment of surfperches. Sharks are particularly plentiful in the bay, and every year a Shark and Stingray Derby is sponsored by local civic groups. Striped bass sometimes are caught in the Southern reaches of the bay in summer. The lower bay also has a small run of coho salmon which are caught trolling during October and November, and some steelhead are taken as they make their way to Papermill Creek to spawn(November to February).

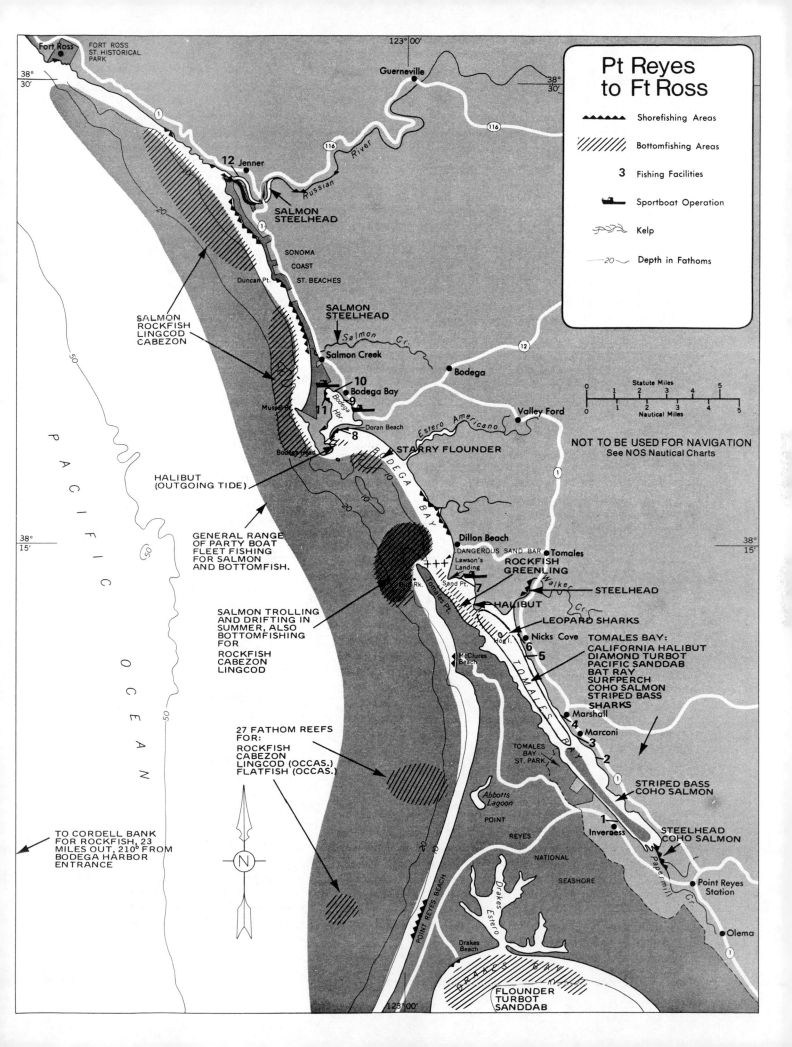

Pt Reyes to Ft Ross

	Shorefishing Areas
	Bottomfishing Areas
3	Fishing Facilities
	Sportboat Operation
	Kelp
20	Depth in Fathoms

NOT TO BE USED FOR NAVIGATION
See NOS Nautical Charts

Statute Miles
Nautical Miles

FORT ROSS
ST. HISTORICAL
PARK

Fort Ross

Guerneville

123° 00'
38° 30'

38° 30'

Russian River

12 Jenner

1

SALMON
STEELHEAD

SONOMA
COAST
ST. BEACHES

Duncan Pt.

116

12

SALMON
ROCKFISH
LINGCOD
CABEZON

SALMON
STEELHEAD

Salmon Cr.

Salmon Creek

Bodega

10

Bodega Bay

9

Mussel Pt.

Bodega Hbr

Valley Ford

Estero Americano

1

HALIBUT
(OUTGOING TIDE)

Doran Beach

8

STARRY FLOUNDER

BODEGA BAY

Bodega Head

38° 15'

38° 15'

GENERAL RANGE
OF PARTY BOAT
FLEET FISHING
FOR SALMON
AND BOTTOMFISH.

Dillon Beach

DANGEROUS SAND BAR

Tomales

Lawson's
Landing

ROCKFISH
GREENLING

STEELHEAD

Walker Cr.

Rk.

Sand Pt.

7

HALIBUT

20

Tomales Pt.

LEOPARD SHARKS

SALMON TROLLING
AND DRIFTING
IN SUMMER, ALSO
BOTTOMFISHING
FOR
ROCKFISH
CABEZON
LINGCOD

Hog I.

Nicks Cove

6

5

TOMALES BAY:
CALIFORNIA HALIBUT
DIAMOND TURBOT
PACIFIC SANDDAB
BAT RAY
SURFPERCH
COHO SALMON
STRIPED BASS
SHARKS

McClures
Beach

TOMALES BAY

Marshall

4

Marconi

3

2

27 FATHOM REEFS
FOR:
ROCKFISH
CABEZON
LINGCOD (OCCAS.)
FLATFISH (OCCAS.)

TOMALES
BAY
ST. PARK

1

STRIPED BASS
COHO SALMON

Abbotts
Lagoon

POINT

1

Inverness

STEELHEAD
COHO SALMON

N

REYES

PACIFIC OCEAN

50

50

50

50

20

10

20

10

20

TO CORDELL BANK
FOR ROCKFISH, 23
MILES OUT, 210° FROM
BODEGA HARBOR
ENTRANCE

NATIONAL

Point Reyes
Station

POINT REYES BEACH

SEASHORE

Drakes Estero

Drakes
Beach

Olema

1

Papermill Cr.

DRAKES BAY

FLOUNDER
TURBOT
SANDDAB

123° 00'

In Bodega Harbor, a narrow channel cuts through this shallow lagoon to the boat basin at the town of Bodega Bay and into deeper water at the harbor's Northwest corner. There is a limited amount of skiff fishing for surfperches and starry flounder in deepwater parts of the lagoon and steelhead occasionally are taken around areas of freshwater seepage.

To the North, skiffs and launching are available at Jenner on the Russian River. In addition to winter steelhead and salmon fishing(September to November), there is skiff fishing inside the tidal lagoon for surfperches and starry flounder. Small boats do not venture into the ocean because the outlet, or "bar," at the Russian River mouth is often too narrow for skiffs.

Shore Fishing: Selected areas of this coast offer many different types of shore fishing, including casting along sandy beaches for surfperches, pier and dock fishing in bays and harbors, stream and river fishing for salmon and steelhead and river fishing for salmon and steelhead, poke-poling and bait casting along rocky shores, and netting smelts around river and creek mouths. Spring and early summer are best for surfperches, steelhead fishing is best in fall and winter following heavy rains, coho salmon appear in the fall from September to November, surf and night smelts are netted March through October, and most rocky-shore fishes are taken year-round.

The sandy beaches along the Point Reyes Peninsula provide good surf fishing. Most of the peninsula is within the boundaries of the Point Reyes National Seashore, and though much of the land is still under the private ownership of ranchers, some beaches are open to the public and it is expected that even more shore areas will be open in the future.

Location	Sport Fishing Boats	Pier Fishing	Boat Rental	Launch Ramp	Jetty Fishing
Inverness (1)			+	+	
Tomales Boat Basin (2)			+	+	
Marconi Cove (3)				+	
Marshall (4)		+			
North Shore Boats (5)		+	+	+	
Nick's Cove (6)		+			+
Lawson's Landing (7)	+	+	+	+	
Doran Park (8)				+	+
Tides Wharf (9)	+	+			
Shaws Marina (10)	+			+	
Westside Park (11)				+	+
Jenner (12)				+	

Along the Tomales Bay shore, pier and dock fishing is available at some of the small-boat harbors and wharves. Jacksmelt and surfperches are the most common pier-caught species. At the very Southern end of the bay, coho salmon are taken near the entrance of Papermill Creek(October to November) and winter steelhead fishing is often productive in deep pools just inside the creek mouth.

On the Eastern shore, near the entrance to Tomales Bay, surfperches are taken by shore casting along beaches North of Sand Point, and fishing is excellent for rockfish and greenlings where the sandy beach gives way to a predominantly rocky coastline North of Dillon Beach. This is also a good place for poke poling monkeyface eels and other crevice-seeking fish. Anglers usually reach this shore area by hiking North from Dillon Beach, since most of the land adjacent to this rocky stretch of coast is privately owned.

The next opportunity for shore fishing as you approach Bodega Bay from the South is found at Doran Beach Park. Most fishing takes place around the East jetty at the mouth of the harbor where the usual fare is shiner and silver surfperches, jacksmelt, starry flounder, rockfishes and greenlings. Anglers also fish from the West jetty on the other side of the harbor entrance for the same species.

In the town of Bodega Bay the public is allowed to fish from the local wharf where the main species taken are jacksmelt, young bocaccio and surfperches. There is some fishing along the breakwater on the Western shore of Bodega Harbor for shiner, surfperches and black rockfishes.

On beaches along the Sonoma coast, anglers catch surfperches, lingcod, rockfishes, and flounder. This stretch of coast also is good for netting surf and night smelts around the mouth of coastal streams. Steelhead and a few salmon sometimes are taken from these streams.

In the Russian River, migrating steelhead are caught just inside the mouth of the river from the South bank, and in selected areas upriver. Striped bass and sturgeons occasionally are landed from boats in the estuary and from the beach adjacent to the river mouth. Surfperches and flounders are taken in the tidal lagoon section, and runs of chinook have occured in the river during late summer and early fall in the last few years.

North of Jenner the coast becomes steep and rugged, and most of the land is privately owned. At Fort Ross State Park and areas to the North where the shore can be reached, anglers cast for rockfishes, greenlings, cabezon, surfperches and occasionally lingcod. This rocky coastline is also very popular with skin divers and shore pickers who hunt for red abalone.

Fort Ross to Cape Mendocino

Here the shoreline is predominantly rocky backed by high grassy bluffs. These rugged headlands are sharply indented with numerous gulches, and public access to shore occurs infrequently because of the steep terrain and the many privately owned areas adjacent to the coast. Most shore fishing occurs at coves and beaches where coastal streams and rivers empty into the sea. Winters are wet and chilly, and in summer the coast is usually fogbound. Fall is the sunniest and most pleasant time of the year.

Most ocean sport fishing takes place out of the town of Fort Bragg and to a lesser extent at Albion, Point Arena and Shelter Cove. Bottom fishing along this rocky coast is excellent and salmon trolling is very popular.

Where the shore can be reached, rock anglers seek lingcod, cabezon and small rockfishes, and where rocky shores are interrupted by stretches of sandy beach, surf casters fish for redtail surfperch during spring and summer(April and May are considered best). Surf netters work the breakers for surf and night smelts around the mouths of streams; best catches of night smelt are made from February to April, and for surf(day) smelt, from April through August. Steelhead run in rivers between early December and end of February, with fishing usually at its peak around New Year's Day.

Location	Sport Fishing Boats	Pier Fishing	Boat Rental	Launch Ramp	Jetty Fishing
Point Arena(1)		+	+	+	
Albion(2)	+		+		
Noyo Harbor(3)	+	+	+	+	+
Shelter Cove(4)			+	+	

Fort Ross to Point Arena: The first access to shore North of Fort Ross is at Salt Point State Park, which has a small bluff protected cove where skiffs can be launched over the beach in calm weather. Fishing is not allowed inside this cove(Gerstle Cove), but when weather and sea are favorable, anglers venture out around the rocky points on either side of the cove in search of lingcod, blue rockfish, kelp greenling and cabezon. From Salt Point to Gualala, all land is part of a private development of houses and rental units, although there is public access to a tiny stretch of rock and driftwood-strewn beach at the Northern end of the development.

The Gualala River has excellent runs of winter steelhead and the tidewater section is a popular fishing area. Access is by way of a dirt road at the North end of the Hwy. 1 bridge that leads out to the gravel bar near the mouth. Small boats can be launched here(no ramp), and the pools near the South bank are considered the most productive.

At Anchor Bay, owners of the property allow anglers access for a fee, and skiffs can be launched over the beach on the North side of the cove in calm weather. Here, skiff anglers catch such rocky-shore species as kelp greenling, blue and black rockfishes, lingcod and cabezon. Because of the steep terrain, access to the shore is limited North of Anchor Bay to the Point Arena area.

Point Arena: The main fishing activities at Point Arena are pier and skiff fishing at Arena Cove. The cove would be a more important fishing port if it were not for its vulnerbility to Southerly and Westerly winds. Skiffs are available for rent at the pier, which also has a boat hoist. Skiff anglers fish over the reef areas for bottomfish, and during July and August there is a limited amount of trolling for salmon out to about 15 fathoms. The small pier at Arena Cove is over rocky bottom, and attracts such rocky-shore species as striped and walleye surfperches, kelp greenling, black rockfish, lingcod and occasionally cabezon. To the North at Manchester State Beach, smelts are netted in the surf along sandy stretches and good rock fishing spots can be found at the North end. About a mile North of the State beach boundary at

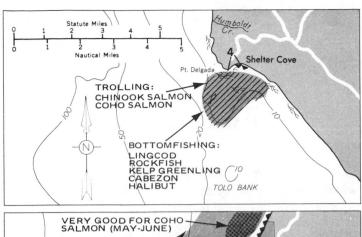

Statute Miles
0 1 2 3 4 5

Nautical Miles
0 1 2 3 4 5

Humboldt Cr.

Shelter Cove

Pt. Delgada

TROLLING:
CHINOOK SALMON
COHO SALMON

BOTTOMFISHING:
LINGCOD
ROCKFISH
KELP GREENLING
CABEZON
HALIBUT

TOLO BANK

N

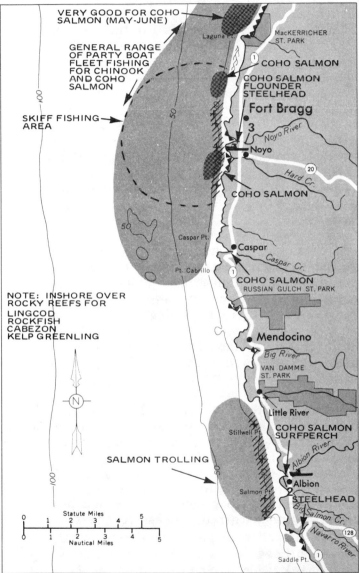

VERY GOOD FOR COHO
SALMON (MAY-JUNE)

Laguna Pt.

MacKERRICHER
ST. PARK

GENERAL RANGE
OF PARTY BOAT
FLEET FISHING
FOR CHINOOK
AND COHO
SALMON

COHO SALMON

COHO SALMON
FLOUNDER
STEELHEAD

Fort Bragg

SKIFF FISHING
AREA

3

Noyo

Noyo River

Hard Cr.

COHO SALMON

Caspar Pt.

Caspar

Caspar Cr.

Pt. Cabrillo

COHO SALMON
RUSSIAN GULCH ST. PARK

NOTE: INSHORE OVER
ROCKY REEFS FOR
LINGCOD
ROCKFISH
CABEZON
KELP GREENLING

Mendocino

Big River

VAN DAMME
ST. PARK

Little River

COHO SALMON
SURFPERCH

Stillwell Pt.

SALMON TROLLING

Albion River

Albion

Salmon Pt.

STEELHEAD

N

Big Salmon Cr.

Navarro River

Saddle Pt.

Statute Miles
0 1 2 3 4 5

Nautical Miles
0 1 2 3 4 5

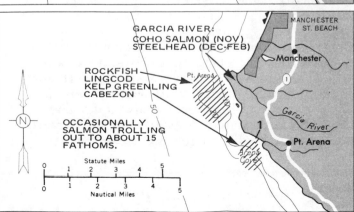

MANCHESTER
ST. BEACH

GARCIA RIVER:
COHO SALMON (NOV)
STEELHEAD (DEC-FEB)

Manchester

ROCKFISH
LINGCOD
KELP GREENLING
CABEZON

Pt. Arena

OCCASIONALLY
SALMON TROLLING
OUT TO ABOUT 15
FATHOMS.

Garcia River

1

Pt. Arena

Arena Cove

N

Statute Miles
0 1 2 3 4 5

Nautical Miles
0 1 2 3 4 5

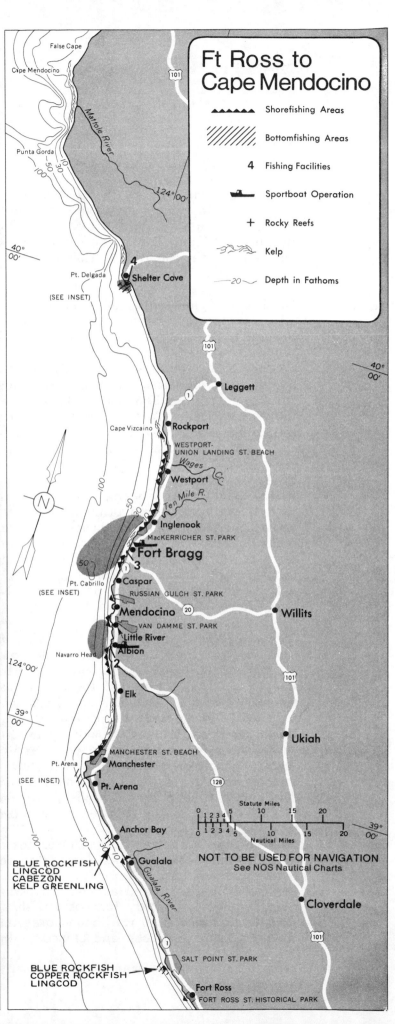

Ft Ross to Cape Mendocino

▲▲▲ Shorefishing Areas

/// Bottomfishing Areas

4 Fishing Facilities

🛥 Sportboat Operation

+ Rocky Reefs

〰 Kelp

—20— Depth in Fathoms

False Cape

Cape Mendocino

101

Mattole River

Punta Gorda

124°00'

40°00'

Pt. Delgada

4 Shelter Cove

(SEE INSET)

101

Leggett

1

Cape Vizcaino

Rockport

WESTPORT-
UNION LANDING ST. BEACH

Wages Cr.

Westport

Ten Mile R.

Inglenook

MacKERRICHER ST. PARK

Fort Bragg

3

Caspar

RUSSIAN GULCH ST. PARK

Pt. Cabrillo

(SEE INSET)

Mendocino

20

Willits

VAN DAMME ST. PARK

Little River

Albion

2

Navarro Head

Elk

Ukiah

124°00'

39°00'

MANCHESTER ST. BEACH

Pt. Arena

Manchester

1

Pt. Arena

128

101

Anchor Bay

BLUE ROCKFISH
LINGCOD
CABEZON
KELP GREENLING

Gualala

Gualala River

Statute Miles
0 1 2 3 4 5 10 15 20

Nautical Miles
0 1 2 3 4 5 10 15 20

39°00'

NOT TO BE USED FOR NAVIGATION
See NOS Nautical Charts

Cloverdale

1

SALT POINT ST. PARK

BLUE ROCKFISH
COPPER ROCKFISH
LINGCOD

Fort Ross
FORT ROSS ST. HISTORICAL PARK

N

Alder Creek, fishing is good for surf smelt, redtail surfperch and migrating salmon and steelhead around the creek mouth.

Fort Bragg and Albion: Sport fishing boats operate out of Noyo Harbor, in Fort Bragg, and in some years, out of Albion when weather permits. Most fishing is during the summer. The rocky reefs along this coast are extremely productive for lingcod, cabezon, kelp greenling and rockfishes. Reef areas around rocky points adjacent to the Noyo and Albion rivers' mouths are excellent spots for lingcod and red rockfish.

Offshore, anglers troll for chinook and coho salmon from May to October in water 10 to 60 fathoms deep. At the height of the season in July and August, coho move inshore to feed over reef areas, and during October and November they congregate around river and creek mouths such as the Ten Mile River, Noyo River, Albion River, Caspar Creek and the Navarro River. During this time skiff fishing reaches its peak around the Noyo River mouth. Most ocean skiff fishing(for both salmon and bottom-fish)occurs within 3 miles of the whistle buoy about a mile West of the mouth of the Noyo River. To the South at Albion River, small-boat anglers are warned that the dangerous bar at the entrance can be crossed only during certain tide stages, and then only during calm weather.

Tidewater fishing takes place in both the Noyo and Albion Rivers. Inside the Noyo River, coho are taken from October to mid-December, and starry flounder are caught year-round with March bringing the best catches. Surfperches are caught in winter and spring(April and May best). Surfperches, jacksmelt and flounders are taken from piers in Noyo Harbor and during the summer and fall there is fishing from the North jetty at the river entrance for surfperches, kelp greenling and small black rockfish. Striped surfperch show around the jetty during spring. The Albion River has tide-water fishing for coho in October and November; surfperches and flounder also are taken here, as in the Noyo River.

Shore anglers looking for spots to fish on the coast around the Fort Bragg-Albion area can try their luck between the towns of Elk and Albion, and at the State parks. Most of these areas have good rock fishing and poke-poling places, and beaches can be good for redtail surfperch and calico surfperch, as well as surf and night smelts. North of Mackerricher Park, smelts are surf netted around the mouths of practically all creeks - especially those between Westport and Rockport(Wages, De-Haven, Hardy and Juan Creeks). Juan Creek and the Ten Mile River also have good surf fishing for redtail surfperches and the Ten Mile River mouth has good fall fishing for coho. North of Rockport, Hwy. 1 turns inland through mountainous terrain and redwood forest, meeting up with U.S. 101 at Leggett. Twenty-seven miles North of Leggett, an access road(not shown on the map) leads to Shelter Cove, the last fishing outpost along this section of coast.

Shelter Cove: Shelter Cove affords reasonably good shelter from Northwesterly winds, but, like Arena Cove, it is exposed to the full force of Southerly and Westerly winds. Skiffs can be rented during the summer. Bait and tackle also are available. Though Shelter Cove is isolated and has no docking or wharf facilities, skiff fishing here is excellent - particularly for bottomfish. Such rocky-bottom types as lingcod, cabezon, greenlings and rockfishes abound over the rocky reefs, and in July and Auguest, skiffs work the cove for coho and chinook salmon. Pacific halibut are sometimes caught by skiffs, and redtail and other surfperches are taken by surf casters on the beach.

Eel River to the Oregon Border

North of Cape Mendocino, dark sand beaches begin to interrupt rocky headlands more frequently, and large rivers, famous for their migrating salmon and steelhead, empty into the sea. The terrain is less steep near the ocean than areas to the South, but the coastline still maintains a rugged beauty of its own. Along this coast, the magnificent coastal redwood trees thrive in the cool and very damp climate of the Pacific Northwest. Salmon is by far the most important game fish in this region, and both chinook and coho salmon are taken during summer and fall. Rockfishes and other bottomfishes also enter the sport catch, especially in the North.

Redtail surfperch are abundant and are available year-round along sandy beaches and in tidewater, with spring and early summer bringing the best catches. Surf smelt are netted from March through September, and night smelt run from February through mid-May. Along the occasional rocky stretches, black and grass rockfishes, and kelp and rock greenlings are taken by rock anglers. In most places there is year-round fishing in tidewater for starry flounder and surfperches, with spring bringing the best catches. Eulachon, or candlefish, are dip netted in the Klamath, Smith and Mad Rivers and in Redwood Creek in April and May. Winter steelhead run in most rivers October through March, with peak fishing in December and January. Summer steelhead run in the Klamath and Eel Rivers from July through September, and sea-run cutthroat trout occur in the more Northerly rivers, fall through spring. Mud flats and beaches along this stretch of coast are famous for their gaper, Washington, littleneck, soft shell and razor clams. Crabbing for Dungeness crab also is popular along this coast during winter and spring, especially at Crescent City, Humboldt Bay and in the Eel River Lagoon.

Location	Sport Fishing Boats	Pier Fishing	Boat Rental	Launch Ramp	Jetty Fishing
Crab Pk. Eel R.(1)				+	
Fields Lndg. Eureka(2)				+	
King Salmon, Eureka(3)	+	+	+	+	+
Ft. of Com.St(4)				+	
Samoa Access(5)				+	
Arcata(6)				+	
Mad River(7)				+	
Humboldt Bay(8)					+
Trinidad Harbor(9)	+	+	+	+	
Stone Lagoon(10)			+		
Klamath R(11)	+		+	+	+
Cresent City Hb(12)	+	+	+	+	+
Smith R(13)	+	+	+	+	

Cape Mendocino to Humboldt Bay: The first coastal fishing area North of Cape Mendocino that is reasonably accessible is at Centerville Beach and around the mouth of the Eel River. In the Eel River lagoon, most fishing is from skiffs, although there is shore fishing also. Steelhead are caught in summer and fall with larger fish landed late in the season. During most years chinook salmon enter the lagoon in August and run through October; coho salmon begin to appear later, around November. Starry flounder and surfperches also are taken in the lagoon. South of the Eel River there is surf netting for surf(day) smelt and casting for redtail surfperch along the sandy beach at Centerville County Park.

North of the Eel River U.S. 101 turns toward the coast as it approaches the town of Eureka, a center of fishing activity during the salmon season. A sizeable party boat and skiff fishery operates out of Humboldt Bay, and boats fish almost exclusively for chinook and coho. Standard fishing methods are trolling and drifting ("mooching") bait close to the bottom. Fishing takes place from May to October with chinook being the first to show. July and August are considered the best fishing months as significant numbers of coho begin to be caught. Salmon move in close to the beaches and around the jetties at the harbor entrance as the season progresses. During this time skiffs venture out into the ocean to join the party boat fleet and the entrance channel soon becomes a favorite spot for chinook fishing. Small-boat fishermen are warned not to negotiate the harbor entrance on an outgoing tide - large breakers form along the bar and make this a highly dangerous area.

Inside Humboldt Bay there is tidewater fishing from skiffs for jacksmelt, sharks, rays and surfperches. Sharks are plentiful in Arcata Bay, and leopard shark fishing is excellent in Mad River Slough during summer. Sturgeons sometimes are taken around the ruins of the old Arcata Channel. South Humboldt Bay is mostly a clamming area, but there also is angling for some of the species mentioned above and rockfishes, which are taken consistently by anglers over the artificial reef during slack tide and when the water is clear. Rockfishes are taken also around the breakwater at Buhne Point.

The ocean beaches adjacent to the Humboldt Bay entrance from the North and South Spits have shore fishing. On the South Spit, anglers cast for surfperches, and net surf and night smelts in the surf. The South jetty is a popular fishing spot for blue and black rockfishes, kelp greenling, lingcod, cabezon, surfperches, jacksmelt and coho and chinook salmon(in summer). Species caught from the North Spit are similar to those taken along the South Spit, but permission from the Coast Guard is needed to fish the tip of the Spit as well as the North jetty where grass rockfish are especially plentiful. Another jetty, on the bay side of the North Spit, is a good spot for lingcod, kelp greenling, cabezon and rockfishes.

A popular shore fishing site on the Eastern side of the bay is at Buhne Point around the electric power plant warm-water outfall, where good numbers of surfperch are taken, as well as other bay fishes. Shore anglers also catch a variety of surfperches around the railroad bridge that spans Eureka Slough. Pier fishing is allowed at a number of docks at Fields Landing, Buhne Point and Eureka, where the catch consists usually of jacksmelt, topsmelt, staghorn sculpin, kelp greenling and surfperches.

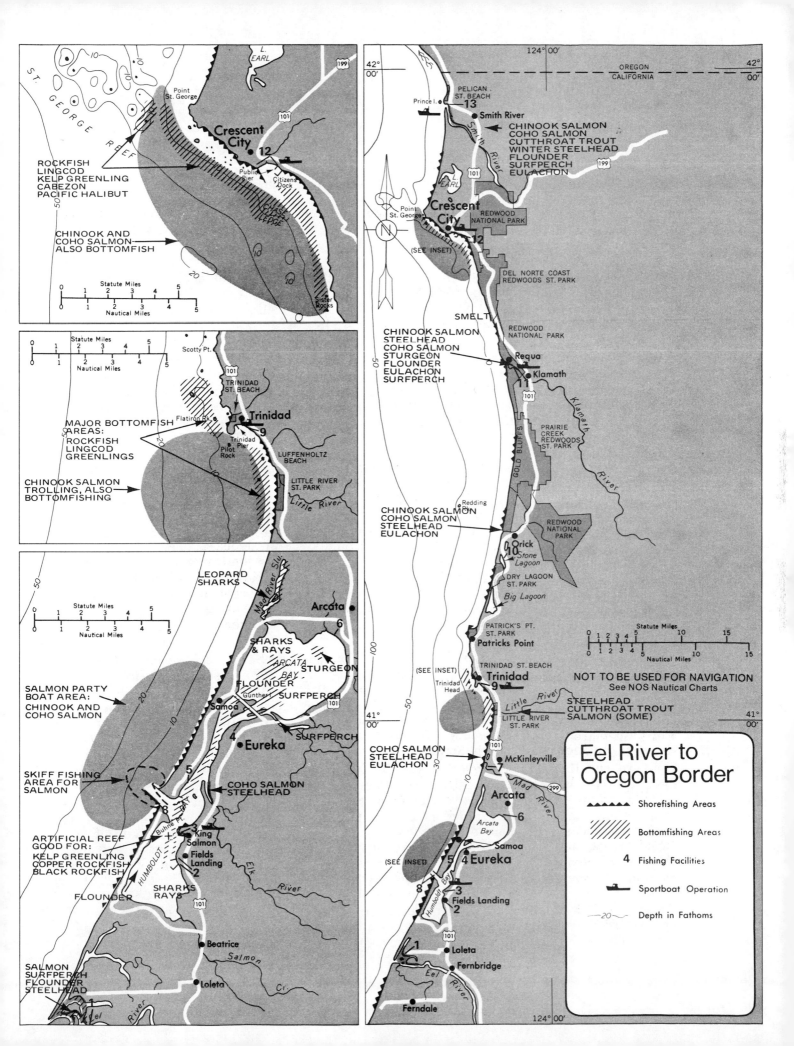

Inset 1 (top left):

ROCKFISH
LINGCOD
KELP GREENLING
CABEZON
PACIFIC HALIBUT

CHINOOK AND
COHO SALMON-
ALSO BOTTOMFISH

ST. GEORGE REEF
Point St. George
Crescent City
Public Pier
Citizens Dock
CHASE LEDGE
Sister Rocks
L. EARL

Statute Miles
0 1 2 3 4 5
Nautical Miles
0 1 2 3 4 5

Inset 2 (middle left):

Statute Miles
0 1 2 3 4 5
Nautical Miles
0 1 2 3 4 5

Scotty Pt.
TRINIDAD ST. BEACH
Flatiron Rk.
Trinidad
Pilot Rock
Trinidad Pier
LUFFENHOLTZ BEACH
LITTLE RIVER ST. PARK
Little River

MAJOR BOTTOMFISH
AREAS:
ROCKFISH
LINGCOD
GREENLINGS

CHINOOK SALMON
TROLLING, ALSO
BOTTOMFISHING

Inset 3 (bottom left):

LEOPARD SHARKS

Mad River Slough
Arcata
SHARKS & RAYS
ARCATA BAY
STURGEON
FLOUNDER
SURFPERCH
Gunther I.
Samoa
Eureka
SURFPERCH

SALMON PARTY
BOAT AREA:
CHINOOK AND
COHO SALMON

SKIFF FISHING
AREA FOR
SALMON

COHO SALMON
STEELHEAD

ARTIFICIAL REEF
GOOD FOR:
KELP GREENLING
COPPER ROCKFISH
BLACK ROCKFISH

Buhne Pt.
HUMBOLDT
King Salmon
Fields Landing
SHARKS RAYS
Elk River

FLOUNDER

SALMON
SURFPERCH
FLOUNDER
STEELHEAD

Beatrice
Salmon Cr.
Loleta
Eel River

Statute Miles
0 1 2 3 4 5
Nautical Miles
0 1 2 3 4 5

Main map (right):

124° 00'
42° 00'
OREGON
CALIFORNIA
42° 00'

Prince I.
PELICAN ST. BEACH
13
Smith River

CHINOOK SALMON
COHO SALMON
CUTTHROAT TROUT
WINTER STEELHEAD
FLOUNDER
SURFPERCH
EULACHON

L. EARL
Point St. George
N
Crescent City
REDWOOD NATIONAL PARK
12
(SEE INSET)

DEL NORTE COAST
REDWOODS ST. PARK

SMELT

CHINOOK SALMON
STEELHEAD
COHO SALMON
STURGEON
FLOUNDER
EULACHON
SURFPERCH

REDWOOD
NATIONAL PARK
Requa
Klamath

GOLD BLUFFS
PRAIRIE CREEK REDWOODS ST. PARK
Klamath River

CHINOOK SALMON
COHO SALMON
STEELHEAD
EULACHON

Redding
REDWOOD
NATIONAL PARK
Orick
Stone Lagoon
DRY LAGOON ST. PARK
Big Lagoon

PATRICK'S PT. ST. PARK
Patricks Point

TRINIDAD ST. BEACH
(SEE INSET)
Trinidad Head
Trinidad
9

Statute Miles
0 1 2 3 4 5 10 15
Nautical Miles
0 1 2 3 4 5 10 15

NOT TO BE USED FOR NAVIGATION
See NOS Nautical Charts

41° 00'
41° 00'

Little River
STEELHEAD
CUTTHROAT TROUT
SALMON (SOME)
LITTLE RIVER ST. PARK

COHO SALMON
STEELHEAD
EULACHON

McKinleyville
7

Arcata
6
Mad River
Arcata Bay
Samoa

(SEE INSET)
Eureka
4
8
Fields Landing
3
2
Humboldt Bay

101
Loleta
1
Fernbridge

Ferndale
Eel River

124° 00'

Eel River to Oregon Border

▲▲▲▲ Shorefishing Areas

///// Bottomfishing Areas

4 Fishing Facilities

⚓ Sportboat Operation

—20— Depth in Fathoms

Mad River: At Mad River, most fishing is in the lagoon section for coho and winter run steelhead(January to March) although a few chinook are landed.   Along beaches adjacent to the river mouth and North to Little River State Beach, there is good shore casting for surfperch and netting for surf and night smelts.   Steelhead run in Little River in winter, sea-run cutthroat trout appear in spring, and salmon occasionally run up the river in fall.

About a mile North of Little River at the Southern end of Luffenholtz Beach(a sandy beach bordered by rock outcroppings), access to shore is difficult in places, but there is good cabezon, and kelp greenling, and excellent smelt netting and surf casting for redtail surfperch along the sandy-shore section.

Trinidad Harbor offers ocean salmon fishing and bottom fishing in summer, and pier and rocky-shore fishing year-round.   The salmon catch is mostly coho, and best fishing is in July and August.   Blue and black rockfishes, lingcod, kelp greenling and cabezon are caught in the salmon fishing areas and inshore over rocky reefs.   There is pier fishing in this harbor for jacksmelt, surfperches, kelp greenling and cabezon.

To the North, rockfishes, greenlings and surfperches are taken from rocky beaches at Trinidad State Beach and Patricks Point State Park.

North of Patricks Point: North of Patricks Point the shore becomes lined with sand dunes, and beaches have excellent runs of surf and night smelts and redtail surfperch.   The large brackish-water lagoons along this section of the coast have sporadic year-round fishing for cutthroat trout and small steelhead.   Big Lagoon and Stone Lagoon sometime break open to the sea during high water, at which time salmon and steelhead move in.   North of Dry Lagoon State Park, beaches backed by evergreen-crowned bluffs have good runs of surf and night smelts and redtail surfperch - paticularly the Gold Bluffs area(reached by way of Fern Canyon Road).

The Klamath River is famous for its excellent runs of chinook salmon and steelhead.   The tidewater section of the river is heavily fished by skiff and shore anglers - there is no skiff fishing in the ocean.   Chinook start running in mid-July or August and continue through October.   Although most fish are landed from skiffs which jam the lower river during the height of the season(August to September), many also are taken by anglers casting from shore around the river mouth.   Coho enter the catch in mid to late September, and the run may last until July and continue to run through November or later, depending on river conditions.   Other fish caught in tidewater include surfperch, starry flounder, white and green sturgeons and eulachon.   Along beaches adjacent to the Klamath River mouth, surf netters strain the breakers for surf and night smelts, and bait casters fish for redtail surfperch and starry flounder.   North of the Klamath, near the South border of Del Norte Coast Redwoods State Park, netters, rock anglers and surf casters fish from shore around the mouth of Wilson Creek.   Within the creek, chinook and coho salmon, summer steelhead and sea-run cutthroat are taken.

Crescent City: The harbor at Crescent City is well protected from sea and weather by extensive seawalls which flank its perimeter and by the Point St. George headland.   The fishing fleet is based at Crescent City Boat Basin between the East seawall and the public fishing pier, an area known as Citizen's Dock. Party boat and skiff anglers fish for salmon and bottomfish, weather permitting. Salmon trolling(mainly for chinook) usually begins in June and continues through September, with best catches made in July and August. Lingcod, cabezon, kelp greenling, rockfishes and Pacific halibut also are taken in the salmon areas, but best bottom fishing is found usually farther inshore close to rocky Sister Rocks to the harbor entrance and along the 10 fathom curve from Chase Ledge North to St. George's Reef. Species of rockfish that enter the catch include black, blue, china, vermillion and bocaccio.

Shore anglers take blue and black rockfishes, lingcod and kelp and rock greenlings from the West breakwater and along rocky shores North to Point St. George. There is pier fishing at Citizen's Dock for starry flounder, kelp greenling, surfperches and jacksmelt. Occasionally, large schools of surf smelt appear around the dock and are taken by snagging; herring are taken during late winter and early spring. Pier anglers also trap Dungeness crab in ring nets during winter and spring. Both surf and night smelts are netted along beaches South of the harbor and North of Point St. George with surf smelt predominating along Northern beaches.

The Smith River: The Smith River mouth and the tidewater lagoon section have considerable skiff fishing during the salmon season. Chinook is the most sought after, and fish weighing 25 to 30 pounds are not uncommon. The season usually extends from September through December; late September and October are peak fishing times in tidewater. Some coho also are taken; most are landed in October and November. Sea-run cutthroat trout are caught from shore and skiffs from September through May, with peak fishing in March and April. A few winter steelhead are caught in the lagoon from December through March, and eulachon are dip netted during their run in spring. Starry flounder, surfperches and cabezon are caught year-round in tidewater, and redtail surfperch and surf and night smelts are taken along the beach South of the river mouth. North along the coast, anglers fish the rocky shores of Pelican State Beach for black rockfish and other rocky-shore fishes, and for night smelt along sandy stretches.

Central Coast Ocean Fishing

Ocean fishing along the Central Coast, from about San Simeon down to about Pt. Conception, is covered in this section. Although this stretch of ocean is actually in the Southern half of the state, fish species and techniques are more akin to those of Northern California. Pt. Conception is often described as an ecological dividing point for marine life. South of the Point is the subropical zone; North of it is the temperate zone. Many coastal pelagic fishes, such as Pacific barracuda and yellowtail that are common to the waters off Southern California and Baja California, Mexico, are taken only rarely North of Pt. Conception. Conversely, some pelagic Northern marine and anadromous species, such as coho salmon, are taken only in small numbers Southeast of Pt. Conception in late winter and early spring.

The coastline alternates between broad sandy beaches and rocky headlands and is backed by low rolling hills. Shore anglers cast from sandy beaches for surfperch and bait cast and poke-pole along rocky shores. Off shore bottomfishing is good year-round, and albacore, salmon and bonito are available seasonally. In some years, white seabass also add to the sport catch. In addition to angling, abalone picking and clamming are very popular in this region, which has one of the heaviest concentrations of pismo clams along the California coast.

Point Sal to Point Buchon: The San Luis Obispo Bay area has offshore bottomfishing for rockfishes and, to a lesser degree, lingcod and cabezon. California halibut are taken over sandy bottom in San Luis Obispo Bay and areas to the South; bonito and white seabass are sometimes taken from summer to late fall. Boats go out for king salmon from early spring to midsummer. Fishing is available at Pismo Beach pier, the county pier in Avila and Port San Luis pier. Surf anglers cast for surfperches at Pismo Beach and lingcod and cabezon at Shell Beach and Avila.

Location	Sport Fishing Boats	Pier Fishing	Boat Rental	Launch Ramp	Jetty Fishing
Pismo Beach Pier(1)		+			
Avila County Pier(2)		+			
Port San Luis Pier(3)	+	+		+	+
Morro Bay (4)	+	+	+	+	+
Cayucos (5)		+			
San Simeon (6)	+	+		+	

Morro Bay Area: Morro Bay party boats operate year-round, many fishing exclusively for albacore when it runs off the coast, best times in September and early October. Inside Morro Bay, skiff anglers catch starry flounder, California halibut, jacksmelt, sharks, rays and surfperches. Outside the Bay the catch consists of rockfishes, cabezon and lingcod. There is pier, dock and bank fishing along the shores of Morro Bay for starry flounder, jacksmelt and surfperches. The powerplant outfall on the North side of Morro Rock is another productive place for surfperches and occasionally striped bass. Ocean shore fishing for surfperch takes place along the sandy spit that separates the bay from the sea. This is also a popular clamming area. Access is by way of a road approaching from the South or by boat.

Areas to the North: North of Morro Bay the shoreline is characterized by sandy beaches interrupted by rock and boulder-strewn shores, affording excellent fishing. Surfperches are taken along sandy shores and bait casting produces cabezon, surfperch, rockfish and kelp greenling. At the Cayucos Pier, jacksmelt, white croaker, queenfish, staghorn sculpin and boccaccio are the usual fare. Cayucos Beach is the Northernmost beach in California with grunion runs, occuring during spring and summer. From Point Estero to San Simeon there is little beach access. At San Simeon, pier fishermen produce starry founder, halibut, skates and surfperches. Stream mouths in this area produce steelhead during years of heavy rainfall. Party boats operate from San simeon during the summer. Along the rocky stretch of coastline from San Simeon North to Pt. Piedras Blancas, shore fishing is excellent for surfperches, kelp greenling, rockfish and cabezon. Most shore areas are open to the public. North of Pt. Piedras Blancas the topography becomes precipitous as Rte. 1 winds its way toward the towering cliffs of the Big Sur coast. There is little access to shore along this majestic route for over 60 miles until one reaches Point Lobos and the Carmel-Monterey Bay area.

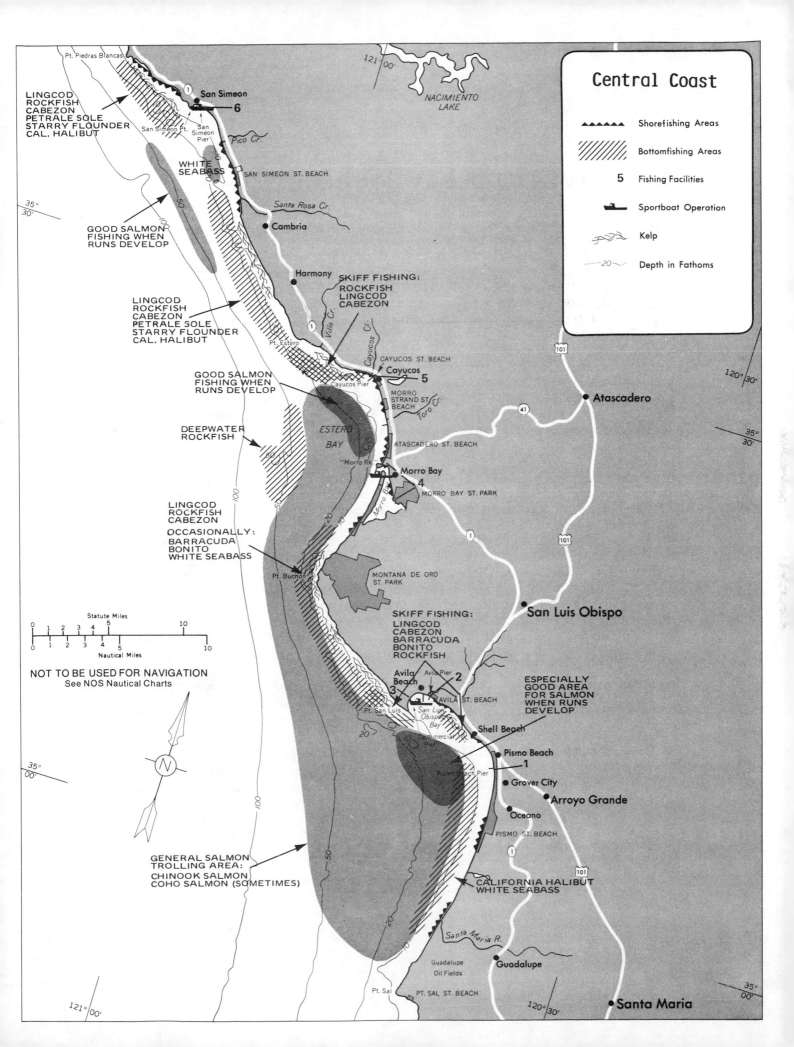

Central Coast

Shorefishing Areas

Bottomfishing Areas

5 Fishing Facilities

Sportboat Operation

Kelp

—20— Depth in Fathoms

LINGCOD
ROCKFISH
CABEZON
PETRALE SOLE
STARRY FLOUNDER
CAL. HALIBUT

WHITE
SEABASS

GOOD SALMON
FISHING WHEN
RUNS DEVELOP

LINGCOD
ROCKFISH
CABEZON
PETRALE SOLE
STARRY FLOUNDER
CAL. HALIBUT

SKIFF FISHING:
ROCKFISH
LINGCOD
CABEZON

GOOD SALMON
FISHING WHEN
RUNS DEVELOP

DEEPWATER
ROCKFISH

LINGCOD
ROCKFISH
CABEZON

OCCASIONALLY:
BARRACUDA
BONITO
WHITE SEABASS

SKIFF FISHING:
LINGCOD
CABEZON
BARRACUDA
BONITO
ROCKFISH

ESPECIALLY
GOOD AREA
FOR SALMON
WHEN RUNS
DEVELOP

GENERAL SALMON
TROLLING AREA:
CHINOOK SALMON
COHO SALMON (SOMETIMES)

CALIFORNIA HALIBUT
WHITE SEABASS

Statute Miles
0 1 2 3 4 5 10
0 1 2 3 4 5 10
Nautical Miles

NOT TO BE USED FOR NAVIGATION
See NOS Nautical Charts

N

Place labels

Pt. Piedras Blancas

San Simeon **6**

San Simeon Pt.
San Simeon Pier

Pico Cr.

SAN SIMEON ST. BEACH

Santa Rosa Cr.

● Cambria

● Harmony

Villa Cr.

Cayucos Cr.

Pt. Estero

CAYUCOS ST. BEACH

Cayucos **5**

Cayucos Pier

MORRO
STRAND ST.
BEACH

Toro Cr.

ESTERO
BAY

ATASCADERO ST. BEACH

"Morro Rk."

Morro Bay **4**

MORRO BAY ST. PARK

Morro Bay

MONTANA DE ORO
ST. PARK

Pt. Buchon

San Luis Obispo

Avila
Beach

Avila Pier

2

AVILA ST. BEACH

3

Pt. San Luis

San Luis
Obispo
Bay

Shell Beach

Commercial
Pier

Pismo Beach

1

Pismo Beach Pier

● Grover City

● Oceano

● Arroyo Grande

PISMO ST. BEACH

Santa Maria R.

Guadalupe
Oil Fields

Pt. Sal

PT. SAL ST. BEACH

● Guadalupe

● Santa Maria

NACIMIENTO
LAKE

121° 00'

● Atascadero

120° 30'

35° 30'

35° 30'

35° 00'

120° 30'

35° 00'

121° 00'

121° 00'

50

100

20

10

20

50

100

50

Highway markers: 1, 101, 41

San Francisco Bay Fishing

San Francisco Bay, California's largest estuary, technically is divided into three connecting bays - San Francisco Bay proper, San Pablo Bay and Suisun Bay. These bays receive runoff from the extensive Sacramento and San Joaquin River systems that drain California's Central Valley and have their source in the Sierra Nevada. In general, most of the San Francisco Bay system is very shallow - the average depth is 20 feet - and there are extensive mudflats in San Pablo Bay and South San Francisco Bay.

The two most sought-after game fishes in the San Francisco Bay area are the striped bass and chinook salmon. Most salmon fishing takes place in the ocean outside the Golden Gate, while San Francisco Bay is practically the unrivaled domain of the striped bass angler. Other fishes such as sturgeon, starry flounder, surfperches, jacksmelt, topsmelt, white croaker, rockfishes, sharks and rays also offer a great deal of sport to Bay Area anglers.

The angler certainly will not find this area lacking in recreational fishing facilities. Piers, skiff rental, concessions and launching facilities are scattered around the bay's perimeter, and scores of party boats operate out of Bay Area ports. There are sizeable sport fishing fleets near Fisherman's Wharf in San Francisco, along the Sausalito waterfront, and at the Berkeley and Emeryville marinas. Many of these boats fish out in the ocean for chinook and coho salmon; some make rockfish trips to the Farallon Islands; and most also fish for striped bass when good runs develop. In the Northern reaches of the bay, party boats operating out of San Pablo Bay and Carquinez Strait ports fish exclusively for striped bass, sturgeon and starry flounder. Charters usually can be arranged at harbors from which boats operate, although in San Francisco, trips are usually arranged through bait and tackle shops because of parking and other logistics problems in the city.

San Francisco, San Pablo and Suisun Bays provide a wonderful year-round fishery. The keys to successful fishing is these bays, beyond using the right techniques, is to fish in the right place and to fish at the right times(see Fishing Tips).

Fishing Seasons   (+=good, -=fair)

Species	J	F	M	A	M	J	J	A	S	O	N	D
Striper			-	-	-	-	-	+	+	+	+	-
Halibut						+	+	+	-			
Sturgeon	+*	+*	+*	-	-	-	-	-	-	-	+	+
Salmon									-	-	-	

*closure in some Bay waters

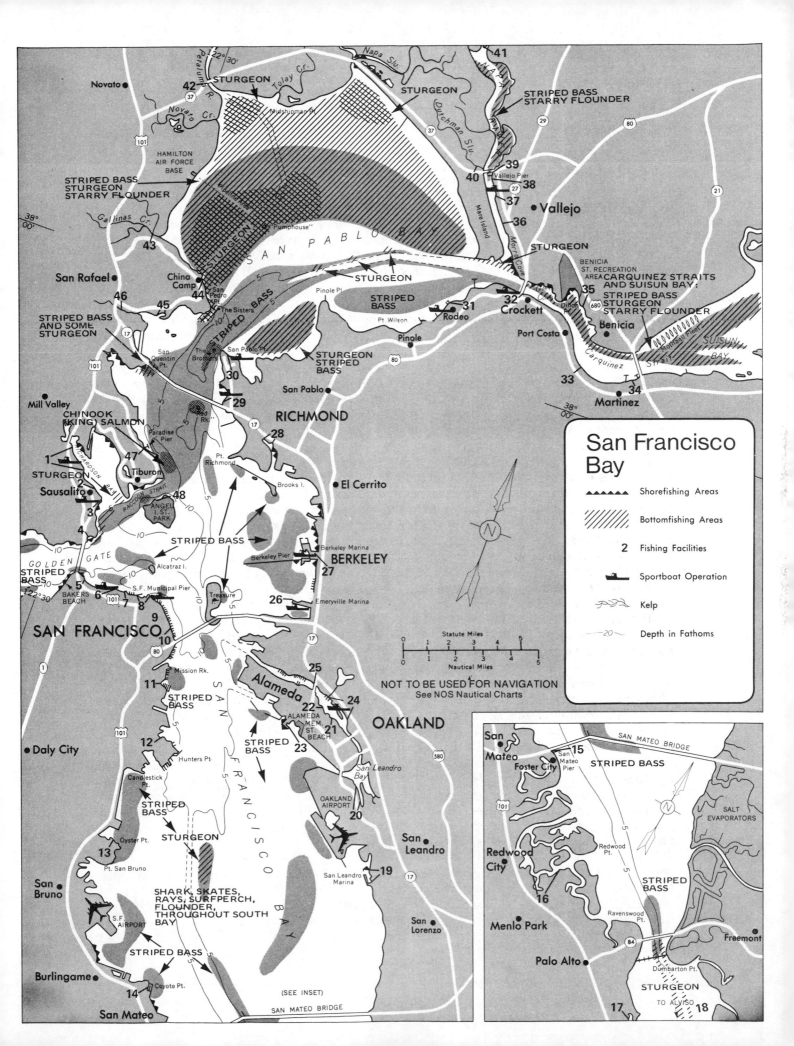

San Francisco Bay

- ▲▲▲▲ Shorefishing Areas
- //// Bottomfishing Areas
- 2 Fishing Facilities
- 🚤 Sportboat Operation
- 〰️ Kelp
- —20— Depth in Fathoms

NOT TO BE USED FOR NAVIGATION
See NOS Nautical Charts

Statute Miles
0 1 2 3 4 5
Nautical Miles
0 1 2 3 4 5

Fishing during the prime tidal movements is extremely important. The best time to fish these Bays is during the two-week cycle of extreme water movement that is a result of the maximum difference between high and low tide. More rapidly moving waters move bait and this produces more active feeding for all game fish in the Bays. Concentrate fishing from the 2-3 hours before the high water slack period until an hour or two after the ebb starts. This will produce the best results. This period is even more productive if it occurs at first light or dusk.

Striped Bass: Striped bass spawn from about April to mid-June in fresh waters of the Sacramento and San Joaquin rivers. After spawning, the fish move back down into the saltwater bays; some venture out into the ocean. They spend most of the summer and fall in salt water before returning once again to brackish-water and freshwater sloughs and rivers. Although best fishing times vary with area, in general, the fishing season extends from March to December, with best fishing from mid- August to November. October has been the best striped bass fishing month consistently since 1969.

In San Pablo Bay, Carquinez Strait, and Suisun Bay, striped bass are caught year-round with best fishing usually in October and November, with a lesser run of fish in June, July and August. Most spring and summer fish are caught trolling in the late afternoon. Fall-run fish are caught still fishing or drifting, primarily with live bait such as staghorn sculpin(known locally as "bullheads").

In the Napa River and nearby brackish-water sloughs along the Northern shore or San Pablo Bay, striped bass are caught throughout the year although weather sometimes restricts fishing during the winter months. Best times are considered to be September, October and November, peaking usually in late October. Fish are taken by bait fishing and trolling from boats; bait casting from shore.

Within San Francisco Bay proper, in such areas as the Golden Gate Bridge(South tower), Raccoon Strait(over Raccoon Shoal), Berkeley flats and off Alcatraz and Treasure Islands, fishing usually starts in June and extends through October into November. Most fish are caught after mid-August, with peak catches in October. A popular fishing method is drifting with live bait(anchovies or shiner surfperch) in areas where an abrupt change in depth occurs and when the current is running swiftest. Anglers also troll for stripers and some will even get out their plug casting gear when a surface-feeding school is located. From Angel Island North to The Brothers, good striped bass fishing can usually be had in September, October and November by drifting live bait and trolling as fish migrate through on their way back to the Sacramento- San Joaquin Delta. Shore and pier fishermen cast lures and bait for stripers from selected spots on both sides of the bay. (See chart for shore-fishing areas and piers).

The striped bass season in South San Francisco Bay extends from June through September, and in some years fishing may last until November or December. Fishing usually reaches a peak around the San Mateo Bridge area in June and July and around the Dumbarton Bridge in September and October. Most striper fishing in South San Francisco Bay is a trolling affair with some plug casting when a school is found. Also, a growing number of anglers are fishing from shore for striped bass in spring and again in late summer around San Francisco Airport and Coyote Point.

Sturgeon: Sturgeon fishing has become very popular in the Bay Area over the years, especially in San Pablo Bay, Carquinez Strait and Suisun Bay. A small but growing sturgeon fishery is also developing in South San Francisco Bay from off Oyster Point(San Bruno Shoals) South to the entrance of Alviso Slough. Both green and white sturgeons are taken; the white sturgeon is the most prized.

Although sturgeons are caught throughout the year in the upper bays, best fishing is usually in the fall and winter when the biggest fish are taken. In San Pablo Bay, they appear to move in over the flats in early fall, and fishing usually lasts from November to May, with best catches from about January to March. The flats along the North side of the bay from the Mare Island ("Rockwall") to China Camp are especially productive at high tide during the winter. Other good spots in San Pablo Bay are the "pump house" and around the odd-numbered bouys that mark the North side of the Main channel with cuts through the middle of the bay. There is also year-round fishing in Carquinez Strait over the flats along the Northern shore. Smaller fish taken are in summer, larger ones in winter.

In Suisun Bay, fishing usually starts in spring around April and lasts until October or November, about the time of the first rains. In summer, most Suisun sturgeon are sublegal size(less that 40 inches long) with about 1 "keeper" out of every 10 caught. Larger fish are taken in the fall. The "mothball fleet" and the channel buoys along the edges of sand bars near the entrance to the bay are good areas to fish. In South San Francisco Bay from San Bruno Shoals South to Alviso Slough, the season extends from about November to March. Early season fishing is usually best in the Northerly areas; late season fishing is usually best in the more Southerly areas along the edge of the channel. Sometimes during the Pacific herring runs, which occur anytime between December and March, sturgeons are taken from boats and shore in the central part of the bay in such areas as Richardson Bay and along the Sausalito waterfront.

Other Bay Sport Fishes: Although most salmon are taken outside the Golden Gate, migrating chinook salmon sometimes are caught deep trolling with whole anchovies in the area from the Golden Gate to Raccoon Strait and off the Tiburon Peninsula North to the Richmond Bridge during late summer. The area off the Eastern side of the Tiburon Peninsula(called "California City" by anglers) is heavily fished when the salmon are running.

Sharks, skates and rays are plentiful throughout the bay; some of the more common types are leopard, brown, smoothhound and sevengill sharks, spiny dogfish, bat ray and big skate. These are especially numerous in South San Francisco Bay all year. Most fishing, however, takes place in summer and fall. Starry flounder are abundant, especially over the flats in San Pablo and Suisun bays and in the Napa River and adjacent sloughs.. An assortment of surfperches are taken, as well as white croaker("kingfish"), jacksmelt, topsmelt, English sole, sand sole, small lingcod and brown and black rockfishes.

Fish Cleaning

There's a syndrome among some anglers that I like to call, "The Fear of Filleting." It's not unlike "The Fear of Flying." But, fortunately, it's a lot easier to overcome. It just takes a little knowledge, a little willingness and an extra sharp filleting knife.

But, don't be mislead, filleting is not the end-all, or be-all of fish cleaning. It's only one of several basic approaches(all are presented here, in detail), and filleting is not even desirable or appropriate for some fish.

Field Dressing

Actually, the word dressing is not accurate, but we're stuck with it, so here goes. Field dressing means removing the entrails and gills of a fish just after catching. This process is generally reserved for large fish(several pounds or more). It's purpose is to preserve the fish at its height of freshness. Field dressing, for example, is quite common among ocean salmon anglers. It's the kind of thing that's desirable but not absolutely necessary. Especially if your catch is kept cold.

Here's how it's done. With the fish pointing away from you, put the tip of your knife in the anal vent and cut through the belly(leaving the intestines as undisturbed as possible) up to where the gills come together under the chin of the fish.

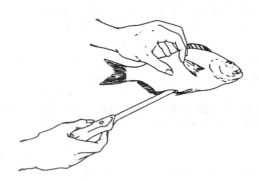

Next, with short cuts, free the bottom of the gills from the chin flesh and from the belly flesh, as illustrated on the top of the next page.

Now, pull open the gill cover on each side of the fish and cut the top of the gills free from the head. The gills and entrails can now be lifted or slid out of the fish in one unit. Now, finally, remove the strip of reddish tissue near the backbone in the intestinal cavity(these are the fishes kidneys). You may have to cut through a thin layer of tissue covering this area. As a last step, rinse off the fish. It is now ready for icing down.

Traditional Fish Cleaning

This approach is basically an extension of field dressing. As a young boy my earliest memory of fish cleaning was the assembly line my Dad set up with my brother and myself to clean a stringer of well over 100 Lake Michigan perch (about ½-1 pound each). Here are the steps;

1) Scaling - Using a knife(not necessarily real sharp) or a fish scaler, scrape from the tail towards the head. This is best done out-of-doors, since the scales fly around. Actually some fish(like salmon and sanddabs) can be scaled with the spray from a garden hose nozzle. It's quick and easy.

2) Gutting - This is actually the same as the beginnings of field dressing. Open the belly from anal vent to gills.

3) Be-Heading - The entrails are slid forward and out of the body cavity, and then with a sharp knife, cut perpendicular to the backbone at the top of the gill cover, cut off the entrails, gills and head.

4) Rinsing - Rinse inside and outside of fish after removing red flesh in body cavity(see Field Dressing above).

5) Fish is now ready for cooking and preserving.

Filleting

Filleting is simple and has many advantages. For example, scaling is not necessary since the skin(and scales) will be removed. It can and often is done without even gutting or field dressing the fish first. It produces boneless or almost bone-free slabs of meat. And filleting works great on fish of all sizes and both round bodied and flat bodied fish.

Here are the steps in filleting;

1) Make the first cut just behind the gills. Cut down to the backbone, then turn the knife toward the tail of the fish and slice above the spine(feeling for it as you proceed) all the way to the tail. One flank of the fish will now be removed. Flip the fish over and repeat the process. This step is illustrated below.

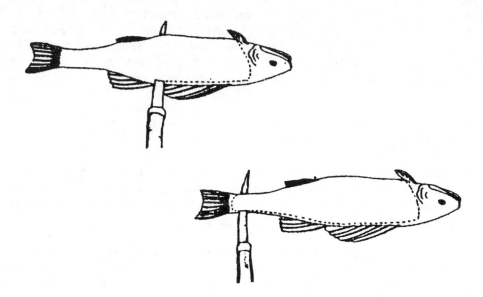

2) Now cut away the rib cage from each fillet. Insert the knife at the top of the rib cage and slice down following close to ribs.

3) Lastly, remove the skin. Lay fillet skin side down on cutting board. Insert the knife just about $\frac{1}{2}$" from the tail and cut down to the skin. Now, firmly holding the tail-end, turn the blade forward and work the knife along the skin, "lifting" the meat from the skin all the way to the large end of the fillet.

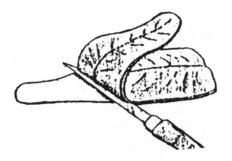

With a little practice, filleting becomes second nature. For a great visual display, watch the pros do it when a party boat docks after a day of fishing. You'll be amazed. Successful filleting depends on two things, once you understand the principles. One: use a good fish fillet knife. Two: keep the knife very sharp.

Steaking

Steaking simply means cutting a fish into similar-sized parts by making parallel cuts that are all perpendicular to the spine! Just joking! I know only math freaks and geometry teachers could understand that definition.

The first step in steaking(which, by the way, is usually reserved only for large fish) is to remove the head(this is done after field dressing), right at the gill cover. Now just lay the fish flat and divide it into about one inch thick pieces. The tail section(where the steaks are small) can be filleted. Some varieties need to be scaled before steaking.

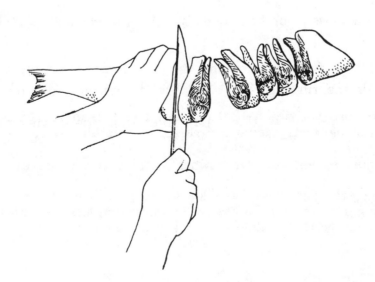

Keeping Fish Fresh

Fish is delicious. But it is also one of the most perishable of foods. So, from the time a fish is caught until it is served, care must be taken to preserve its freshness.

Freshness on the Water

If possible, the best way to keep a fish fresh, while continuing to fish, is to keep your catch alive. This can be done in several ways;

- For pan fish, use a collapsible basket. A fully submerged burlap bag also will serve the purpose.

- The best stringers are those that have large safety pin type clasps, and some type of swivel mechanism so fish are less likely to get twisted up.

- The proper stringing technique is to run the stringer through both the upper and lower lip. This allows the fish to open and close its mouth, thereby forcing water through its gills to breathe. Never run a stringer through the fishes gills. This prevents it from closing its mouth and therefore starving it of oxygen.

- Let out the full stringer. Even add a rope, if extra length is needed to keep the fish down deep in the water. The water is cooler and more oxygenated down deeper.

- If you move your boat quickly, lift the stringer out of the water during a short trip.

- Surf and river anglers, who use a stringer, move the fish along with them, always placing them back into the deepest water available.

- When using a creel, bed and surround fish in dry grass. Canvas creels or fishing vests should be moist to maintain coolness.

There are some cautions to watch when keeping fish in water;

- Stringered fish have been known to have been eaten by turtles. Never string fish in warm water. Summertime surface water temperatures in some Northern California lakes are in the 80's!

. Stringers are taboo in salt waters. It's just feeding the sharks. Rather, use a cooler or fish-box, preferably with ice in it.

Freshness During Travel

If you're traveling for any length of time, follow these simple steps to insure freshness;

. Field dress the fish.

. Dry the fish thoroughly.

. Cover each fish with foil or plastic.

. Surround each package of fish, in a cooler, with crushed ice or cubed ice.

Refrigeration

Fish do not do particularly well under prolonged refrigeration. So it's best to either eat fresh caught fish, or freeze them. Refrigerated fish should be covered with heavy foil, freezer paper or plastic to prevent moisture from escaping.

Freezing

There are basically two ways to freeze fresh fish. With either approach you can freeze whole-field cleaned fish, fish fillets, steaks or chunks.

The first method is more conventional. Wrap fish in packaging materials with high barriers to moisture and vapor transmission. A good quality freezer wrapping paper or heavy foil is recommended. Wrap tightly and tape securely. This method is adequate. Defrost slowly in a refrigerator. Better flavor and preservation can be achieved by repeatedly dipping and freezing unwrapped fish in water until a layer of ice is formed. Then wrap securely.

Actually, the best and simplest way to freeze fish is to utilize old milk cartons or similar liquid holding containers. Fresh and well-cleaned fish can be placed in the container up to an inch from the top. Now, simply fill the container with water(or a brine solution of 1/3 cup of table salt to one gallon of water) and shake to make sure there are no air bubbles. Seal up container and freeze. Thawing is best done on a drain rack so fish does not sit in cold water.

Date fish packages you put in your freezer. Store it at 0°F or lower and plan to use it within two months, for best flavor.

Cooking Fish

There are numerous fish cook books jam-packed with recipes. But matching your favorite catch to an unfamiliar or inappropriate recipe often leads to less than enjoyable eating. Rather than special recipes, successful fish cooking depends on adhering to two simple principles;

1) Know when the fish is done - too often fish is over-cooked.

2) Match cooking method to the fish flavor, fish size and fat level.

First, let's address the "when fish is done" issue. Fish, by its very nature is more tender than red meat or poultry. It doesn't contain fibers that need to be broken down by extensive cooking. Some cooking experts say fish should be considered more like egg, than like meat. So, as in cooking egg, just enough heat need be applied to firm-up the protein. Over-cooking makes eggs tough and dry; it does the same for fish.

So how do you tell when fish is cooked for just the right length of time? It's easy. Fish is cooked properly when it flakes when probed with a fork. By flaking, I mean separated into its natural layers or divisions. This test should be done often, at the center, or thickest part of the fish fillet, steak or whole fish.

Matching Fish to Cooking Method

Now the second key principle of successful fish cooking. That is, matching the specific fish to the specific cooking method. Fish caught in Northern California have a wide variety of flavor levels, fish size and fat level. Typically, all fish is considered a low-fat source of protein. But there are pronounced differences in fat content that do affect taste and texture. Flavor level also varies generally from very mild to quite pronounced. This influences cooking method and seasoning selection. Fortunately, all these fish can be grouped into four cooking categories

Category One: Here are the delicate, mild flavored, lean and generally small cuts of fish. Specific examples include sole, sandabs, flounder and halibut. Cuts of fish in this category are generally thin and oval shaped. The exception is halibut which is thicker and has a heavier texture.

Category One fish are very good sauteed. Sole fillets are so delicate that some only need to be cooked on one side. A flour coating promotes browning. Thicker cuts can have a flour, crumb, cornmeal or egg-wash coating before frying. Oven frying or foil baking also works well, as does poaching.

Category Two: Fish here are generally of medium density, yet still light in flavor. We're talking about lingcod, the whole family of rockfish, surfperch, salmon, trout, catfish, striped bass and steelhead. Both steaks and fillets from larger fish in this category are good poached, cooked in foil or oven-fried. Pan frying is good with a coating like crumbs or egg-wash to add flavor, texture and enhance browning. Small, whole fish are good baked or foil cooked. The most oily fish in this category, salmon, is very good barbecued.

Category Three: Here we have the Northern California fish that are more dense with a darker meat and more pronounced flavor. Three ocean going fish - the tunas(albacore, yellowfin, etc.), bonito and mackerel - make up this third category. To be honest with you many fishermen don't even like the robust (some say strong) flavor of these fish. But those who do usually barbecue them. Fresh caught barbecued tuna is quite tasty, but some would say that it's not as good as "good old Charley-the-Tuna."

Category Four: Now we're into the large fish that result in thick cuts(1-1½") of dense meat. Northern California fish in this category are the sturgeon and shark (leopard and blue). Cuts of these fish brown nicely in a frying pan without any coating and you can barbecue them directly on a greased grill. In fact, cubes can be skewered for kabobs. Meal-sized pieces are good baked, poached or cooked in foil.

The above categories and guidelines have wide latitude. That's why for each fish covered in the "How To Catch..." section in the book, we give specific cooking information.

Sauteing

This method is often called frying, but frying is quite distinct. More on this in the pan frying section below. Sauteing is cooking fish in a frying pan, usually in a small amount of melted butter, over moderate or high heat.

This is one of the fastest and simplest ways to prepare fish. And, it is well-suited for either lean or fat fish. The fish is sprinkled with salt and pepper and dipped in flour on both sides. Cooking time per side varies from 1 minute to 3 minutes. A sauce can be prepared in the pan after the fish are removed to a warm platter.

Frying(both Pan and Deep)

Frying fish means emersing either partially or completely in cooking oil. This process results in a thicker, more crusty covering of the fish than with sauteing or oven-frying. Frying usually involves a batter made with a beaten egg and a small amount of milk. The dipped fish pieces are rolled in bread crumbs, cracker crumbs or a purchased coating mix.

1/8 inch of shortening or salad oil should be heated to between 350° and 375° in a substantial frying pan. Or, if deep-frying, use enough shortening or salad oil in a deep fryer, to cover the fish. Heat to the same temperature. Finished fish should be golden brown and flake when tested.

Some pitfalls to avoid. Don't let the oil temperature fall. It results in a greasy or soggy coating. Too much fish put in the oil at one time can lower cooking temperature too much. Too high an oil temperature will result in dark coating or burnt flavor. If batter falls off, the fish pieces may have been too wet. So, pat dry before battering.

Oven Frying

Everybody knows how to oven-fry chicken, so everybody knows how to oven-fry fish. This method is simple and doesn't cause fat-spattering, if that's a problem with you.

Fish should be in serving-sized pieces. Dip each piece in milk, drain, sprinkle with salt and pepper, then roll in bread crumbs or cracker crumbs. Melt enough butter or margarine in a shallow baking pan to generously coat the bottom. Now, turn the crumb coated fish over in the melted butter or margarine and arrange the pieces in the pan. Bake in a hot oven(about 500°) until the fish flakes(from 5 to 15 minutes). Turn each piece one time so it browns evenly.

Baking

Foil wrapped or covered-dish oven cooking is the typical fish baking approach. The covering or enclosure is needed to prevent the fish from drying out. This is an ideal method for baking fish with vegetables, herbs or tomato sauce. The steam that is developed helps produce a tasty sauce. Oven temperature is usually about 450°.

Barbecuing or Grilling

Rich, full-flavored fish such as salmon, trout or tuna are most desirable for barbecuing, since they're fatter and the smoke enhances the taste. Milder-tasting fish might be overcome by the smoke flavor. Serving-sized fillets, steaks and whole fish can be barbecued.

Some people like to grill directly over the coals, while others put the fish on a sheet of heavy aluminum foil. The foil method works well in a covered grill because it prevents any sticking or turning problems.

Some helpful hints. Make sure the coals are hot and the grill is hot. Fish stick like magnets to a cold grill. Start fillets skin side up(if no foil is used) and turn only once. If foil is used, fillet skin should be down(that is, touching foil). While cooking, the fish is basted with melted butter or your favorite sauce.

Broiling

Broiling, of course, is much akin to barbecuing, except that the heat is above the fish. Any fish can be broiled, but leaner fish must be basted often to prevent it from drying out. Fillets are often broiled on only one side, while steaks are turned once. Broil 2-3 inches from the heat.

Poaching

Poaching is simmering fish gently in a flavorful liquid. The liquid is never boiled, however. Fish prepared this way is very good served hot with a fish sauce made from the poaching liquid. Any fish with a low fat content, and salmon, of course is delicious prepared this way. And, as an extra bonus, cold, poached fish, like tuna, is great.

Pieces of fish are often poached in cheese cloth while large, whole fish are done in a poaching pan that has a special rack for lowering and removing the fish. Again, the flake test will reveal when the fish is cooked properly. Fillets should be tested after about 5 minutes.

An easy way to poach a steak or fillet is to put it in lightly salted water in a wide saucepan or skillet on top of the stove(it's much less fuss than the classic oven poach). Frozen fish pieces can even be defrosted and poached at the same time. Poaching is complete(for frozen or fresh fish) when the meat has turned from translucent to opaque, and it feels somewhat springy, rather than squishy. Cooked pieces are patted dry and served with melted butter, or in other more elaborate ways.

Smoking

Many avid, and some not so avid, anglers own and use fish smokers. They are simple to use and quite modestly priced. And they produce delicious smoked fish. All commercially available smokers come with detailed instruction manuals. It is also possible to convert such items as 55 gallon drums, or a discarded refrigerator and a hotplate. Instructions for these do-it-yourself projects can be found in smoking-oriented cook books in your local library.